The Performance of Small Firms

THE PERFORMANCE OF SMALL FIRMS

Profits, Jobs and Failures

David Storey, Kevin Keasey, Robert Watson
and Pooran Wynarczyk

CROOM HELM
London • Sydney • Wolfeboro, New Hampshire

© 1987 David Storey, Kevin Keasey, Robert Watson
and Pooran Wynarczyk
Croom Helm Ltd, Provident House, Burrell Row,
Beckenham, Kent BR3 1AT
Croom Helm Australia Pty Ltd, Suite 4, 6th Floor,
64-76 Kippax Street, Surry Hills, NSW 2010, Australia

British Library Cataloguing in Publication Data
The Performance of small firms.
　　1. Small business — Great Britain —
　　Finance
　　I. Storey, D.J. (David John), *1947*-
　　658.1′592′0941　　　HG4027.7
　　ISBN 0-7099-4411-X

Croom Helm, 27 South Main Street,
Wolfeboro, New Hampshire 03894-2069, USA.

Library of Congress Cataloging-in-Publication Data
The Performance of small firms.
　　Includes bibliographical references.
　　1. Small business. 2. Business failures. 3. Small
business — Government policy. I. Storey, D.J.
HD2341.P399　1987　　　658′.022　　86-29052
ISBN 0-7099-4411-X

Typeset in Times Roman by Leaper & Gard Ltd, Bristol, England
Printed and bound in Great Britain
by Billing & Sons Limited, Worcester.

Contents

Foreword

In this book we address two audiences. The first half of the book is directed towards those interested in public policy designed to create economic activity within the small business sector. Within that group we include local and national government officials, business pressure groups and our fellow academics. To this group we emphasise that small businesses are not simply 'scaled down' versions of large businesses.

The fundamental problem in accounting for the differing performance of small and large firms is that many small firms exist only for a very short period. Failure rates are more than ten times as high for new small firms as for large well established firms. It is for this reason that the second half of the book is devoted to a study of failure which, in our view, is the central characteristic of the small business sector. In studying failure it has been our intention to demonstrate that it is possible to predict failure in advance. This research is therefore designed to be of practical assistance to banks and other private sector financial institutions. It may also help entrepreneurs in assessing their own business, but ultimately it is firmly targeted towards makers of public policy in order to demonstrate that selective assistance, either to prevent failure or to promote further growth, is technically feasible.

In undertaking this work we have been assisted by many organisations. Our prime source of finance came from the Economic and Social Research Council (ESRC) on a project called 'Failed and Non-Failed Firms'. Finance for clerical assistance was provided by the Manpower Services Commission. The financial data was initially assembled by David Floyd and Tom Manley under the supervision of Patrick Steele. Maintenance of the employment data file has been the responsibility of Audrey Crow.

The material included within the book has been tested on numerous audiences including seminars of the ESRC Industrial Economics Study Group and Staff Seminars at the Universities of Leicester, Glasgow and at Hatfield Polytechnic. Presentations have also been made at the Universities of Umeå and Karlstadt in Sweden. Two presentations have been made to the Institute of Credit Management, and to the Northern Society of

Chartered Accountants. Particular thanks go to Norman Strong of the Economics Department at Newcastle University and Paul Geroski of Southampton University whose most useful comments have led both to a substantial reduction in the size of the volume and, hopefully, a sharpening of the argument. Finally, we would like to thank our typists, particularly Betty Robson and Denise Rainford at CURDS and Janet McKibben at New College Durham. Their work has been consistently excellent.

As joint and equal authors we are most grateful for all the comments, help and encouragement which we received from all our colleagues, particularly during those many dark moments when at least three of us were convinced the book would never be written. We thank them all, but we alone are responsible for what follows.

1

Introduction

The small firm has increasingly become the focus for public policy designed to increase employment and to decrease unemployment in the developed countries (Binks and Coyne, 1983). It is now widely believed that small firms contribute to economic vitality partly by increasing the level of competition in the economy through competing with large firms and party by providing inputs to large firms, enabling the latter to be competitive in world markets.

The startling results obtained by Birch (1979), showing that 66 per cent of the increase in employment in the United States between 1969 and 1976 was in firms employing less than 20 workers, ensured that the small firm would be a focus of attention for public policy makers — especially in times of recession. Subsequent work by Armington and Odle (1982) and Teitz *et al.* (1981) in the United States and the considerable European literature (reviewed in OECD, 1985 and Storey and Johnson, 1987) has shown that the original results obtained by Birch were significant overestimates. Nevertheless it is clear that small firms are creating jobs at least as fast as other sizes of enterprise, and perhaps somewhat faster. They therefore demand to be the subject of public policy during times of high unemployment.

Unfortunately many public policy makers both in Europe and North America have made the unwarranted assumption that because small firms are significant creators of new employment they should therefore be actively encouraged. It has been pointed out, however (OECD 1985; Storey, 1982) that any special treatment for small firms requires a much deeper understanding of the processes by which jobs are created. It requires an analysis of the market failures which require public intervention and an understanding of any externalities created by policies to assist small businesses.

It is the purpose of this volume to obtain a better insight into the process of job creation in smaller businesses, so that decisions may be made on the appropriate form of public policy and upon an appropriate mechanism for its delivery. As industrial economists and accountants we recognise that, even if the ultimate purpose of public policy is job creation, this has to take place through the expansion of individual firms. Small firms will expand only if it is financially worthwhile although, as we shall demonstrate, even if it is financially worthwhile some firms may choose not to expand. The ultimate focus of our attention will therefore be upon employment, but the process of job creation will be traced through the Balance Sheets and the Profit and Loss Accounts of more than 600 small manufacturing businesses.

It is our contention that public policies to promote the development and growth of small firms have been developed, particularly in Western Europe, rather faster than our knowledge about small firms. The fact that the shares of large companies are publicly traded means that information on their performance has to be available and so the large company sector has been extensively studied and its performance monitored. Even without examining individual companies directly it is possible, through sectoral analyses, to identify the contribution of the major producers.

This is not the case with small firms where data availability is a much more serious problem for several reasons. First, data on the financial performance of small firms are so closely connected to the income of the proprietor that public divulgence is thought to constitute an unwarranted loss of privacy to those individuals. Secondly in most major industries more than 90 per cent of all firms are defined as small[1], even though they only produce between 25 and 50 per cent of national output. Consequently a data base would need to be very large if coverage were to be complete, and so it is clearly more efficient to study a few relatively large firms, which have a major effect upon economic aggregates such as output and employment. Thirdly it has to be recognised that interest in small firms amongst politicians and public policy-makers is relatively recent. In the 1960s, and for much of the 1970s, the thrust of industrial policy in many countries was to ensure that large firms were able to reap the benefits of scale economies by raising the levels of industrial concentration, either through positive encouragement for mergers and acquisitions or by allowing anti-trust legislation to be set aside.

For all these reasons the small firm sector is now in the unusual position of being poorly understood, whilst being the focus of political attention. Perhaps the most dangerous development, however, is that because of our relatively clear understanding of the large firm sector there has been a tendency to assume that empirical results derived from this sector apply to small firms. It is our contention that this is not the case. The small firm is not simply a scaled down version of the large firm. It has different objectives and aspirations. It faces different problems and it responds to different incentives. Indeed throughout this volume it is our intention to highlight those characteristics, other than scale, that distinguish small firms from large.

The fundamental characteristic which distinguishes small firms from large is their relatively high probability of failure. This is shown in Table 1.1 which presents British data on failure rates according to the turnover (sales) of the business. From the table it is clear that failure rates are substantially higher for the smaller business than for the large.

In fact it appears that businesses with very small sales, i.e. less than £13,000 have a failure rate which is six times as high as the largest businesses, whilst those with a turnover of between £50,000 and £99,000 have a failure rate which is twice that of the larger businesses. It is a crude, but nevertheless helpful, rule of thumb to assume that one full time employee is approximately equal to £10,000 and so those businesses in the largest size category are those with 200 or more employees.

Table 1.1: Failure rates by size of turnover

Turnover size in 1980 £'000	Number of businesses	Failures	Failure rates %
1-13	172,976	43,321	25.0
14	19,870	3,209	16.1
15-49	424,106	50,955	12.0
50-99	237,230	17,185	7.2
100-499	277,239	12,299	4.4
500-1,999	64,769	2,306	3.6
2000 +	22,389	871	3.9

Source: Ganguly (1985)

The central importance of failure in the study of small businesses is the reason why we have chosen to sub-divide this book into two parts. Part 1 deals with conventional measures of firm performance in a way designed to facilitate comparisons with similar types of studies which have been conducted on large firms. However in making valid performance comparisons we are constantly hampered by the high rates of failure amongst small firms. For example in comparing whether profitability and size are related, much depends on the length of time over which the comparisons are made. In essence the longer the period, the greater the emphasis placed upon surviving small firms which are a biased sample from the small firm population.

Part 2 of the book therefore makes an explicit study of failure and asks whether it is possible to identify, in advance, the characteristics of those firms which will fail over, say, the following three-year period. In attempting to answer this question we have used the techniques developed in the numerous failure prediction models for the large firm sector, but again these have to be modified to take into account differences in the characteristics and availability of data for small firms.

To conduct this study several methods could have been used. The first technique would have been to conduct structured or unstructured interviews with the owners of small firms in order to obtain an insight into their motivations, aspirations, background etc. A number of such studies have been undertaken (Lloyd and Mason 1985; Oakey, 1984; Storey, 1982) and have yielded useful insights. However the results have now become increasingly predictable, and we have judged there to be sharply decreasing returns from undertaking another such study. We were also well aware of the subjective nature of the responses provided and of the reluctance of the owners to provide full and accurate financial information. Finally it is only possible to interview businesses which are still in operation and since it has been shown that failure is a major factor which distinguishes small from large businesses interviews with existing businessmen offer no insight into this key matter.

A second research method would have been to use a very large data base, such as the Dun and Bradstreet used by Birch and by Armington and Odle. This however would not have suited our purposes for several reasons. First, much of the debate between Armington and Odle on the one hand and Birch on the other concerned the extent to which essentially dirty data could be cleaned up. Both the US and the UK data bases are so large that it is not feasible to check individual records for their validity. Instead computerised matching techniques and scanning for extremes have to be used. This is recognised to be error-prone. Secondly even the Dun and Bradstreet data do not have adequate details on the financial performance of small companies and have little coverage of factors which we find to be important determinants of small company performance, such as the numbers and backgrounds of directors, and changes on the board of the company. Hence, although we believe that large data sets serve a potentially valuable function in quantifying the contribution of different sized units to employment change, they are less helpful in leading to an understanding of the process by which that change occurs or could be encouraged to occur by public policy.

Our approach has been to identify, from a population of manufacturing firms in an area, those for which it was possible to obtain both financial and employment data for a single plant. We describe in Chapter 2 the derivation of the 636 companies used, together with their financial and employment characteristics. Chapter 3 describes, for a sample of the 636 companies, some of the more qualitative aspects of their operations which appear to be related to the performance of the firm. It outlines data on factors such as the number of directors, their backgrounds, and changes in the ownership structure of the company over time. It also identifies the presence of floating charges and the holders of such charges. Finally it directs attention to the role of auditors particularly in terms of their likelihood of qualifying the published accounts. It is these qualitative factors which are used as predictors of small firm failure discussed in Chapter 9 of this book.

The two remaining chapters in Part 1 discuss the performance of small companies. Using data on all 636 companies, Chapter 4 compares the relationship between profitability and growth in this collection of small firms with the numerous studies which have been undertaken of the performance of large companies. It shows that some significantly different relationships exist and that young small firms perform very differently from old small firms.

In Chapter 5 we begin to approach the key issue raised at the start of this chapter by OECD (1985) of whether it is possible, even if it is deemed desirable, to assist the growth of small firms.

We note that government small firm policy, particularly in the UK, has been directed towards increasing the level of trading profit in the small company sector, through a variety of assistance measures, in the belief that this will lead to increased employment. If this belief is valid it would be expected that those companies which experienced increases in trading profit would, *ceteris paribus*, experience a faster rate of increase or slower rate of decline of employment than those with no increases or a fall in trading profit. In Chapter 5 we attempt to address this hypothesis.

Comparisons between performances of small and large firms and any appraisal of the effectiveness of small firm policy always encounters the problem that the small firm population is highly transient. In all years more than 12 per cent of all businesses in the UK cease to trade and are replaced by new businesses. We also know that of the 309,102 businesses which registered for VAT payment in 1975, only 37 per cent had survived until 1980.

It is to this question of failure we return in Part 2, and begin by noting the absence of carefully argued analyses of the role of business failure in the process of economic development. In fact the subject of business failure appears to have produced two rather differing strands of work. The first is a description of the characteristics of the firms that fail, based primarily upon case study material, and with only modest efforts made to generalise or to use this to predict failure in other firms. The second type of work is statistically-derived predictive failure models which attempt to identify relationships between financial ratios and failure/non-failure. Unfortunately there appear to be few links between these two types of studies with the prediction models appearing to be based exclusively on statistical search procedures, rather than upon theoretically well-grounded selection of appropriate ratios. Finally, almost all the failure prediction models and the case-study material appear to have been conducted for the large company sector where data are more plentiful and yet where failure is less common.

Part 2 is devoted to an attempt to use this experience of building predictive models of large firm failure in constructing similar models from a selection of small firms. The client group for statistical models for predicting small firm failure differs from the client group for the large firm studies. The latter are primarily of interest to those trading in the shares of the company and to a much lesser extent to the providers of credit. The client group for failure prediction models of small firms is the commercial banks which provide overdraft or loan facilities, the directors themselves and those providing trade credit. There is no requirement that the results of models should be public knowledge (Keasey and Watson, 1987). In this work we have only used statistical search procedures to select ratios when ratios have either been shown to be important in other studies or where there is a strong *a priori* case for their inclusion. In Chapters 6-8 we employ the full package of statistical techniques which have been used in the large firm models. Chapter 6 uses univariate analysis; Chapter 7 uses multiple discriminant analysis whilst factor and logit analysis are used in Chapter 8. The main problem encountered in constructing these models is that many failing companies do not submit accounts in the years immediately prior to failure. Consequently it is difficult to observe changes in key ratios in these years.

The merits of a model of small firm failure are best identified by its predictive powers, and in each of the chapters we conduct rigorous hold-out tests. Broadly it appears that, despite the additional difficulties of producing a small firm predictive model, the best of the present models perform as well, but no better than many of the models of large firm failure.

The analyses in Chapters 6-8 use financial data drawn from the Balance Sheets and Profit and Loss Accounts of companies to construct predictive models of failure. Publicly available data on companies in the UK as reviewed in Chapter 3, however, also provide a set of qualitative information on company directors, accountants etc. Throughout this book we have noted that a major problem in constructing a model of small firm failure is that, despite their legal responsibilities, many failing companies do not submit accounts in their final years. Chapter 9 uses a variety of such 'qualitative' factors in assessing their contribution, either independently or in conjunction with the financial data, towards the production of an improved model of failure prediction in small companies.

Even from this introduction it should be apparent that there are unique problems in a study of small firms, and that the 'results' obtained can be highly sensitive to the procedures used for selecting firms included in the analysis. Most studies have concentrated upon existing small businesses, even though many may have only a short life. This is because so many studies of small firms have been conducted using interview techniques, and it is difficult to obtain interviews with ex-businessmen. The better studies of this type, however, have endeavoured to ensure that the sample of firms derived is in some respects 'representative' of the population under survey. Unfortunately even this is a far from universal practice and a number of shoddy studies have been conducted on easily-derived lists of small businesses, such as those represented on courses at a research institution or members of small-business clubs. In no way can such studies purport to reflect the small-business population. Similarly, studies of new firms are subject to particular biases since there is no population of new firms from which to sample, and all the major data sets have deficiencies (Birley, 1985a).

In the present study we have been keenly aware of these problems and it is for this reason that we offer no apologies for devoting considerable space both to a full articulation of how the sample of companies was derived, and to comparing their characteristics with those included in the major existing studies of small firms.

NOTE

1. There are considerable variations in definitions of a small firm. As Cross (1983) shows, there are more than 40 different definitions used by government of a small firm in the UK alone. These differences multiply at an international level (Ganguly, 1985; Heartz, 1982).

Part One

The Small Company: Profits and Jobs

2

The Small Manufacturing Company: Employment and Financial Characteristics

INTRODUCTION

The derivation of a sample of small businesses which is representative of the population of small firms is a truly formidable problem. The small firm sector fluctuates markedly from year to year with, in the UK, more than 10 per cent of the stock changing annually. Furthermore, business failure rates are disproportionately high for the youngest firms. Of those firms which fail within ten years of starting business, 50 per cent of failures occur in the first $2\frac{1}{2}$ years, 33 per cent in the next $2\frac{1}{2}$ years, and only 17 per cent in the following five years (Ganguly, 1985). If the dynamics of the small firm population are to be modelled over a period of time, in order that public policy towards the sector can be made more effective, then the collection of firms analysed has to include both substantial numbers of new firms and those which have ceased trading. It is wholly misleading to concentrate upon survivors, although as we shall demonstrate 'missing' data do present considerable problems in making comparisons.

Unfortunately, too little emphasis is placed, within small business research, on satisfying these conditions. There is a somewhat cavalier tendency for researchers to conduct interviews with an easily identifiable group of small businesses and infer that the results are generally applicable to the small business sector. For example business schools or public agencies frequently report the results of interviews with their own client group, planners tend to interview firms on industrial estates and small business pressure groups place great weight on the views of their members. The typical small businessman, at least in the UK, however, has never been near a university business school, does not have a plush new factory and belongs to no pressures groups whatsoever. Those able to afford a new factory, or with the self-confidence even to approach a university business school are thus atypical of the population of small firms and the results of studies of such firms risk being sample-dependent. Furthermore there is a tendency to accept, without question, the answers obtained by interviews, with this being particularly suspect when respondents are required to make future projections, primarily because in three years time 30 per cent of those businesses will not be trading. Even where future projections are not required there are often marked discrepancies between formal audited statements and information obtained by interviews. There can be little doubt that statements for which the directors of a business and its auditors are legally responsible are likely to be closer to the truth than hurriedly conducted interviews. For the above reasons, we devote the whole of this chapter to a discussion both of the construction of the data set and of its general characteristics.

This chapter is divided into four sections. The first is a detailed description of the methods used for collecting the companies to be included in the data base, detailed analysis of which is undertaken in the remainder of the book. A second section is devoted to a preliminary statement of the characteristics of the included companies. In particular the age, sectoral composition and size of companies are discussed. In the third section, some comparisons are undertaken between the financial characteristics of companies included in the data base and those of other collections of small UK manufacturing companies. Finally any study of smaller companies has to address the question of failure and so the fourth section discusses both the derivation and characteristics of those businesses which are classified as having 'ceased to trade' or 'failed'.

DERIVING A SAMPLE OF SMALL MANUFACTURING COMPANIES

In assembling the data to be examined in this book three characteristics of a small firm which were identified by the Bolton Committee (1971) have to be borne in mind. Bolton argued that the small firm generally had a small share of the market, that it was managed by the owners and that it was legally independent. Translating these considerations into a statistically operational definition of a small business has created problems for governments throughout the world, since the typical firm which satisfies these conditions in, for example, the chemical industry is likely to be much larger than the typical firm in retail distribution. Definitions of 'a small firm' by government statisticians and policy-makers even within the same country therefore differ markedly. Cross (1983), quoting from Beesley and Wilson (1981) shows that in the UK alone there were more than 40 different definitions of 'the small firm' which were in use by the central government in 1982. Hertz (1982) shows that these problems multiply when undertaking international comparisons.

Although there is considerable variety, in the UK there is general agreement, since the days of the Bolton Committee, that a small manufacturing firm is defined as having less than 200 employees, whereas in most other sectors definitions are based upon the value of turnover of the business. As will be shown later 98 per cent of the firms in the present study have less than *100* employees and are therefore well within the official definition of a small manufacturing firm.

The present data base was established with two prime objectives:

(1) to obtain financial data upon a selection of small manufacturing businesses;
(2) to compare the financial performance of small manufacturing firms with the creation of employment in those enterprises.

In the UK it is possible to obtain financial data upon those businesses which trade as limited companies. Such businesses are legally required to submit annual accounts to Companies House in pre-specified format, at which time it becomes public information upon payment of a fee of £1 per company. In the event of a business choosing or being required to trade either as a sole proprietorship or partnership, i.e. without the benefit of limited liability, then the accounts of that business remain a private matter between the owner and the Inland Revenue.

The current study, because it concentrates on manufacturing *companies*, provides an extensive yet nevertheless incomplete coverage of the performance of manufacturing *businesses.* Restrictions on data availability, however, mean that such problems are unlikely to be overcome in the future.

To satisfy the Bolton Committee definitions of a small firm it was decided to exclude all businesses which were not legally independent. One of the objectives of this research was to 'match' employment and financial performance at the level of the individual small company. Hence it was felt that to include companies which were linked in any way to other companies, about which there was incomplete knowledge, would lead to bias. A highly restrictive definition of independence was therefore employed. Any company which was found, in any year, in the annual accounts to be either a lender to, or borrower from an associated company was deemed not to be independent. Furthermore any company where *any* shares were owned by another company was also *not* included in the financial data base.

To satisfy the criteria outlined above the financial data base to be used in this book was constructed by examining only:

(1) companies which remained independent throughout the period 1965-78;
(2) companies which remained single-plant throughout the period 1965-78;
(3) companies which were classified as manufacturing;
(4) companies located in the counties of Durham, Cleveland or Tyne and Wear in Northern England;
(5) companies in existence at some stage between 1965-1978; and
(6) companies providing financial data to Companies House for more than one year between 1970 and 1980.

From work undertaken in conjunction with the Department of Employment and the County Councils of Durham, Cleveland and Tyne and Wear a data base existed in 1982 which included all manufacturing *establishments* which had existed in those three counties at any stage between *1965* and *1978.*[1] The data base containing ownership and annual employment data for 4880 establishments was used to identify legally independent single-plant establishments. Since only data on limited companies were publicly available sole proprietorships and partnerships were excluded, as were establishments which were independent but had been acquired by 1981.

Once these exclusions had been made the data base contained the records of 636 single-plant independent manufacturing companies which provided more than a single year of financial data (Balance Sheet and Profit and Loss Account) at some stage between 1970/71 and 1980/81. The nature of this information is shown in Table 2.1 and to this was added employment data for the same establishments (companies) for the period 1965-1981.[2]

In most of the subsequent analysis the financial records of the 636 companies which were single-plant independent Northern manufacturing companies existing at some stage between 1965 and 1978, but providing financial data for more than a single year between 1970 and 1980, will be used. Where it is thought to be particularly relevant the data on the 70 single-plant independent Northern manufacturing companies, which either provided no financial data or provided only one year's financial data, will also be included.

Table 2.1: Information on companies available from Companies House

---

1. Name of company.
2. Registered office and date of incorporation.
3. Names, occupation, addresses of Directors and Secretary of Company.
4. Other Directorships held.
5. Share allocations.
6. Articles of Association.
7. Mortgage or Charge Documents.
8. Annual Profit and Loss, Balance Sheet and Source and Application of Funds Statements.

   For companies which are voluntarily wound-up there may be:
   (a) Date of Creditors' Meeting (if creditors' voluntary liquidation).
   (b) Date of appointment of Receiver/Liquidator.
   (c) Liquidator's Statement.

   For companies which are compulsorily wound-up there may be:
   (a) Date of Court Order.
   (b) Date of appointment of (generally) the Official Receiver.
   (c) Liquidator's Statement.

   For companies which are dissolved there will be:
   (a) Date of dissolution.
   (b) Dates and copies of letters sent to the last known address of the company.

THE CHARACTERISTICS OF THE DATA SET

Sectoral composition

The sectoral composition of the three Northern Region manufacturing data sets is shown in Table 2.2 The first pair of columns show the sectoral composition of 2537 manufacturing establishments taken to be single-plant and independent. It shows concentration in mechanical engineering (16%), timber and furniture (15%), printing and paper (11%) metal goods (10%) and food and drink (10%). The virtual absence of so-called 'high tech' industries such as instrument engineering (2%) and electrical engineering (4%) is also clear.

The 636 companies in the financial data base (second pair of columns) appear to reflect the sectoral distribution amongst the Regional population of single-plant independent manufacturing establishments, with a slightly higher concentration in mechani-

Table 2.2: Sectoral composition of independent Northern Region manufacturing businesses

Sector (Standard Industrial Classification, 1968)	Number of single-plant independent establishments in employment data set		Number of single-plant independent companies in employment and financial data set		Companies not providing accounts data 1970-80	
	Number	%	Number	%	Number	%
Food, drink & tobacco	252	10	39	6	—	—
Coal & petroleum	6	—	1	—	—	—
Chemical & allied	74	3	24	4	—	—
Metal manufacturing	64	3	13	2	1	(1)
Mechanical engineering	400	16	125	20	6	(9)
Instrument engineering	59	2	18	3	2	(3)
Electrical engineering	104	4	34	5	1	(1)
Shipbuilding	41	2	14	2	5	(7)
Vehicles	64	3	15	2	3	(4)
Metal goods not elsewhere specified	263	10	85	13	6	(9)
Textiles	51	2	10	2	3	(4)
Leather	16	1	3	—	2	(3)
Clothing	154	6	34	5	9	(13)
Bricks, pottery etc	115	5	26	4	6	(9)
Timber & furniture	375	15	77	12	13	(19)
Printing & paper	280	11	63	10	5	(7)
Other manufacturing	125	5	33	5	3	(4)
Not known	94	4	22	3	5	(7)
Total	2537	(100)	636	(100)	70	(100)

cal engineering (20%) and metal goods (13%) and a consequent slight under-representation amongst timber and furniture (12%) and food and drink (6%). It is assumed that this is a reflection of the larger minimum efficient scale in mechanical engineering/metal goods businesses compared with those in timber/food, thus providing an incentive to the owners to opt for corporate status.

The third pair of columns provide a sectoral breakdown of the 70 companies which submitted either no accounts or only one year's accounts during the 1970-80 period. These businesses are known to have traded, and employed workers, but many are 'twilight' businesses. Indeed we are aware of several where legal proceedings either have been undertaken or where litigation is pending. Not surprisingly the sectors which are well represented are the clothing trade, and timber and furniture.

Employment size

Whilst financial data are available during the 1970/71 to 1980/81 period, employment data are available for the period 1965-1981. It must also be recalled that at no stage during the whole of the period 1965-1981 were *all* these companies actively trading. Furthermore even when they were trading there is no certainty that, despite their statutory responsibilities, the companies would provide either financial or employment data. It is therefore possible to provide only an incomplete view of either the financial or the employment characteristics of most companies in the data set trading in any given year.

Given these provisos the first row of Table 2.3 shows employment data for single-plant independent firms in the Northern Region in 1978. It then compares this distribution with that of companies included in the financial data base.

The table shows that 50 per cent of single-plant independent manufacturing establishments in Northern England in 1978 employed less than ten workers. No distinction is made between part-time and full-time work, so employment in terms of full-time equivalents is significantly lower. The penultimate row of Table 2.3 shows that in 1978 single-plant independent companies in the data base contain rather fewer of these very small businesses than the 'population', but a compensating higher proportion of slightly larger establishments in the 10-49

Table 2.3: Employment size of Northern single-plant independent establishments in 1978 and financial data base companies in 1965, 1969, 1971, 1974, 1978 and 1981

		Employment size (total number of employees)					Total number of cases	Total number of jobs
		1-9	10-24	25-49	50-99	100+		
All single-plant independents:								
Employment in 1978	No.	716	420	184	89	36	1445	
	%	(50)	(29)	(13)	(6)	(2)	(100)	
Companies on financial data base:								
Employment in 1965	No.	111	110	59	32	16	328	9378
	%	(34)	(33)	(18)	(10)	(5)	(100)	
Employment in 1969	No.	112	107	49	29	18	315	9111
	%	(35)	(34)	(16)	(9)	(6)	(100)	
Employment in 1971	No.	109	133	62	32	12	348	9252
	%	(31)	(38)	(18)	(9)	(4)	(100)	
Employment in 1974	No.	143	156	78	30	12	419	10134
	%	(34)	(37)	(19)	(7)	(3)	(100)	
Employment in 1978	No.	206	165	85	37	13	506	11263
	%	(41)	(33)	(17)	(7)	(2)	(100)	
Employment in 1981	No.	171	103	55	28	11	368	8076
	%	(47)	(28)	(15)	(7)	(3)	(100)	

category. Companies with more than 50 employees included in the financial data base appear to reflect the population accurately. By 1981, however, 47 per cent of the companies included had less than ten workers.

The overall employment size distribution of companies accords with our expectations since it contains rather fewer very small businesses which are less likely to reap the financial benefits of incorporation. Table 2.3 also provides an interesting insight into the performance of this group of companies in creating jobs. It shows that the total number of companies on the financial data base with more than 100 employees in 1965 was 16. They provided 5 per cent of the total of 9378 jobs. By 1978 only 13 companies had more than 100 employees, with this constituting 2 per cent of the total number of companies in the data base employing workers in that year, and by 1981 this had fallen to 11 companies. Furthermore although the total number of companies employing workers rose from 328 in 1965 to 506 in 1978, total employment in the sector rose only to 11263 in 1978 and fell back to 8076 in 1981. Indeed the striking feature of the final column of the table is that total employment in the sector shows very little increase over the period until 1978 at a time when new firms were being formed, with this being followed by a major decline in the following three-year period.

The age of companies

A number of businesses trade either as sole proprietorships or partnerships before they obtain corporate status, so that in these cases the incorporation date is an imperfect guide to the date at which the business started. Amongst the companies included in the data base, for example, two were incorporated in 1979, even though they are known to have employed workers in 1978.

Broadly speaking, however, the date of incorporation is a satisfactory guide to the age of business, and the spectrum of ages of companies in the financial data base is shown in Figure 2.1. The histogram shows the number of Northern company incorporations in that year surviving to be included in the data base. Unfortunately regional data on company incorporations do not exist, but James Foreman-Peck (1985) has kindly provided us with UK incorporation data for the inter-war years for

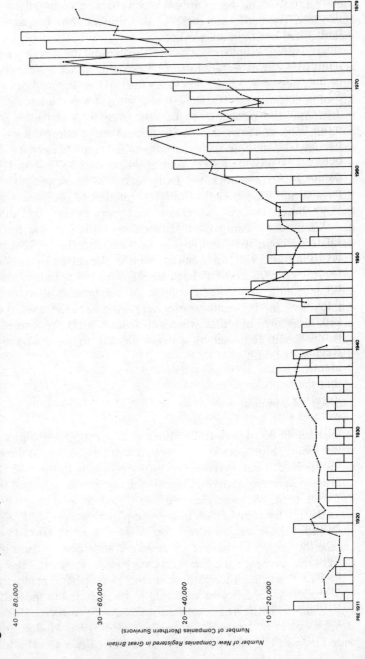

Figure 2.1: Incorporation years for Northern single-plant independent manufacturing companies

all sectors and post-war data is published. National data is shown in Figure 2.1 as a dotted line. It will be recalled from the discussions of the sampling frame that the companies in the data base are those which satisfied the conditions that they were single-plant Northern Region independent manufacturing companies trading at some stage between 1965 and 1978. Bearing in mind this sampling 'bias' it is somewhat surprising that only 52 per cent of companies were incorporated after 1965. In fact 7 per cent of the stock were incorporated before 1930, i.e. were more than 40 years old, 13 per cent were incorporated before the Second World War and 25 per cent were incorporated before 1950. Hence whilst approximately one-third of all companies in the data set are 'new' in the sense of being incorporated during the 1970s, a further quarter are at least twenty years old.

Figure 2.1 also offers interesting time series observations. First, it shows that amongst the early peak years for company incorporations are 1919 and 1946 when soldiers were returning from the World Wars and establishing businesses. This is clear for both Northern Region 'survivors' and for the UK national data. Indeed it is remarkable that more than 60 years later, 1919 can be identified as being an 'exceptional' year in this context. It is noteworthy that, after 1919, the next peak year for Northern Region surviving incorporations is 1937 with this being almost identical to the 1936 peak for the UK data. This might suggest that the depression years of the 1920s and much of the 1930s were not great incubators of Northern Region businesses that were to survive for a long period, but it must be recalled that only businesses which were single-plant independents throughout the 1970s are included. Hence it could be that a number of businesses formed during the 1920s and 1930s had grown into group companies or had 'spawned' new plants by the 1970s and would therefore have been excluded from the analysis.

Nevertheless it is interesting that 1937, when the UK and the Northern Region economies were starting to pull out of recession, is a peak year for surviving incorporations. This is then followed by a slump in incorporations over the years followed by a substantial formation rate in 1946, after which incorporation numbers are fairly stable until 1960. Here again there is a strong similarity of pattern between Northern manufacturing survivors and all UK company incorporation data.

After 1960 Northern Region companies included within the

data base rise in most years until 1976. In part this is likely to reflect the actual number of incorporations in the Region and partly it reflects the fact that newly formed companies have not had enough time to die. The relatively few companies formed in the period 1977-79 is because only companies employing workers at some stage between 1965 and 1978 were included in the sample selection. Subsequently 1981 employment was added for these companies. It does not reflect a real reduction in formations in these years, but merely the normal lag between incorporation and appearing in the Employment Census. Nevertheless, as noted earlier, there are two companies which were not incorporated until 1979 but which were providing employment in 1978. These companies would have been trading in 1978 either as sole proprietorships or partnerships but indicated to Department of Employment a corporate status which at that stage had not been granted. With the exception of the years 1977-79 there is again a striking similarity of pattern between numbers of surviving Northern Region manufacturing companies and UK totals of all company incorporations.

THE FINANCIAL CHARACTERISTICS OF NORTHERN COMPANIES: COMPARISONS WITH OTHER DATA SOURCES

The Northern Region of England has a number of characteristics which appear to distinguish it from the remainder of England. It has experienced significantly higher rates of unemployment than any other English Region for more than 50 years and, partly as a consequence, has the lowest income per head of any English region. It has fewer businesses per head of population and conversely a high proportion of total employment is in large, externally-owned branch plants. Finally it has one of the lowest rates of new firm formation in the United Kingdom (Ganguly, 1985). For these reasons the Region is generally viewed (from outside) as lacking an 'enterprise culture' and it might be expected that the small businesses located in the Region would differ from those of the UK as a whole. This, in turn, might suggest that a detailed study of such businesses is only marginally relevant to the national policy towards smaller firms. It is likely that the performance of small businesses in the more prosperous areas of Britain is superior to that in the less prosperous area. It may also be true that variations in small company performance vary between urban and rural areas (Fothergill *et al.* 1984) but even this is challenged by Bayldon, Woods and Zafiris (1984) who are unable to identify significant differences in trading profit between otherwise similar firms in an inner city and a New Town context.

Lloyd and Mason (1985), in comparing businesses in (prosperous) South Hampshire and (less prosperous) Merseyside summarise the position well when they state that the contrasts between businesses in the two areas were not individually sharp, although there were broad regional differences.

This section will demonstrate that whilst the choice of companies only from the Northern Region of England may be a source of bias, it is difficult to quantify its importance vis-à-vis the UK small business sector as a whole. This is illustrated in the comparisons between the financial structure of the 636 Northern companies and the major sources of financial data on UK smaller companies. A comparison is undertaken of the size, profitability, growth and balance sheet structure of Northern companies with analyses of smaller companies from four other sources: Wilson Committee (1979), Business Monitor (MA3), ICFC (1983), and the unquoted companies examined by Hay and Morris (1984). Each of these studies or statistical tabulations was concerned with different aspects of smaller companies and so the selection of companies to be included in the analysis differed somewhat from that used in the current study. Nevertheless it is important to place the present work in the context of existing material on the small company.

General characteristics of financial studies of small companies

Table 2.4 shows the general characteristics of the major UK studies and sources of data on smaller unquoted companies. The Wilson Committee was established to review the functioning of the financial institutions and devoted considerable resources to an investigation of whether small firms were at a disadvantage in obtaining short or long-term financing. To assess whether there was any bias by the institutions against

23

Table 2.4: Characteristics of financial studies of small companies

Study Characteristics	Northern Region	Wilson Committee	MA 3	ICFC	Hay and Morris Large Sample	Hay and Morris Small Sample
Unquoted companies	Yes	Yes	Yes	Yes	Yes	Yes
Time period	1970-80	1972-1975	1977 to date	1970/71-1979/80	1970-75	1966-79
Source of data	Companies House	Companies House	Companies House	Accounts of Assisted Companies	Jordans 1000	Jordans 1000 and Companies House
Sample size	636	31	Approx 120	687	1018 in 1975	45
% of companies in manufacturing	100	100	not specified	65	35	80
Geographical coverage	Counties of Durham, Cleveland and Tyne & Wear	Great Britain	Great Britain	Great Britain	Great Britain	Great Britain
Size % of companies with capital employed in 1975 of	ICFC defin. / MA 3 defin.					
(a) Less than £100,000	85% / 84%	Not known	100%	21%	Zero	Zero
(b) Less than £250,000	95% / 94%	100%	100%	47%	Zero	Zero
Sample selection method	All single-plant independent manufacturing companies in the study area are included	Stratified random sampling based on MA 3 frame. Stratification based on capital employed in 1975	1:360 random sample of very small companies	All companies assisted by ICFC are included	All companies appearing in Jordans 1000 list of largest UK unquoted companies	From Jordans 1000, undiversified companies providing continuous financial data between 1966 and 1979
Other information		In total 296 unquoted companies were examined	National statistical data which includes non-manufacturing companies and a full survey of larger companies	Companies assisted by ICFC generally perform significantly better than the 'average' small companies		

smaller businesses, and if so whether it was 'justifiable', the Committee examined the Profit and Loss and Balance Sheets of 296 small manufacturing companies. Only 31 of these businesses could be regarded as small i.e. having a capital employed in 1975 of less than £250,000.

In 1982 the Business Monitor published the first results of a new analysis of the accounts of what it called 'a fully representative sample of companies'. The series, MA3, started with data for 1977 and contained an analysis of nearly 3000 companies. The sample was, however, highly stratified and based upon a sampling of 1:360 for the very small companies and a complete enumeration for the top 500 companies. For the purposes of MA3 data, company size was defined according to the capital employed (i.e. issued share capital and reserves, minority shareholders' interest, deferred taxation, long-term loans — including debentures and mortgages — plus bank loans and overdrafts, short-term loans and indebtedness to directors and group members, less amounts due from members). According to this criterion a small company was defined as having a capital employed of less than £100,000, a medium company as having a capital employed of between £100,000 and £4.16m and a large company as having a capital employed of more than £4.16m. All these figures were at 1975 prices.

MA3 data presents a balance sheet, income and appropriation account and sources and uses of funds statements for small manufacturing companies, thus facilitating a comparison with Northern Region data. In total MA3 estimates there are 44,298 small manufacturing companies and so, assuming a 1 : 360 sample has been taken this suggests a total of 123 companies were sampled in 1977.

The Industrial and Commercial Finance Corporation is a subsidiary of the 3i group which is owned by nine English and Scottish clearing banks and the Bank of England. ICFC has a distinguished record of successful investment in smaller businesses. Very broadly its portfolio of start-up businesses grow (at least in terms of employment) at a rate which is more than double that of the typical new firm (Storey, 1982, p. 146). ICFC also has a failure rate among its assisted businesses which is approximately half that which would be expected from a random sample of new businesses.

The main thrust of the study by Hay and Morris is to examine the differences between quoted and unquoted compan-

25

ies. In order that any differences are not attributable exclusively to size, and recognising that on balance quoted companies are significantly larger than unquoted companies, Hay and Morris examine the financial characteristics of only the largest unquoted companies. Since the early 1970s these have been compiled by the private data company, Jordans, who provide accounts on a standardised basis for the 1000 largest unquoted companies.

It should be clear that although all the above data sets and studies are of unquoted companies the purposes for which they were derived differ markedly. These differences are reflected in the study characteristics identified in Table 2.4. The table shows that the Hay and Morris small sample study covers the longest period, 1966-79, whereas the Wilson Committee data cover only three years, 1972-75. Whilst all studies, with the exception of ICFC, use Companies House information the sample sizes vary markedly. The Wilson Committee study includes only 296 companies compared with 636 in the current study and 687 in the ICFC study. However, when an examination is made of manufacturing companies the Wilson Committee included only 104 manufacturers, ICFC only 447 and the Hay and Morris large sample only 356, compared with the 636 in the current study.

In the current study the prime area of interest is small manufacturing companies. Here the numbers of such companies examined in other studies reduce further. If the definition of small used by the Wilson Committee is used (having a capital employed of less than £250,000 at 1975 prices) then only 31 companies in that category were examined by Wilson, when the results were published. *None* of the unquoted companies examined by Hay and Morris could be classified as small according to these definitions, whilst less than half (47 per cent) of ICFC companies were small. Unfortunately ICFC do not provide any significant disaggregation of their data to facilitate a distinction either between manufacturing and non-manufacturing or between small and medium sized.

In short the table shows that, with the exception of the 31 companies examined by the Wilson Committee, it is difficult to make exact comparisons between the financial characteristics of small manufacturing companies in Northern England included in the data base and the significantly larger businesses, many of which are not in manufacturing, which are included in the other studies outlined in the table. It certainly prevents any examination of the question of whether there is any specific regional influence upon the companies included in the analysis in the sense of having lower profitability or efficiency than otherwise similar companies located elsewhere in the UK.

Recognising these differences it is insightful to compare the sizes, profitabilities, growth and balance sheet structures of companies included in the Northern data set with the other studies. But bearing in mind the small size of the Northern businesses, it is worthwhile to begin by explicitly comparing the size structures of the companies in each of the studies.

The size of Northern Region companies

The companies included in the Northern data are significantly smaller than those examined in either studies or statistical material on unquoted companies. None of the companies included in the Northern data base is large enough to be included in the Jordans 1000. Hence the companies studied by Hay and Morris are markedly larger than those included in this study yet, on the basis of size, the current study is a more accurate reflection of the 'typical' unquoted companies since 85 per cent of all companies had a capital employed in 1975 of less than £100,000.

It is not only in comparison with the Hay and Morris study that the Northern companies studied are small. Table 2.5 shows that in 1975/76, 52.5 per cent of companies financed by ICFC had a capital employed in excess of £250,000 and only 21.2 per cent had a capital employed of less than £100,000. Using the ICFC definitions of capital employed (which includes bank overdrafts in current liabilities) Table 2.5 shows that these percentages are almost reversed, with more than 85 per cent of Northern Region companies having a capital employed of less than £100,000.

Neither the Wilson Committee nor MA3 data provide a detailed statement of the sizes of companies included in their sample, although we do know that the Wilson Committee regarded a small manufacturing company as having a capital employed of less than £250,000, whereas MA3 data on small manufacturing businesses include only companies with a capital employed (in 1975 prices) of less than £100,000. They also

Table 2.5: Size of companies: capital employed in 1975

Capital employed/ Net assets	ICFC definition in 1975	Wilson/MA3 definition in 1975	ICFC (1975/76)	Wilson (1975)	MA 3 (1975)
			Northern Region		
Less than £4,999	14.0	10.1			
£5,000-£14,999	24.6	22.3			
£15,000-£24,999	14.4	15.0	12.1		
£25,000-£49,999	17.9	19.2		100.0	100.0
£50,000-£99,999	14.2	16.7	9.1		
£100,000-£249,999	10.3	10.9	26.3		
£250,000+	4.6	5.8	52.5		0.0
Total	100.0	100.0	100.0	100.0	100.0

Note: Definitions of Capital Employed
Wilson Committee: Total capital and reserves and minority shareholders *plus* deferred tax *plus* bank loans and overdrafts, long-term and short-term loans *plus* net amount due to other group members.
MA 3: Shareholders' interest (issued share capital and reserves), minority shareholders' interest, deferred taxation, long-term loans (including debentures and mortgages) plus bank overdrafts and loans, short-term loans and indebtedness to directors and group members, less amounts from group members.
ICFC: Minority interests, long-term loans, loans from directors, HP and mortgages, deferred taxation, issued share capital and capital and revenue reserves.

distinguish, for sampling purposes, so-called 'very small' companies with a capital employed of less than £50,000. Using the MA3 definition of capital employed which is also that used by the Wilson Committee, Table 2.5 shows that 66.6 per cent of companies included in the Northern Region sample would be classified as very small.

Profitability

There are a number of possible different definitions of profitability but for most purposes in this book the definition that will be used is pre-tax profit, which will be normalised by total assets.

Since the companies included in the Northern data base are meant to be representative of smaller unquoted companies, it would be surprising if their profitability levels were as high as those of the companies selected for investment by ICFC or of those large unquoted companies examined by Hay and Morris.

ICFC present data on the profitability of 590 of their companies drawn from the manufacturing and non-manufacturing sectors over the period 1975/76 to 1978/79. In their tables they provide a profitability rate averaged over the four years, since there are marked year-to-year fluctuations in rates. The results are shown in Table 2.6 and are contrasted with the results of 373 Northern independent manufacturers over the same period. The upper half of the table shows that on average ICFC companies were nearly twice as profitable as those in the Northern sample, but much of this is due to the freak results of 1975/76 when massive losses for one Northern company resulted in an overall negative figure for the sample as a whole.

There was also a substantial difference in mean profitability rates in 1978/79 but for the two intermediate years the means did not differ markedly. The upper half of the table also illustrates that whilst there is some year-to-year variability in the mean profitability amongst ICFC financed companies the amplitude of the swings is nowhere near as great as that of the Northern Region companies. Two possible explanations for this are the differences in sample size and the different size of company included. It could be argued that since the ICFC sample is significantly larger, the performance, either bad or good, of an individual company, is unlikely to have such an impact as in the Northern sample. However the fact that 373 companies provided data in the Northern sample suggests that any differences are more likely to reflect 'real', rather than sampling bias effects.

This is demonstrated in both the lower half of Table 2.6 and the histogram shown in Figure 2.2. These show that differences in the means are due to the presence within the Northern Region sample of a much higher proportion of companies either making losses or making very low profits. Table 2.6 shows that for the lower quartile of Northern companies profitability was 4.9 per cent compared with 10.2 per cent for the ICFC companies. Alternatively Figure 2.2 shows that only 3.5 per cent of ICFC companies made losses over that period compared with 14 per cent of Northern companies.

It was postulated above that some of these differences between the ICFC and Northern companies could be due to differences in the average size of company. In Chapter 4 it will be shown that in the Northern sample, the larger companies were generally more profitable than the very smallest, but it

Table 2.6: Profitability of ICFC companies and Northern companies

Year	Mean profitability (%)	
	Northern (373 companies)	ICFC (590 companies)
1975/76	− 1.2	16.1
1976/77	11.8	15.4
1977/78	14.4	16.1
1978/79	4.0	15.9
Overall mean	8.5	15.9

Average of profitability ratio 1975/76 to 1978/79

	Northern	ICFC
Upper quartile	+17.8	+21.2
Median	+10.9	+15.3
Lower quartile	+ 4.9	+10.2

seems likely that the prime explanation for these differences is that ICFC is particularly good at avoiding investments in unprofitable companies. Of equal interest, both to ICFC and to those formulating small business policy, is that there were a substantial number of small manufacturing companies in Northern England which achieved a rate of return which would offer ICFC and other investors a satisfactory return on their investments. It suggests that, in principle, there are a number of potentially satisfactory investments for venture capitalists even in a supposedly unprosperous Region such as the North, and in the unfashionable manufacturing sector, although the risks are also high because of high failure rates.

There is, of course, a considerable gulf between observing relatively high rates of profitability amongst a group of firms and inferring that there are opportunities for institutions such as ICFC which specialise in relatively long term investment in smaller businesses. For example, some of the highly profitable companies may have no wish to grow since this presents problems of looking for new markets. In particular they may have no wish to grow by selling a share of the equity to an outside institution. Finally, since we are examining pre-tax profits, the directors may choose not to reinvest the profits but to use them to pay themselves relatively high dividends and so increase their own standard of living.

Figure 2.2: Distribution of profitability: ICFC and Northern manufacturing companies 1975/76 to 1978/79

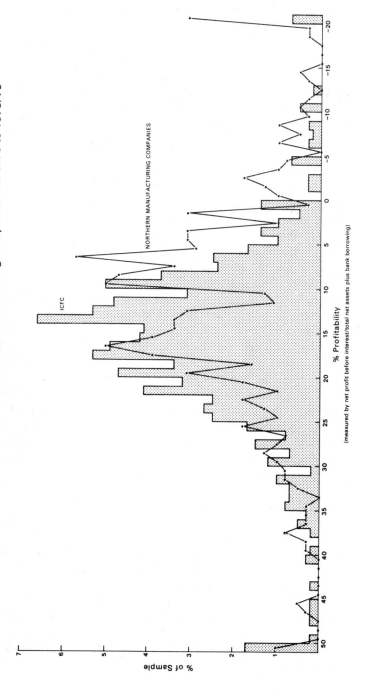

% of Sample

ICFC

NORTHERN MANUFACTURING COMPANIES

% Profitability

(measured by net profit before interest/total net assets plus bank borrowing)

Balance sheet structure

The balance sheet structure of Northern manufacturing companies included in the data base over the 1970-80 period can be compared with the other studies. Two broad questions are posed in this analysis. Firstly, are the balance sheet characteristics of Northern companies significantly different from those examined in other studies, and secondly have these characteristics changed significantly over the period 1970-80?

Table 2.7 compares the balance sheet structure for those Wilson Committee companies with a capital employed in 1975 of less than £250,000, with Northern Companies providing data for that year. All figures in the table are expressed as a percentage of total assets, and it is clear that the balance sheet structures of the two groups are strikingly similar. In both cases Fixed Assets constitute about 30 per cent of Total Assets, whilst the structures of current liabilities are also very similar. On the other hand whilst the Wilson Committee smaller manufacturing firms in 1975 were marginal receivers of trade credit (Creditors > Debtors) those in the Northern sample were marginal extenders (Debtors > Creditors). However the Committee also presented data on trade credit for their sampled firms for the 1972-75 period and this showed that in the years 1972-74 smaller manufacturing companies were net extenders of trade credit. The table also demonstrates that for both the Wilson Committee and the Northern Region companies, Share Capital and Reserves plus Directors' Loan Account constitutes approximately 45 per cent of Net Assets. Perhaps the major difference is the greater importance of long-term loans amongst Northern Companies with this probably reflecting the greater importance of government loans and public financing in the Region.

To be satisfied that these similarities were real, rather than a freak observation for 1975, it would have been helpful if the Wilson Committee had also presented an aggregate balance sheet for small manufacturing companies for the years 1972-74. Unfortunately it published only selected items and a full balance sheet was presented only for *all* 296 small companies, i.e. including both companies in the service sector and those with a capital employed of between £250,000 and £4m in 1975. These inclusions have prevented the undertaking of valid comparison between the two samples for other years. Nevertheless it is clear that the balance sheet structure of small manufacturing

Table 2.7: Balance sheet analysis: comparison of Northern Region and Wilson Committee companies

	Cleveland, Durham and Tyne and Wear single-plant independent manufacturing companies	Wilson Committee small manufacturing companies
No. of companies	(382)	(31)
Fixed Assets:		
1. (a) Net Tangible Assets (i.e. NBV of land & buildings + NBV of plant & machinery + NBV of motor vehicles)	27.6	29.4
2. (b) Intangible Assets	0.3	0.4
Total Net Fixed Assets	(27.9)	(29.8)
Current Assets:		
3. (a) Stock & Work in Progress	24.6	21.5
4. (b) Debtors & Pre-payments & Other Current Assets	33.7	34.8
5. (c) Investments	3.6	3.5
6. (d) Cash & Bank Deposit Account	10.4	10.4
Total Current Assets	(72.1)	(70.2)
Total Assets	100.0	100.0
Current Liabilities		
7. (a) Short Term Loans and Bank Overdrafts	8.1	9.4
8. (b) Creditors and Accruals	32.0	35.7
9. (c) Other Current Liabilities	1.1	0.5
10. (d) Current Taxation	3.3	3.8
Total Current Liabilities	(44.5)	(49.4)
Net Assets financed by:		
11. (a) Share Capital & Reserves + Directors' Loan Account	45.0	43.4
12. (b) Deferred Taxation	6.8	6.1
13. (c) Long-term Loans (Hire Purchase & Mortgages + other loans + Govt. loans)	3.7	1.1
Net Assets	(55.5)	(50.6)

Notes: 1. All figures are percentages of total assets.

2. Wilson Committee sample (i.e. 31 companies) was taken from a population of approximately 0.25 million companies. Northern sample was taken from Northern single-plant independent manufacturing establishments with a population of approximately 2500.

3. (a) Companies selected by Wilson Committee include a few companies registered during the period 1973-1975 which did not provide accounts for the full period under study (i.e. 1973-1974-1975).

   (b) There were no companies in the Wilson Committee sample which were in operation during 1973 or 1974 but which had ceased to trade by 1975. The exclusion of these companies probably introduced some bias into the results for the earlier years because failed companies usually have lower retained profits and are more highly geared (see Chapters 6 and 7).

companies examined by the Wilson Committee is strikingly similar to those companies included in the Northern Region data base. It suggests that, since the Wilson Committee small manufacturing company is both national and yet the nearest in terms of company size to the Northern sample, the latter may be taken to reflect the financial structure of small UK manufacturing companies adequately and *not* simply those of the Northern Region of England alone.

Table 2.8 compares the aggregate balance sheet of companies financed by ICFC with that of Northern Region companies. In both groups of companies tangible fixed assets constitute 58 per cent of total net assets, although ICFC companies have considerably more intangible assets than Northern companies. Differences in the extent to which companies in the two samples rely on trade credit are also apparent from the table and in many respects are surprising. It can be seen that although Northern companies are substantially smaller than the ICFC funded companies their debtors exceed their creditors in 1978/79. On balance they are net extenders of trade credit by a substantial margin. For ICFC companies debtors exceed creditors only by 3.5 per cent of net assets, whereas for the Northern companies the comparable figure is 6.2 per cent. In fact in all years between 1970 and 1980 Northern companies included in the data set were net extenders of trade credit, as were the ICFC sample in 1978/79, yet the Wilson Committee companies were net recipients. Finally, as would be expected, the financing of net assets differs between the Northern companies and those financed by ICFC; in particular, long-term loans are of considerably greater importance amongst ICFC companies than among Northern Region companies. Accordingly a lower proportion is financed by share capital and reserves among ICFC customers (even though the profitability of ICFC customers is high), with the proportion financed through deferred taxation being broadly similar in both groups.

In Chapter 7 of their study of unquoted companies Hay and Morris (H/M) also conduct a detailed comparison of the financial characteristics of quoted and unquoted companies. They present some interesting time-series analyses of changes in the balance sheet structure of unquoted companies and of their profitability. They conclude that the two groups became increasingly similar over the period 1967-78. In particular they found for unquoted companies:

Table 2.8: Balance sheet analysis: comparison of Northern Region and ICFC financed companies in 1978/79

	Northern single-plant independent manufacturing companies	ICFC financed companies
No of companies	(382)	(590)
Fixed Assets:		
1. (a) Net tangible assets (i.e. NBV of land & buildings + NBV of plant & machinery + NBV of motor vehicles)	58.0	58.1
2. (b) Intangible assets	0.4	6.4
Total Net Fixed Assets	(58.4)	(64.5)
Current Assets:		
3. (a) Stock & work in progress	43.4	50.4
4. (b) Debtors & prepayments & other current assets	65.1	51.6
5. (c) Investments	2.0	0.3
6. (d) Cash & Bank Deposit Account	11.5	5.1
Total Current Assets	(122.0)	(107.4)
Total Assets		
Current Liabilities:		
7. (a) Short Term Loans & Bank Overdrafts	17.2	19.0
8. (b) Creditors and Accruals	58.9	48.1
9. (c) Other current liabilities	4.3	4.8
Total Current Liabilities:	(80.4)	(71.9)
Net Assets	100.0	100.0
Financed By:		
10. (a) Share Capital & Reserves + Directors Loan Account	76.3	68.9
11. (b) Deferred Taxation	16.1	16.3
12. (c) Long Term Loans (Hire Purchase & Mortgages + other loans + Gov. loans)	7.6	14.8
Net Assets	(100.0)	(100.0)

Note: All figures are percentages of Net Assets/Capital Employed.

(a) the ratio of issued equity to total long term funds had fallen (p. 191).

(b) the proportion which both debtors and creditors constituted of capital employed had also fallen (p. 198).

Figures 2.3 to 2.6 are constructed to test the H/M hypotheses.

35

Figure 2.3 is taken from Hay and Morris and Figure 2.4 plots the comparable Northern data. The Northern data set is insufficiently disaggregated to test hypothesis (a) fully, since it combines share capital with reserves. However, H/M note that reserves appear to consistitute a constant proportion of net assets and furthermore it is widely recognised that the distinction between the two is somewhat arbitrary. Hence the two are aggregated in Figure 2.4. H/M data show clearly that between 1970 and 1978 a major change took place in the financing of net assets among unquoted companies. Share capital and reserves which in 1970 constituted virtually 90 per cent of financing had fallen to 76 per cent in 1978. The Northern data set as illustrated in Figure 2.4 also identifies this change very clearly. These developments, however, reflect the increased relative importance of deferred taxation, due partly to the introduction of stock relief in 1974-75, compounded by the effects of high rates of inflation. Indeed the setting aside of deferred taxation balances, which are generally not paid over to the Inland Revenue, might reasonably be treated as equity and be included with share capital and reserves. Conversely the increasing importance of deferred taxation, noted by H/M is also a feature of companies in the Northern data base. Indeed by 1978, 16 per cent of net assets are financed by deferred taxation. Long term loans appear to constitute between 6 and 8 per cent of net assets throughout the period in both studies. It is our belief, however, that the composition of these loans is significantly different in the two data bases. For H/M companies it is more likely to include debentures whereas the importance of government loans in Northern companies has already been noted.

The second hypothesis presented by H/M is that the proportion which both debtors and creditors constitute of capital employed has declined for unquoted companies. Examination of Figure 2.5 shows that H/M found debtors constituted 92 per cent of capital employed in 1970 compared with only 55 per cent in 1978. Similarly, creditors constituted 107 per cent in 1970 and 68 per cent in 1978. No such trend is apparent from the data on debtors or creditors amongst companies in the Northern Region data base which is shown in Figure 2.6. Except for 1970 there is no evidence of a downward trend amongst debtors which constituted 58.5 per cent in 1971 and 61 per cent in 1978, having reached a high point of 63.6 per

Figure 2.3: Change in composition of sources of long-term funds for sample of unquoted companies 1968-78

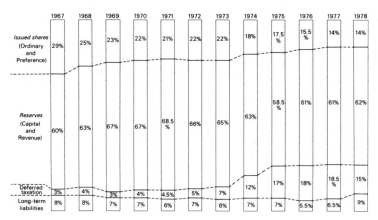

Source: Hay and Morris, *Unquoted Companies.*

Figure 2.4: Composition of long-term funds: Northern unquoted companies

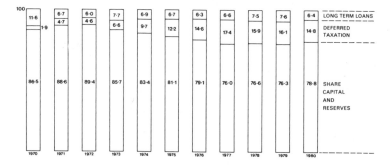

cent in 1974 and a low of 55.8 per cent in 1972. Indeed it appears that during the period 1975-77 H/M data correspond closely with the Northern data, with the creditors following a similar pattern to that of the debtors. H/M identify a downward trend which is not apparent amongst Northern companies after 1970, although the data for that year are significantly higher than for any subsequent year. No such trends occur in the time series analysis of the structure of Northern companies' balance sheets.

It is our belief that these differences between the unquoted companies examined by H/M and those included in the

Figure 2.5: Changes in composition of use of funds for sample of unquoted companies, 1967-78

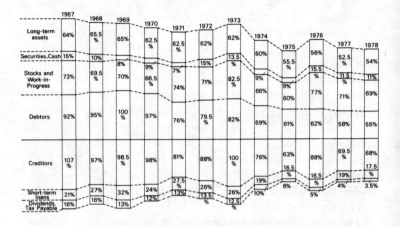

Note: All figures are percentages of capital employed. Total assets are shown above the line. Short-term liabilities are shown below the line. Total assets minus short-term liabilities may not equal 100 per cent due to rounding.

Source: Hay and Morris, *Unquoted Companies*, p. 196.

Figure 2.6: Balance sheet structure: Northern unquoted companies

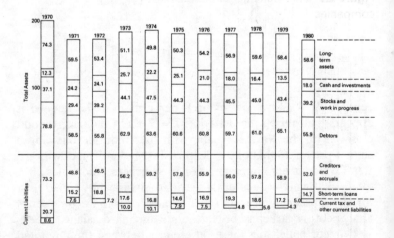

Note: All figures are per cent of capital employed.

Northern data base stem from the sampling technique by H/M. In order to obtain a satisfactory time series H/M initially selected 20 sectors, (ultimately reduced to 15) in which they identified three unquoted companies (all of which were amongst the largest 1000 unquoted companies) which provided continuous financial records to Companies House between 1966-79 *and* which operated exclusively within one sector i.e. they were not diversified but for unquoted companies were also very large. Twelve of the 15 sectors were in manufacturing. H/M note that their sampling procedure meant that the companies included were large, relative to the average size of unquoted companies. H/M, however, do not point out how exceptional these companies are. They do not make it clear that a company which both survives for 13 years *and* presents data to Companies House over that period is truly exceptional and, *in no way* can be regarded as being typical of unquoted companies.

The closest time series comparison of balance sheet structures which could be made between the H/M small sample and the Northern Region companies would be to examine only those Northern companies which not only survived for the whole of the period 1970-80 but which also submitted accounts to Companies House for each year. This is shown as Figure 2.7 and, again in contrast to the Hay & Morris studies, there is no clear time trend on any items in the balance sheet with the

Figure 2.7: Balance sheet structure: long-life Northern companies

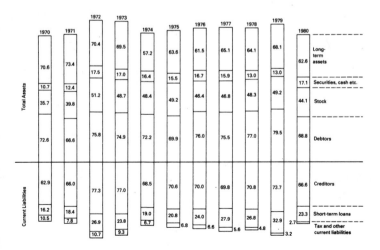

39

exception, because of legislative changes, of a relative decline in the proportion which tax and other current liabilities constitute of all current liabilities. Indeed the consistency of the various items over time is quite striking. This suggests that any differences in a time series analysis of the balance sheet structure of Northern companies, compared with that of H/M, is not due to differences in the age of the companies. It seems more likely that it is associated either with the size of the companies or with their growth rates, or both.

Summary

This section has shown that Northern companies included in this analysis are substantially smaller than the unquoted companies which have been the subject of study by Hay and Morris, ICFC or the Wilson Committee or those which are described as 'small' in the MA3 data.

It shows that the profitability of Northern companies was generally lower than that of either the Hay and Morris or the ICFC companies, but in Chapter 4 we will show that profitability in the Northern sample is positively related to size. Hence the smaller size of Northern companies 'explains' a proportion of these lower rates of profitability. It is likely, however, that real differences in profitability exist between Northern companies and those financed by ICFC, because of the latter's selection policies.

Finally the balance sheet structure of Northern companies is broadly similar to that of those selected in the Wilson Committee, but little support is provided for the changes over time in the equity/long-term loan ratio or the trade credit/capital employed ratios observed by Hay and Morris. Indeed the most striking feature of Northern company balance sheets is, at least until the end of the 1970s, the stability of the major components.

COMPANIES WHICH CEASED TO TRADE: FAILURES

This section outlines the problems of determining, from incomplete secondary information, the date at which small companies *effectively* ceased trading, i.e. the date at which they failed. It compares the results obtained with national data on UK company registrations and deregistrations. It is important to specify the date of 'failure' correctly since if the performance of failed firms deteriorates as failure approaches then, by implication, it is significantly more difficult to distinguish failed from non-failed firms five years, rather than one year, prior to failure. 'Correct' dating of failure is therefore of considerable importance.

National data comparisons

The document 'Companies in 1983' provides data on the stock of companies in the United Kingdom and of gains and losses to that stock for each year between 1970 and 1983. For 1983 Table 2.9 shows that a total of 43,023 companies were removed from the Register, of which 17,214 (40 per cent) were liquidations. Of all removed companies 11 per cent were compulsory and 29 per cent voluntary liquidations (9 per cent members' and 20 per cent creditors').

A very different picture is obtained when the Northern companies included in the financial data base are presented. Two-thirds of all 'failed' companies were liquidated, compared with only 40 per cent in the national sample. Furthermore a much higher proportion of all removals are creditors' voluntary liquidations (44 per cent compared with only 20 per cent nationally).

Several explanations may be advanced for these differences. Firstly it will be recalled that all the Northern companies were

Table 2.9: Companies ceasing to trade (removed from the Register)

	England and Wales 1983		Northern data set		Northern counties no accounts 1970-80	
	No.	%	No.	%	No.	%
Liquidations: all types	17214	(40)	117	(66)	27	(53)
Compulsory	4807	(11)	20	(11)	8	(16)
Voluntary:	12407	(29)	97	(55)	19	(38)
Members'	3808	(9)	19	(11)	3	(6)
Creditors'	8599	(20)	78	(44)	16	(31)
Dissolved	25809	(60)	60	(34)	24	(47)
Total removed from register	43023	(100)	177	(100)	51	(100)

Note: Figures in parenthesis show the percentage of the total removed from the register in each sub group. Totals may not sum up to 100 due to rounding.

either exclusively or primarily manufacturers. Manufacturing companies are more likely to have purchased fixed assets in order to operate their business. Businesses in the service sector may have less clear-cut tangible assets and self-employment may be a more appropriate vehicle for taxation purposes.

Secondly, and probably more importantly, it will be recalled that all the companies selected for investigation were known to have been actually trading at some stage between 1965 and 1978, in the sense of employing workers other than the director(s). They would also have to have been of sufficient size to have been included in the Annual Census of Employment, at least for one year. *In short we know that these companies were truly in business,* as opposed to companies which were created perhaps in anticipation of trading.

A third possibility is that Table 2.9 is identifying a Regional effect i.e. that the high proportion of creditors' voluntary liquidations is a reflection of poor management of businesses in the North compared with elsewhere in the UK. Since Regional data on company registrations or dissolutions are not provided it is impossible to reach a fully informed judgement on this matter, but the similarity of the balance sheet structures of Northern and the Wilson Committee companies suggests this is unlikely to be the major cause of the difference.

The final column of Table 2.9 shows that a further 51 Northern Region manufacturing companies were either liquidated or removed from the Register without ever having submitted any accounts to Companies House during the period 1970-80. They were therefore *not* included in the data base and were relatively short-lived companies with 60 per cent having a corporate life of five years or less. The table shows that such companies are significantly more likely to be dissolved than those included in the data base which ceased to trade. Thus of the short-lived companies not submitting any accounts between 1970-80, 47 per cent were dissolved, compared with 34 per cent of those included in the data base. Nevertheless even this is a substantially lower proportion than that for UK companies in aggregate.

It seems likely that the prime reason for the low proportion of liquidations in the total number of companies ceasing to trade (removed from the Register) in the national data is the large numbers struck off under Section 353 of the Companies Act 1948. If the Northern experience is typical then many were never, in fact, genuinely operating businesses. Whilst such businesses may have had corporate status they rarely exercised it to the extent of trading, or at least employing a sufficient number of workers in order to appear in employment statistics. It should, however, be noted that some companies may have traded on a very modest scale since not *all* establishments are included in the Employment Data Base, but it is most unlikely that a company of significant size would have been consistently omitted and such ommissions are unlikely to be of significance in aggregate. If the Northern Region, in this context, is not significantly different from England and Wales as a whole and ignoring any differences between manufacturing or non-manufacturing businesses, it suggests that perhaps up to 20,000 businesses removed from the National Company Register never in fact traded at all or never traded at any significant level.

Information on failure

The existing failure prediction literature (Steele, 1984), because it has dealt almost exclusively with large quoted companies, has not needed to address the problems of identifying the date at which a company ceased trading. With smaller companies and using only secondary publicly available information that date can be very unclear, yet if a failure prediction model is to be effective then correctly classifying the date at which the business failed is most important.

The definition of a failed company in this context is one that has ceased to trade. Such a company will either have been struck off the Register at Companies House or will be removed at some stage in the future if its circumstances remain the same. In fact only about 10 per cent of companies in the data set have been formally dissolved.

The sources of information used in determining either whether a small company has ceased trading (failed) and, if so, the selection of the most appropriate year, are the microfiche Companies House records, the Employment Data Base, the telephone directories and contact with the company's accountants. The choice of a suitable year to represent the date at which the company ceased to trade, however, requires some judgement to be exercised by the researchers since none of the above sources of information is definitive.

Dating the closure of small companies

Armed with information from the sources above it became clear that whilst in some cases apparent closure dates from each source were compatible with each other, in other cases the dates conflicted. To overcome this problem a number of decision rules were devised and these are shown in Table 2.10 together with the number of cases to which they referred.

The decision rules outlined in Table 2.10 stem from a belief that the telephone directory is, subject to the qualifications outlined in Storey and Wynarczyk (1985), the best indication of whether or not a business has ceased to trade. In decision rule 1, where the appointment of the liquidator or the date of a court hearing for a compulsory wind-up coincides with the final date at which the company appears in the telephone directory, then the liquidator/court appearance year is chosen as the closure date. In no case does this conflict with the final year in which either financial or employment data are provided.

It has been established that it takes Companies House several years before companies which cease to trade are struck off. Such companies were those which had ceased to provide recent financial or employment data and which had disappeared from the telephone directory but where no dissolution date was provided. Nevertheless our enquiries led us to the belief that these companies had ceased to trade and, in time, would be struck off the Register. For these cases covered in decision rule 3 the year of failure was taken to be the most recent year in which either financial or employment data were provided, or the last year in which the company appeared in the telephone directory.

It was also noted above that several companies effectively cease to trade for some time before they are compulsorily or voluntarily wound-up. In some cases the directors, recognising the company is insolvent, realise that further trading would be illegal. There therefore remains a gap in time between ceasing to trade and the decision to wind-up. In these cases the firm ceases to provide financial or employment data and disappears from the telephone directory. Where this gap is more than one year we have assumed that the company has *not* traded in that time and that the last year in which it provided either financial or employment data, or the last year in which it appeared in the telephone directory was a *better* indication of the year of

Table 2.10: Decision rules on classifying date at which a company ceases to trade

	Not Liquidated	No. of Cases Liquidated		Compulsory
		Voluntary		
		Members'	Creditors'	
1. Closure year in telephone directory compatible with date of appointment of Liquidators or date of compulsory wind-up.	0	14	72	13
2. Accounts state company is ceasing to trade. This is compatible with telephone directory.	9	0	0	0
3. Dissolved companies with no liquidation date. Here the most recent date for the provision of financial or employment data or appearance in telephone directory is used.	26	0	0	0
4. Companies wound-up compulsorily but where Court date is more than one year after last appearance in telephone directory, or last financial or employment data. Here the most recent date is chosen *not* the date of Court appearance.	0	0	0	7
5. Companies wound-up voluntarily but where appointment of Liquidator is more than one year after last appearance in telephone directory, employment data or financial data. Hence the last date is chosen i.e. *not* appointment of Liquidator.	0	5	6	0
6. Companies which have disappeared from telephone directory and provide no recent financial or employment data but where there is no dissolution date or appointment of Liquidator. Here last date is chosen.	20			
7. Contact with accountants confirmed that the company had ceased trading.	5	0	0	0
Total	60	19	78	20

failure than the date of a decision to wind-up compulsorily or voluntarily. These cases are dealt with under decision rules 4 and 5 respectively.

The clearest case for dating a failure is where in the accounts of the company the directors state that because either of 'adverse trading conditions' or 'the death of one of our dear colleagues' that the company is to cease trading from this date. Unfortunately, as can be seen from Table 2.10 such unambiguous statements are infrequent, but these are covered in decision rule 2.

In other cases the company has not only disappeared out of the telephone directory but has also ceased to provide any employment or financial data. It has all the hallmarks of a failed company but without any evidence of an appointment of a liquidator or of its affairs being wound up. Where we believed that the resources of the business were probably insufficient to justify the appointment of a liquidator we have assumed the business failed at the time of either its last appearance in the telephone directory or the date at which it last supplied employment or financial information — decision rule 6.

Finally in a few cases we felt that the only possible way to confirm or deny our suspicions that the company had ceased trading was to speak to the company's accountants. These cases are covered in decision rule 7.

Time series description

In this final section data are presented both on the lifespan of the failed companies and the years in which they ceased to trade.

Table 2.11: Age of companies which ceased to trade

Age of Companies in Years	Numbers	% of Failures	Cumulative %
0 – 4.9	40	22.6	22.6
5 – 9.9	46	26.0	48.6
10 – 14.9	19	10.7	59.3
15 – 19.9	10	5.6	64.9
20 – 24.9	11	6.2	71.2
25 – 39.9	30	16.9	88.1
40+	21	11.9	100.0
Total	177	100.0	100.0

Table 2.12: Time series analysis of failed companies

Reason for failure	1972		1973		1974		1975		1976		1977		1978		1979		1980		1981		1982		1981	
	No.	%	No.	%	No.	%	No.	%	No.	%	No.	%	No.	%	No.	%	No.	%	No.	%	No.	%	No.	%
Compulsory Liquidation	—	—	—	—	—	—	2	29	4	31	4	20	3	13	3	18	3	9	—	—	—	—	1	20
Members' Voluntary	1	20	—	—	—	—	1	14	3	23	4	20	2	9	1	6	6	19	4	12	2	12	—	—
Creditors' Voluntary	1	20	1	50	2	50	2	29	4	31	6	30	9	39	5	31	16	50	20	61	9	51	4	80
Dissolved	3	60	1	50	2	50	2	29	2	15	6	30	9	39	7	44	7	22	12	36	6	35	—	—
Total	5	100	2	100	4	100	7	100	13	100	20	100	23	100	16	100	32	100	33	100	17	100	5	100

The table clearly demonstrates that the data base contained significantly more long-life failures than would a random selection of small business failures. For example Ganguly (1985) finds that half of companies which were registered for VAT and which failed after 1974 were less than two and a half years old. The comparison is imperfect because companies did not have to register before 1974 so that included in Ganguly's data were a substantial number of long-life companies. Nevertheless it is clear that from companies registered for VAT for the first time in 1978, for example, 42 per cent had failed to survive until 1982.

This emphasis upon relatively long-life companies in the Northern data set stems primarily from the selection procedure, since the company name was initially identified from employment records and then the company was required to have submitted at least one year's accounts to Companies House. It may also be due, to a lesser degree, to sectoral composition since the Ganguly results cover all sectors whereas the financial data base contains primarily manufacturing firms. Ganguly does provide data for what he terms the 'production' sector but this contains industries other than manufacturing.

Finally we provide in Table 2.12 a time series analysis of failed companies with a distinction being made between compulsory and voluntary liquidations and between these and dissolved companies. It shows that 103 of 177 failures identified on the data base occurred in or after 1979. In this sense they are a reflection of a period in which a Conservative government was elected to office and during which time there has been a substantial change in emphasis in macro-economic conditions and policies.

In short, the analysis emphasises the failure in the late 1970s and early 1980s primarily of manufacturing companies that had been in business for a number of years.

CONCLUSION

This chapter has described the procedures by which the financial records of single-plant independent manufacturing companies in Northern England have been processed and collected onto a single data base. These have been combined with existing records on employment in such enterprises.

The chapter has also described the characteristics of the companies in terms of their size, sector, age, balance sheet structure, profitability and growth. Finally it has analysed those companies which ceased to trade ('failed'). It has discussed the problems of identifying a date of failure and the different types of failure.

It is our view that several major studies purporting to be about small firms have yielded conclusions which reflect the nature of the study sample rather than the population of small businesses as a whole. To highlight, if not overcome, the problem of sample bias this chapter has described the derivation and characteristics of 636 companies which qualify, under almost any definition, as small businesses. In charting their financial performance over the period 1970-71 to 1980-81 we believe that, subject to certain caveats, they reflect more general trends within UK small manufacturing companies.

It would, however, be misleading not to re-emphasise the limitations of the sample since this will be used in all the remaining analyses. We believe that the sample contains an under-representation of short-life businesses, i.e. those where the period between incorporation date and ceasing to trade is three years or less. We also believe that there is an under-representation of rapid growth firms since only single plant independents are included, and it seems likely that many rapidly growing companies will expand either by acquiring or establishing new plants or enterprises and so also be excluded. The geographical concentration of our sample in Northern England may also give rise for concern but the similarity of the balance sheet structure of our companies and that of those of the Wilson Committee suggest this is not a key problem for generalising the results to elsewhere in the United Kingdom.

NOTES

1. The employment characteristics of the full population of establishments are examined in Storey (1985).

2. Note that only companies which employed workers in the period 1965-78 are included in the total of 4880 establishments and the 636 companies in the financial data base. However after the selection of companies had been made, employment data for 1981 became available and these were appended where appropriate.

3

The Small Company and Financial Reporting in Context

INTRODUCTION

Chapter 2 described the derivation of a sample of 636 single-plant independent manufacturing companies and the financial characteristics of those companies. It was found that the high failure rates unique to small companies created considerable data and analysis problems. In this chapter the non-financial information filed at Companies House by 146 of these companies is analysed to highlight other unique aspects of small companies which need to be taken into consideration when making an assessment of their past performance and future prospects. The chapter includes details of the economic, financial and legal constraints within which the small company operates. These environmental factors may explain many of the unique features characteristic of small companies such as high failure rates, lack of sustained growth and paucity of reliable data.

From this work it should become clear that the small company is far from being merely a scaled-down version of a large public quoted company. Rather, it is an entirely different creature with its own characteristic mode of organisation, financial structure and financial practices. Differences between the large and small company sectors are considerable and many of the observations and conclusions drawn from previous studies of large corporate enterprises are irrelevant or misleading. In order to interpret and evaluate the financial and employment performance of small businesses adequately, an understanding of their unique characteristics and the business milieu within which they operate is essential.

This chapter is organised into a number of sections. The next describes the sample and data to be used in the following sections, whilst the third examines the ownership and management structure of the small company. It includes analyses of the position of the small company within company law, the relationship between the membership (shareholders) and the directors and, finally, changes in the board of directors and the occupational backgrounds of directors.

The fourth section examines a number of issues relating to the preparation of the financial accounts. It begins with a discussion of the role of the auditor within company law. This provides the context for the following sub-sections on compliance with the disclosure requirements embodied within company law and the professional accounting standards. The major areas examined relate to the disclosure of the company's accounting policies, the incidence of audit qualifications and the time lag between the accounting year end and the submission of the accounts to Companies House. These issues necessarily involve an analysis of the small company auditor/client relationship. The section concludes with a discussion of this relationship and includes some empirical results concerning the independence of the auditor vis-à-vis the small company management.

The penultimate section presents an analysis of the major sources of long-term finance utilised by the small company sector. The relative importance of the issue of new share capital and/or secured loans as the primary sources of finance for the small company forms the basis of this section. Finally, there is a summary of the findings of this chapter and an indication of their importance for the remaining chapters of this volume.

THE SAMPLE AND DATA

This chapter analyses the financial returns and supporting documents filed at Companies House for 146 small manufacturing companies, all of which are included in the employment and financial data-base described in Chapter 2. The sample used in this analysis is a 'paired sample' in the sense that it consists of an equal number of randomly selected failed and non-failed companies. Whilst no attempt at matching companies by any other characteristic was attempted, the resulting sub-samples of failed and non-failed companies do not exhibit any statistically significant differences in respect of either age or industrial classification[1].

The empirical findings presented in this chapter give figures for both the full sample of 146 companies and for the two sub-samples of failed and non-failed companies. Whilst an analysis of the importance of small company failure is left to Part Two of the book, clear differences between the characteristics of failed and non-failed companies will be discussed here.

The purpose of drawing the sample and analysing the results in this way was twofold. First, the small company sector includes a large proportion of failing companies. Thus, given a study period of five years and a (not unrealistic) failure rate of 10 per cent per annum (Ganguly, 1982 1983), a researcher can expect 50 per cent of a random sample of small companies to fail within the period. Second, these 'qualitative' factors not only reflect important environmental features of small companies generally, but also, as demonstrated in Chapter 9, provide a number of important 'company-specific predictors' of small company failure.

The qualitative information for the 73 failed companies has been taken from the final three years of annual accounts available before failure. Table 3.1 analyses the dates of failure for the sample and shows that the first failure occurred in 1975 and the last in 1983. The table also shows that, in comparison to the full sample, the 73 failures are primarily those which took place in the late 1970s and early 1980s rather than in the earlier period. The numbers falling into each of the major categories of business failure are also shown in the table and the figures indicate that, in common with the complete data base, the largest group consists of creditors' voluntary liquidations. For the non-failed companies, the three consecutive years of data were randomly chosen from the Companies House documents covering the same period (from 1975 to 1983).

Table 3.1: Analysis of failure

Type of failure	Present Sample		Full Data Base	
	No.	%	No.	%
Court winding-up	12	16.4	20	11.0
Creditors' voluntary	39	53.4	78	44.0
Members' voluntary	5	6.8	19	11.0
Ceased trading/dissolved	17	23.3	60	34.0
Total	73	100.0	177	100.0

⊞ Failed companies in full data set
■ Failed companies in qualitative data set

THE OWNERSHIP AND CONTROL OF SMALL COMPANIES

The legal framework

In unincorporated business enterprises such as sole traders and partnerships, each member has an inalienable right to participate in the management of the enterprise. In addition, each member also has a right to a share of any profits made, an unlimited share of any losses incurred and to a veto concerning the introduction of new members whatever the preferences of his fellow participants. Thus, the possibility of conflicts of interest arising due to separation of ownership from the day-to-day management of the enterprise is usually small and, if they do

53

occur, may be resolved simply by the dissolution of the association by the aggrieved member.

The major disadvantages of these unincorporated associations are those concerning the unlimited liability of each member and the lack of legal continuity of the business. Unlimited liability often restricts access to new capital and partners, so restricting the growth of some small businesses. Because the business is not recognised as an entity distinct from the owners themselves, it lacks legal continuity and so there is a legal requirement to renegotiate the terms of association after every change in membership, no matter how trivial.

The act of incorporation overcomes these problems to some degree[2]. The liability of members is limited to the amount of share capital invested. This considerably eases the problems of raising new capital for expansion by placing an upper limit on the possible loss incurred by any new investor. In contrast to the laws of bankruptcy, where almost all of the personal assets of the individual owners are deemed to be part of the trading assets of the enterprise in the event of business failure, creditors of a company can only seek repayment of debts from the assets of the company and not from the individual shareholders[3].

Upon incorporation the enterprise becomes a legal entity distinct from the shareholders whose investments created the company. This has two major consequences. Firstly, the continuity of the business is facilitated as ownership in the enterprise may be simply transferred by the sale of the members' shares without affecting the legal status of the entity in any way. Secondly, the ownership and the management of the enterprise become, in legal terms, separate and distinct activities. Unlike an unincorporated business, no shareholder has an automatic right to participate in the management of the company. The day-to-day control of the company is vested in the board of directors elected by the shareholders.

The precise terms of and periods in office for the directors are determined by the company's Articles of Association. However, UK company law allows the participants in business enterprises considerable flexibility in determining the basis of their association. As Hadon (1977) points out, with the exception of the principle of 'majority rule', which appears to be the one sacrosanct principle, participants may come to almost any contractual arrangments they wish to govern their internal relations. Major issues, such as the allocation of profits and risks and the power of control over the day-to-day running of the business, are thus capable of being settled in any number of ways in order to effect virtually any distribution of rights and liabilities amongst participants. In this respect, UK company law often allows the small business entrepreneur, upon incorporation, the flexibility more usually associated with sole traders and partnerships whilst seemingly granting the privilege of limited liability.

However, irrespective of the formal legalistic position, the questions which now need addressing are:

(a) to what extent do small incorporated businesses exhibit the classic separation of ownership from control typical of large corporate enterprises?

and,

(b) is it more correct to view the majority of small companies as merely sole traders and partnerships taking advantage of the benefits of company status?

The empirical results presented below attempt to address these questions.

Small company shareholders

Table 3.2 presents frequency distributions detailing the number of living shareholders for the 146 companies in the present sample[4]. As may be seen from the table, slightly over half of the companies had less than three members and only four companies (2.7 per cent) had ten or more members. The non-failed companies have a slightly larger number of shareholders than the failed companies. However, these differences are small as the median number of shareholders for the failed and non-failed companies are two and three respectively.

Given the small average number of part-owners it would seem that any separation of ownership from control is likely to be minimal. With such small numbers involved it would be comparatively easy (indeed probably essential) for all shareholders to take an active part in the management of the enterprise. This observation is generally confirmed by the figures shown in Table 3.3 which details the number of shareholders who are not also directors of the company. In over two-thirds of

Table 3.2: Number of shareholders per company

No. of shareholders	All companies		Non-failures		Failures	
	No.	%	No.	%	No.	%
≤2	74	50.7	36	49.3	38	52.1
3	26	17.8	9	12.3	17	23.3
4	19	13.0	12	16.4	7	9.6
5	9	6.2	5	6.8	4	5.5
6	4	2.7	2	2.7	2	2.7
7	6	4.1	3	4.1	3	4.1
8	2	1.4	1	1.4	1	1.4
9	2	1.4	1	1.4	1	1.4
≥10	4	2.7	4	5.5	0	0.0
Total	146	100.0	73	100.0	73	100.0
Total no. of shareholders	509		289		220	

Table 3.3: Number of shareholders who are not directors

No. of non-director shareholders	All companies		Non-failures		Failures	
	No.	%	No.	%	No.	%
0	100	68.5	50	68.5	50	68.5
1	22	15.1	12	16.4	10	13.7
2	8	5.5	3	4.1	5	6.8
3	3	2.1	1	1.4	2	2.7
4	3	2.1	1	1.4	2	2.7
5	4	2.7	1	1.4	3	4.1
6	2	1.4	2	2.7	0	0.0
7	2	1.4	1	1.4	1	1.4
≥8	2	1.4	2	2.7	0	0.0
Total	146	100.0	73	100.0	73	100.0
Total no. of non-director shareholders	No.	%	No.	%	No.	%
	141	27.7	85	29.4	56	25.5

all companies there are no non-director shareholders. A further twenty-two companies (15.1 per cent) have only one non-director shareholder and an analysis of these companies revealed that the majority of these shareholders consisted of the spouses of other members/directors. In total, out of the 509 shareholders for the full sample of companies only 141 (27.7 per cent) were not also directors. The comparable splits between non-failed and failed companies were 29.4 and 25.5 per cent respectively. The differences between the non-failed and failed companies are almost totally due to two non-failed companies which between them accounted for 36 non-director shareholders.

The directors of small companies

Table 3.4 presents the frequency distributions detailing the sizes of the boards of directors and the total number of directors involved. These figures are virtually identical to those shown in Table 3.2 showing the size of membership. For the whole sample, both the mode and median number of directors is two per company. Again, the non-failed companies tend to have a slightly larger board of directors than failures. Some 85 per cent of all failed companies had three or fewer directors as against only 73 per cent of non-failed companies. However, only 9 non-failed companies (12.3 per cent) have 5 or more directors and the most common figure (the mode) is still only two directors (43.8 per cent).

Of the 69 companies which have only two directors, 37 or one-quarter of the total sample, were controlled by a 'husband and wife' team (20 of which were non-failed and 17 failed companies). Of the remainder of companies with only two directors, the vast majority consisted of two males (frequently either brothers, father and son, or men with similar craft-based skills) with equal shareholdings in the enterprise. This suggests that, whatever the corporate legal form suggests to the contrary, for these companies the basis of association may be more accurately characterised as essentially a partnership.

Table 3.4: Number of directors per company

No. of directors	All companies		Non-failures		Failures	
	No.	%	No.	%	No.	%
1	5	3.4	1	1.4	4	5.5
2	69	47.3	32	43.8	37	50.7
3	42	28.8	21	28.8	21	28.8
4	17	11.6	10	13.7	7	9.6
5	6	4.1	2	2.7	4	5.5
6	5	3.4	5	6.8	0	0.0
7	2	1.4	2	2.7	0	0.0
Total	146	100.0	73	100.0	73	100.0
Total No. of directors	411		222		189	

The extent of family connections and non-member directors

Table 3.5 presents the estimated number of family connections on the board of directors. These results were obtained by an analysis of directors' names and addresses in order to determine the extent to which small companies are controlled by members of the same family. Whilst these estimates are likely to under-state the actual number of family connections[5] they show clearly that more than two-thirds of all companies have at least two members of the same family on the board of directors. In addi-tion, of the total of 411 directors some 232 or 57 per cent have at least one other member of their immediate family on the board of directors.

The Articles of Association of many large quoted companies often specify that directors must also be shareholders of the company. This, however, may not be the case for the small company sector where the founder(s) and immediate family may wish to retain 100 per cent ownership of 'their' company. Table 3.6 gives the number of directors without shareholdings in the company. All but 43 of the 411 directors (10.5 per cent) have some form of shareholding in the company they manage and for 79.5 per cent of all companies every director has some equity interest in the company. Of the 30 companies which do have one or more directors without an equity interest in the company, two-thirds have only one such director. Further analysis of these 20 non-shareholder directors indicated that 12 (60 per cent) of these were the wives of the principal share-holder/director and, furthermore, generally occupied the posi-tion of company secretary. No company had any identifiable representative of loan or other creditors sitting on the board of directors and the few remaining non-shareholder directors appeared to consist solely of other employees (i.e. production manager, foreman, etc.).

Changes in the management

The above results suggest that the overwhelming majority of small companies draw their executive directors from the founders and their immediate families and there is litle evidence to suggest that 'outsiders' with specific management skills are either common or even encouraged. From this, one might

Table 3.5: Family ties on the Board of Directors

No. of family ties per company	All companies No.	%	Non-failures No.	%	Failures No.	%
0	47	32.9	20	27.4	27	37.0
2	76	51.4	37	50.7	39	53.5
3	14	9.6	8	11.0	6	8.2
4	8	5.5	7	9.6	1	1.4
5	0	0.0	0	0.0	0	0.0
6	1	0.7	1	1.4	0	0.0
Total	146	100.0	73	100.0	73	100.0
Total no. of family ties as a % of all directors	No. 232	% 56.4	No. 132	% 59.5	No. 100	% 52.9

Table 3.6: Number of companies with non-shareholder directors

No. of non-shareholder directors per company	All companies No.	%	Non-failures No.	%	Failures No.	%
0	116	79.5	61	83.6	55	75.3
1	20	13.7	7	9.6	13	17.8
2	8	5.5	4	5.5	4	5.5
3	1	0.7	1	1.4	0	0.0
4	1	0.7	0	0.0	1	1.4
Total	146	100.0	73	100.0	73	100.0
Total no. of non-shareholder directors as a % of all directors	No. 43	% 10.5	No. 18	% 8.1	No. 25	% 13.2

expect the composition of the boards of directors of small companies to be stable over time with very few changes in personnel apart from inevitable generation movements — i.e. the occasional introduction of an offspring and the death or retirement of older family members.

This observation is confirmed when an analysis of changes in the personnel of the directors is made. All the changes in the personnel of the board of directors for each company over the three-year period examined are shown in Table 3.7. These results indicate that over 80 per cent of the full sample of companies experienced no change in directors over the three year period. Twenty-one companies involving 29 individuals had a director leave, whilst 16 companies with 23 individuals involved elected a new director to the board. However, the

Table 3.7: Changes in directors

	All companies		Non-failures		Failures	
	No.	%	No.	%	No.	%
No. of companies with no changes in directors	117	80.1	61	83.6	56	76.7
No. of companies with directors leaving the company	21	14.4	9	12.3	12	16.4
No. of directors involved	29	7.6	11	5.0	18	9.5
No. of companies with new directors	16	11.0	7	9.6	9	12.3
No. of directors involved	23	5.6	12	5.4	11	5.8
Net change in directors	−6		+1		−7	

overall figures hide possibly significant differences between the non-failed and failed companies. Only twelve of the non-failed companies had any changes in personnel over the three year period examined (16.4 per cent), the net change (new directors less the number of directors leaving) was only +1 and the number of directors involved was only 10.4 per cent of all directors of non-failed companies. The comparative figures for the failed companies were as follows: 17 companies experienced some change in the composition of their board of directors (23.3 per cent); this amounted to a net change of −7 and involved some 15.3 per cent of all directors of failed companies.

It would appear from the above that whereas the management of the small company sector as a whole is remarkably stable, a somewhat larger minority of the failed companies experienced some form of change (particularly an outflow) in the managerial personnel in the years leading up to failure.

The occupational backgrounds of directors

As we have seen, the management of the typical small company is usually in the hands of the founder(s) and their immediate families. The question which now arises is how so small a board of directors can possibly possess the portfolio of managerial skills necessary to run a successful business. An examination of the occupational backgrounds and other directorships held by the directors is obviously the first step in attempting to answer this question. Table 3.8 presents an analysis of the occupational backgrounds of the 411 directors for the 146 companies covered by this study, the analysis being based on information supplied to Companies House by the directors themselves.

From the information obtained from the Companies House documents, four broad occupational groupings were identified. These are shown in Table 3.8. One striking feature is that only 8 or 1.9 per cent of directors claim to have any form of accounting or financial background.[6] However, this is likely to be an under-estimate of the actual numbers with financial training since others may be included in the 'Director' group. The occupational group labelled 'other' mainly consists of the spouses of the principal shareholder/director (except when they indicated that they fell into one of the remaining categories).

Table 3.8: Occupational backgrounds of directors and other directorships held

	All companies		Non-failures		Failures	
	No.	%	No.	%	No.	%
No. of companies with one or more technical/craft directors	107	73.3	60	82.2	47	64.4
No. of directors involved	196	47.7	113	50.9	83	43.9
No. of other directorships	48	33.6	18	29.0	30	37.0
No. of companies with one or more professional directors	57	39.0	25	34.2	32	43.8
No. of directors involved	109	26.5	45	20.3	64	33.9
No. of other directorships	79	55.2	36	58.1	43	53.1
No. of companies with one or more accounting/finance directors	7	4.8	3	4.1	4	5.5
No. of directors involved	8	1.9	3	1.4	5	2.6
No. of other directorships	16	11.2	8	12.9	8	9.9
No. of companies with one or more 'other' directors	72	49.3	44	60.3	28	38.4
No. of directors involved	98	23.8	61	27.5	37	19.6
No. of other directorships	0	0.0	0	0.0	0	0.0
Total no. of directors	411		222		189	
Total no. of other directorships	143		62		81	

Table 3.8 shows that slightly over one-quarter of all directors (109 individuals) simply describe themselves as 'Directors'. This form of self-assessment adds nothing to what was already known about these individuals, i.e. that they are directors, and is of little use in aiding our understanding of the occupational skills and business experience of small-company management. However, three points are worth mentioning concerning this group. Firstly, whilst these 109 individuals comprise only 26.5 per cent of the total number of directors, between them they account for 55 per cent of all posts on the boards of other companies held by the total sample of 411 directors. This would seem to indicate that some of these directors are not solely dependent for their livelihood upon the fortunes of the one small company actually studied, i.e. they have a portfolio of investments in several small companies and are perhaps more experienced in business mangement than the other groups of directors. Secondly, this group tends to be concentrated in a relatively small number of companies as only 57 companies (39 per cent) have one or more such members on the board. Finally, this professional director group appears to be associated with failed companies to a far greater extent than any of the other occupational groups. A greater proportion of the directors of failed than of non-failed companies are professional directors (33.9 and 20.3 per cent respectively). Furthermore, a greater proportion of failed than of non-failed companies have at least one such director (43.8 and 34.2 per cent respectively).

The largest occupational group of directors, almost half of all directors, is the 'technical/manufacturing' group which consists of those individuals who described their present/former occupation in a way which indicated that they possessed some relevant practical-based technical/craft skills.[7] Nearly three-quarters of all companies have at least one such director and 58.2 per cent (85 companies) of all companies had either solely technical/craft based directors or these directors and spouses.

Slightly over half of all directors of non-failed companies possessed technical/craft based skills and 82.2 per cent of these companies have at least one such director. The comparative figures for the failed companies are 43.9 per cent of all directors and 64.4 per cent of companies. For the overall sample, relatively few of these directors have other directorships, a mere 48 other directorships spread amongst 196 directors. However, the difference in this respect between failed and non-failed companies is marked and shows the same asymmetry evident in the professional director group. For the non-failed companies, less than one director in six has any other directorships whilst for the failed companies the comparative figure is slightly over one director in three.

One possible explanation for the large number of other directorships held by directors of failed companies could be that these directors in some way lack commitment to the company. In this respect, some company failures may be no more than a reflection of these 'diversified' directors restructuring their corporate 'portfolios'. Thus, for a minority of the failed companies, failure may be analogous to a large company's divestment of a loss-making plant or subsidiary. However, in Chapter 5 we shall demonstrate that high-growth companies are also characterised by directors with an equity interest in other companies.

THE PRODUCTION OF THE FINANCIAL STATEMENTS

The auditor and company law

Both limited liability and the possibility of a divergence of interests between shareholders and directors are generally seen to be open to potential abuse. The history of the moral hazards associated with the privilege of limited liability have been well documented by Hadon (1977) and the unscrupulous have not been slow to recognise this potential, as instances of such abuse have been detailed as long ago as the very first limited companies.

The accounting profession has traditionally referred to the responsibility of possible abuse of limited liability imposed upon shareholders, directors and management, by the generic term 'stewardship'. Owing to the growth of a separation of ownership from day-to-day management control in many large enterprises, the idea that stewardship should also incorporate some assessment of how well the company has been managed has become generally accepted in the business world.

The initial solution to the problems associated with possible abuse of stewardship was achieved by individual contractual arrangements between shareholders and management. The more successful of these early private arrangements soon became custom and practice within business and many were eventually enshrined in company law (Watts and Zimmerman, 1983). Thus, since the middle of the last century, a framework of company law regulations designed to make companies and their managements accountable both to their shareholders and to society has been developed.

The major feature of these regulations, and one progressively extended in a succession of Companies Acts since 1844, is that each company should prepare a set of annual financial accounts which have been audited by a professionally qualified firm of accountants elected by the shareholders at the company's annual general meeting (AGM). The auditor has an overriding obligation to report to the members of the company whether, in his opinion, the accounts comply with the provisions of the Companies Acts and whether they present 'a true and fair view of the financial position of the company'. The role of the auditor is thus to provide an independent verification of the accuracy of the figures shown in the accounts. The audited financial statements are then issued to each individual share-holder prior to the AGM and a further copy has to be deposited with the Registrar of Companies within nine months of the accounting year end. This copy is then made available for public inspection.

A clear legal definition of a 'true and fair view' has proved difficult to achieve and so the law courts have generally left this to the accountancy profession itself to decide. Thus, the major UK professional accountancy bodies now issue 'statements of standard accounting practices' (SSAPs) which are authoritative rulings on which practices are deemed to be true and fair. Therefore, if an auditor is unsure whether an accounting practice is true and fair he must consult, firstly, the relevant accounting standard issued by the professional accounting bodies and secondly, the generally accepted accounting practices of the profession. Thus, the notion of a 'true and fair view' has been interpreted to mean that accounts should be drawn up in conformity with generally accepted accounting principles and practices.

Financial reporting submission lags

The Companies Acts require companies to submit their audited financial accounts to the Registrar of Companies within nine months of their accounting year end. This requirement is supposed to enable anyone with an interest in the financial performance of the company to obtain this information on a timely basis. Financial information that relates to past performances seems likely to be progressively less useful for most purposes as time passes. The timeliness and usefulness of small company financial accounts will tend to be highly correlated in the eyes of the majority of account users such as loan creditors, customers and suppliers.

Figure 3.1 presents the 3-year average reporting lag distribution (in months) between the accounting year end and the date on which the accounts were received by Companies House for the full sample of 146 companies. The distribution is heavily skewed to the right with a pronounced 'bunching' around the legal limit of nine months for the submission of the accounts. A small minority of companies (six cases) took on average more than two-and-a-half years to submit their accounts. The median submission lag is 9.5 months which indicates that over the three year period, on average, less than 50 per cent of the present sample of companies complied with the Companies Act regulations concerning the submission of their financial statements.

The separate distributions of failed and non-failed companies, whilst being skewed to the right, are far less skewed than the distribution of the full sample. The major reason for this is differences between the reporting behaviours of the two sub-samples. The average submission lag for the failed companies is 14 months with an average spread (as measured by the standard deviation) of 8.3 months. This contrasts strongly with the results obtained for the non-failed companies which indicate that these companies have both a smaller mean reporting lag (9.3 months) and a smaller spread (5.9 months). Both the mean and variance of the reporting lags between failed and non-failed companies are large and statistically significant from one another at 99 per cent confidence levels. This would tend to suggest that financial information on many companies experiencing financial difficulties is likely to be considerably out-of-date by the time it finally reaches the public realm.

Figure 3.1: Reporting lag distribution

Section 1: Full sample, three-year average submission lag

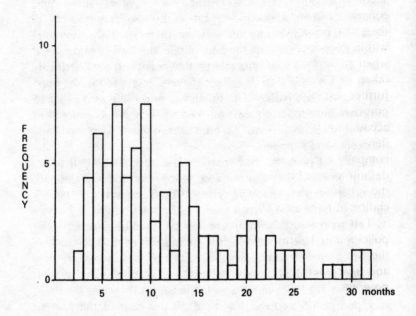

Section 2: Three-year average submission lag, summary statistics

	All companies		Non-failures		Failures	
	x̄	σ	x̄	σ	x̄	σ
	11.8	7.6	9.3	5.9	14.0	8.3
Median lag —	9.5		7.8		12.7	

*t-value — 3.67   Sig.> .001

*Separate variance estimate

Accounting policies

The UK Companies Acts (1948 to 1981) require that all companies keep proper books of accounts in respect of sales, purchases, assets, liabilities and monies received and expended. These books must present a 'true and fair view of the state of the company's affairs' and explain its transactions adequately. In 1971 the Accounting Standards Committee (ASC) issued the 'Statement of Standard Accounting Practice Number Two'

(SSAP2) which requires the disclosure of the accounting policies actually adopted by the company. These policies must be justified in terms of generally accepted, or 'fundamental accounting concepts'. SSAP2 lists four such concepts: going concern, accruals, consistency and prudence. A discussion of these concepts, the usefulness of the resulting information within the historic cost framework and the problems this creates when attempting to make inter-company comparisons is undertaken in Chapter 9. The concept of a 'going concern' will be further examined in the following subsection. For present purposes, however, we are primarily interested in the actual accounting policies adopted by small companies. The major items in the published accounts which may materially affect a company's reported performance and which require some definite choice between various acceptable alternatives are: (a) the valuation of stocks and work-in-progress and (b) the depreciation of fixed assets.

Table 3.9 lists the number of companies and the accounting policies adopted in respect of the provision for depreciation for the two major classes of fixed assets (land and buildings, plant and machinery) and the valuation of stocks and work-in-progress. The most striking feature shown in the table is the

Table 3.9: Accounting policies for fixed assets and stock and work-in-progress

Land and Buildings	All companies		Non-failures		Failures	
	No.	%	No.	%	No.	%
Missing/not applicable	123	84.2	62	84.9	61	83.6
Straight line	21	14.4	10	13.7	11	15.1
Reducing balance	2	1.4	1	1.4	1	1.4

Plant and Machinery	All companies		Non-failures		Failures	
	No.	%	No.	%	No.	%
Missing	73	50.0	38	52.1	35	47.9
Straight line	21	14.4	11	15.1	10	13.7
Reducing balance	51	34.9	24	32.9	27	37.0
Other	1	0.7	0	0.0	1	1.4

Stocks & Work-in-progress	All companies		Non-failures		Failures	
	No.	%	No.	%	No.	%
Missing	44	30.1	22	30.1	22	30.1
Director's valuation	17	11.6	7	9.6	10	13.7
Lower of cost or NRV	84	57.5	43	58.9	41	56.2
Other	1	0.7	1	1.4	0	0.0

large proportion of missing values. Some 123 companies did not indicate their accounting policies in respect of land and buildings. One reason for this is that many of these companies may not have owned any land or buildings. However, this is extremely unlikely to be the case as far as plant and machinery is concerned where only 50 per cent of companies actually disclosed their accounting policies on the depreciation of plant and machinery. Much the same may be said in respect of the valuation of stocks where only 69.9 per cent of companies made the relevant disclosures. There are no apparent differences between failed and non-failed companies in either the propensity not to disclose their accounting policies or in the policies actually utilised.

One distinctive feature of small company financial reporting which may explain this lack of disclosure of accounting policies is that, unlike large quoted companies, the majority of small companies have their financial accounts audited by small firms of accountants. From the figures presented in Table 3.10, it appears that those companies which had their financial statements audited by large national/international firms of accountants had a far greater propensity to disclose their accounting policies than companies whose accounts had been audited by local firms of accountants.[8] For instance, only one company out of the 20 companies audited by the large firms of accountants did not disclose its accounting policies in respect of the depreciation of plant and machinery and only two of these 20 did not disclose

Table 3.10: Disclosure/non-disclosure of accounting policies by type of auditor

Plant and Machinery		Local auditors	Top 20 auditors	Total
Not disclosed	No.	72	1	73
	%	57.1	5.0	50.0
Disclosed	No.	54	19	73
	%	42.9	95.0	50.0
Total		126	20	146
Stocks and work-in-progress		Local auditors	Top 20 auditors	Total
Not disclosed	No.	42	2	44
	%	33.3	10.0	30.1
Disclosed	No.	84	18	102
	%	66.7	90.0	69.9
Total		126	20	146

their accounting policies for the valuation of stocks and work in progress. The figures for companies audited by local firms of accountants and which did not disclose their accounting policies for plant and machinery and stocks and work in progress are 57.1 per cent and 33.3 per cent respectively. Chi-squared values of 18.8 and 4.5 (with 1 degree of freedom) for plant and machinery and stocks and work-in-progress indicate that these differences are statistically significant at 99 per cent and 95 per cent levels of confidence respectively. It would appear that large firms of auditors are far more likely to prepare their clients' financial statements in conformity with the provisions laid down by the Companies Acts and the profession's own SSAPs than are local firms of accountants.

Returning to Table 3.9, the results for those companies which did provide the relevant information concerning their accounting policies for land and buildings indicate that all but two companies used the straight-line or equal instalment method and that approximately 30 per cent of disclosing companies depreciate their plant and machinery by this method. All but one of the remaining 70 per cent utilise the reducing balance method for depreciating their plant and machinery. The accounting policies in respect of stocks also provide little in the way of useful information by which to make meaningful inter-company comparisons. As may be seen from the table, 101 of the 102 companies that actually mention their accounting policies merely state that stocks are 'valued at the lower of cost or net realisable value' or, what amounts to the same thing, 'are shown at the directors' valuation'.

These general phrases obviously do not provide any useful information to an outside observer wishing to know how the company's stock valuation has been calculated. Neither do they reduce the scope of the directors' ability to manipulate the financial results of the company via an under- or over-valuation of the companies' investments in stocks and work-in-progress. As may be seen from section 2 of Table 3.11, 33 of the 51 audit qualifications received in the final year of accounts relate to either stock valuations or the lack of adequate information by which to verify the figures shown in the accounts.

In addition to the disclosure of the company's accounting policies, SSAP2 also requires that companies disclose any changes in their accounting policies from those followed in previous years. No company claimed to have altered any

Table 3.11: Audit qualifications

Section 1

	All companies		Non-failures		Failures	
No. of companies with audit qualifications to:	No.	%	No.	%	No.	%
Final year of accounts	34	23.3	12	16.4	22	30.1
Previous 2 years accounts	22	15.1	12	16.4	10	13.7

Section 2: Analysis of final year's audit qualifications

	All companies		Non-failures		Failures	
Nature of qualification	No.	%	No.	%	No.	%
Going concern	8	5.5	1	1.4	7	9.6
Stock valuation	11	7.5	3	4.1	8	11.0
Insufficient information to form an opinion	22	15.1	10	13.7	12	16.4
Lack of independent confirmation	5	3.4	1	1.4	4	5.5
Other	5	3.4	0	0.0	5	6.8

of its accounting policies over the three years covered by the survey. This result is hardly surprising given the lack of disclosure of actual accounting policies.

Audit qualifications

If the auditor doubts any of the figures presented in the accounts he must 'qualify' his report to the shareholders which accompanies the financial statements and state the nature of these doubts. The Auditing Standard on 'Qualifications in Audit Reports' (APG 1980) states that the auditor:

> should qualify his report by referring to all material matters about which he has reservations. All reasons for the qualification should be given, together with a quantification of its effect on the financial statements if this is both relevant and practicable . . .
> A qualified audit report should leave the reader in no doubt as to its meaning and its implications for an understanding of the financial statements . . .

Depending upon the nature of the circumstances giving rise to the qualified report, the qualification will fall into one of the following two categories:

(a) where there is uncertainty which prevents the auditor from forming an opinion on a matter (uncertainty); or
(b) where the auditor is able to form an opinion on a matter but this conflicts with the view given by the financial statements (disagreement).

Each category may be further sub-divided depending upon whether the uncertainty or disagreement is considered to be fundamental so as to undermine the view given by the financial statements taken as a whole.

The forms of qualification which should be used in different circumstances are shown in Figure 3.2.

The Auditing Standards of the profession are intended to apply 'to all reports in which the auditor expresses an opinion'. However, the Auditing Standards explicitly recognise the problems associated with auditing the accounts of small companies, notably having to rely on the assurances of the directors that all transactions are entered in the books. In such cases, provided that the directors are able to give the necessary assurances and that there is no evidence that these assurances are inaccurate, the Auditing Guidelines recommend the issue of a small company qualified Audit Report.

None of the companies in the present sample had any qualifications that indicated that the auditor had disagreed with the

Figure 3.2: Forms of qualification

Nature of circumstances	Material but not fundamental	Fundamental
Uncertainty	'SUBJECT TO' opinion	DISCLAIMER OF OPINION
Disagreement	'EXCEPT' opinion	ADVERSE OPINION

In a disclaimer of opinion the auditor states that he is unable to form an opinion as to whether the financial statements give a true and fair view.

In an adverse opinion the auditor states that in his opinion the financial statements do not give a true and fair view.

In a 'subject to' opinion the auditor effectively disclaims an opinion on a particular matter which is not considered fundamental.

In an 'except' opinion the auditor expresses an adverse opinion on a particular matter which is not considered fundamental.

figures presented in the financial statements. This is hardly surprising because the general lack of accounting expertise amongst small company managers means the auditors themselves also prepare the annual accounts for all but a tiny proportion of their clients.

All of the audit qualifications amongst our sample referred to matters of uncertainty. Table 3.11 presents an analysis of the major categories of 'subject to' audit qualifications. Only a small proportion of companies, 15.1 per cent received any form of audit qualifications to their accounts in the two earlier years covered by this study. On the face of it, this may be somewhat surprising since, for these companies, the 'system of control will be dependent upon the close involvement of the directors' and 'independent confirmation of the accounting records' is not generally available. However, this figure rises to 23.3 per cent in the final year of financial statements examined and is wholly accounted for by the increased number of failed companies receiving qualifications. The non-failed companies remain remarkably stable in this respect and receive fewer qualifications than the failed companies in all categories of audit qualification. This suggests that, for a proportion of companies, as failure approaches, the company's financial records tend to become less satisfactory and increasingly inadequate in the opinion of their professional auditor.

Probably the most 'serious' type of audit qualification in the eyes of most account users will be the 'going concern' qualification. The financial accounts of companies are drawn up on the assumption that the business entity will continue to operate as an on-going business in the foreseeable future. Thus, the accounts will not show any provisions for losses caused by winding up or for the forced sale of a substantial part of the business to raise finance to support what remains.

However, the going concern principle must not be applied if the auditor believes that the company is in serious financial difficulties which render this assumption unrealistic. As may be seen from Table 3.11, less than 10 per cent of failed companies received going concern qualifications from their auditors in the final set of financial statements issued prior to actual failure. The small proportion of going concern qualifications in respect of failed companies seems not to provide account users with much of an 'early warning' system of impending failure.

This lack of going concern qualifications for companies close to failure could reflect a genuine belief of viability on the part of auditors, but this seems unlikely given the financial situation of many of these companies. More possibly the auditor may be unwilling to risk precipitating a company's collapse by issuing a going concern qualification, since it is conceivable that creditors might demand immediate repayment of debts and refuse to renew the credit facilities which most small businesses rely upon for their working capital requirements. In addition, customers worried about ensuring future inputs might look elsewhere for their supplies. As this belief that disclosure of financial problems could in fact intensify a company's difficulties has wide currency in the accounting profession, the apparent reluctance of auditors to disclose their doubts is hardly surprising.

It must be noted, however, that whilst a 'going concern' qualification may hasten a failing company's demise, there is no evidence that an otherwise healthy company has been forced into liquidation by the issue of a going concern qualification. In our view, the possibility that a qualification will bring forward the date of failure hardly seems a strong enough reason for the auditor to renounce his professional duty to prepare financial statements that present a 'true and fair view' of the financial position of the company. The fact that less than one-third of all failures received any form of audit qualification in their last set of accounts suggests that outside users of accounts are not being adequately informed.

The independence of the auditor vis-à-vis the small company

This clear reluctance of auditors to issue any form of qualification to the accounts of their clients, particularly going concern qualifications to small companies on the verge of failure, raises a number of related issues, chief of which are

(a) the significance the user of the accounts should attach to an audit qualification, and
(b) the independence and professional judgement of the auditor.

The suggested small company audit qualification has, as we have seen, been used only in a small number of cases. What is the user of these financial statements to infer from such a qualification?

Page (1985) believes the difficulty in interpreting an audit qualification is primarily due to the differing policies adopted by individual auditors and the doubts concerning the circumstances in which the qualification is issued. However, this begs the question of why there should be such a wide diversity in practice between auditors. An examination of the economic relationship between the auditor and the small company may provide an explanation of this diversity and, in particular, the general reluctance of auditors to qualify their audit reports.

As noted earlier, because most shareholders are also directors, ownership and day-to-day management of small companies is closely linked. Thus, if the concept of stewardship is limited to providing shareholders with information concerning the possible abuse of their funds by management, then the auditor will be irrelevant to companies where he is appointed by the same group of people, the directors-shareholders, that he is supposed to be auditing. However if the auditor takes this limited view of his stewardship duties then the interests of other outside users such as creditors, customers and employees are necessarily overlooked.

The professional standard and reputation of the auditor and the requirements of the Companies Acts to some extent ensure that the auditor cannot merely 'rubber stamp' whatever figures the directors produce. However, in practice, the absence of 'outside' shareholders means the auditor is not really independent from the small company's directors as they, effectively, appoint and pay him. An auditor who asks too many probing and awkward questions may well not be reappointed in subsequent years.[9]

A priori, one would expect that a lack of independence would be more marked in the case of small, local firms of accountants who, unlike large national/international firms, rely upon a limited local market for their services. A major feature of this reliance upon a local market is that a local reputation for providing low cost accounting services and remaining on 'good terms' with one's clients is essential if the accountant is to remain in business. By far the major source of new clients for the accountant's services are introductions from existing (satisfied) clients, i.e. friends, relatives and business contacts. Clients are extremely unlikely to be willing to bear the additional costs associated with complying with statutory regulations, accounting standards and the conduct of a 'thorough' audit.[10] Furthermore, they cannot be expected to be appreciative of the resulting qualification to the accounts (especially if they can obtain a cheaper service elsewhere). In this situation, 'turning a blind eye' not only makes good business sense, but also allows the auditor to remain *de jure*, if not *de facto*, independent of his clients.[11]

In contrast, the large accountancy firms will be more concerned with their reputation for thoroughness and reliability than the possibility of lost fees from their few small clients. This good reputation is generally their major asset and forms the basis of the demand for their services. The possibility of incurring expensive litigation costs brought by aggrieved, and often sophisticated, investors who rely on the audited figures for investment decisions is a further constraint upon any 'selective myopia'. Thus, most large firms of accountants have evolved a sophisticated system of audit procedures which the individual auditor must follow and which leaves very little scope for personal preferences. For these reasons we would hypothesise that the large firms of accountants will be more willing to:

(1) insist upon the disclosure of the information required by the Companies Acts and the relevant accounting standards,

(2) apply greater pressure upon the directors to submit the accounts to Companies House within the required legal limit, and,

(3) qualify the accounts of small companies.

Empirical evidence as to (1) has already been detailed above and Tables 3.12 and 3.13 present empirical evidence as to (2) and (3) respectively.

Table 3.12 indicates that the mean submission lag of 9.5 months for companies audited by the 'Top 20' is significantly smaller than that for companies audited by local firms of auditors (12.2 months). The variance of the companies audited by the Top 20 is also significantly less than that for the locally audited companies (4.4 and 8.0 months respectively).

Table 3.13 shows that, whilst only 13.7 per cent (nine non-failed and eleven failed companies) of the companies in the present sample were audited by the Top 20 firms of accountants, 13 of these companies (65.0%) received some form of audit qualifi-

Table 3.12: Three-year average submission lag by type of auditor

Top 20 auditor			Local auditor		
N	X̄	σ	N	X̄	σ
20	9.5	4.4	126	12.2	8.0

*t-value — 2.15   1-tail sig. — .02

*Separate variance estimate

Table 3.13: Audit qualification by type of auditor

Section 1: All qualifications

	All companies		Unqualified		Qualified	
	No.	%	No.	%	No.	%
Top 20 auditors	20	13.7	7	35.0	13	65.0
Local auditors	126	86.3	105	83.3	21	16.7
Total	146	100.0	112	76.7	34	23.3

Section 2: Going concern qualifications for failures

	All failures		Unqualified		Qualified	
	No.	%	No.	%	No.	%
Top 20 auditors	11	15.1	6	54.5	5	45.5
Local auditors	62	84.9	60	96.8	2	3.2
Total	73	100.0	66	90.4	7	9.6

cation to their accounts. The comparable figures for companies audited by local auditors indicate that out of the 126 companies involved, only 21 (16.7%) had their accounts qualified. Turning to the going concern qualifications, five of the eleven failed companies (45.5%) audited by the top 20 received going concern qualifications whilst a mere two out of the 62 failed companies (3.2%) audited by the local auditors received these qualifications.

FINANCING THE SMALL COMPANY

Share capital

Most small companies begin life with an initial paid up share capital of often only a few pounds. The vast majority of the remainder of the necessary capital tends to come from trade creditors (primarily to finance the company's short-term working capital requirements), and loan creditors for the fixed capital costs required to commence the business. These loan creditors, whilst being primarily the banks, often include the directors themselves. Rather than purchasing a greater number of their own company's shares with their available funds, many founders take the prudent precaution of introducing the necessary funds into the new company via directors' personal loan accounts. Given the inherently risky nature of starting up a new company, this has a number of advantages from the director's view point.

It is cheaper because the scale of fees charged by the Registrar of Companies to register a company is based upon the authorised share capital of the proposed venture. More importantly, this method of finance gives these funds a much greater degree of liquidity as share capital can only be repaid in the event of the winding up of the company and then only after all other creditors' claims have been met in full. Directors' loan accounts, on the other hand, may be withdrawn at any time, subject of course to whatever contractual arrangements pertain to the loan agreement and the availability of sufficient funds in liquid form.[12] In addition to the above considerations, interest on debt is an expense deductable for corporation tax purposes and it is thus often more 'tax efficient' than paying dividends.

Once the company is established it may be able to finance expansion out of retained earnings, further loans or through the issue of new share capital. However, for the directors, the disadvantages of issuing new share capital still stand. Unless for some particular reason, such as the introduction of new members, new shares are expressly required, there is little incentive for the issue of further shares once the business is established. As already noted, the introduction of new members is a relatively unusual occurrence for most small companies.

In our sample, over the three-year period covered only six of the 146 companied issued any new shares but only one of the six companies had any change in membership over the period. Further analysis of the six companies that issued new shares revealed that five of these companies subsequently failed. All six companies had a floating charge on their assets held by a bank.

Whilst it is an obvious advantage to the directors to minimise their investment in permanent share capital, no such advantages accrue to the other providers of funds who will have to incur proportionately greater costs in the event of failure. Therefore, it seems likely that if the bank perceives that the company is in difficulties, either when it reviews its existing loan agreements or when the directors negotiate for additional funds, it may insist upon the introduction of additional permanent share capital in order to reduce the risks associated with lending to what it perceives to be a poor credit risk. In our cases we cannot be certain that the bank was the moving spirit behind the increased share issues in all cases. Nevertheless, as the banks are often the sole source of finance available to the small company, they are in a powerful position and thus are usually able to apply pressure on the directors of small businesses. In none of these six cases, however, was the strategy successful.

Secured loans

As small business ventures are inherently risky undertakings, financial institutions usually ensure that any loans granted to small companies are covered by adequate security. This is normally achieved either by obtaining personal guarantees from the directors themselves (usually a mortgage on the private homes of the directors) or by creating a fixed or floating charge on the company's assets.

The extent to which financial institutions utilise personal guarantees is impossible to determine from the published accounts, as this information is not generally disclosed. However, forms of security on the assets of the company are required to be registered at Companies House. Table 3.14 presents frequency distributions of the number of companies with a fixed/floating charge, mortgage or an otherwise secured creditor against the company's assets registered at Companies House. The secured creditors are also identified in Table 3.14.

Over half of all the companies examined had a secured creditor. 65 of these 78 companies had floating charges held by the banks. The next largest category of secured creditors, consisting of a mere five cases, were the Local Authorities, followed by three cases where another company held the floating charge. Building societies, commercial/public agencies and the directors/members held the remaining five floating charges.

The differences between failed and non-failed companies is marked both in terms of the relative proportion actually having

Table 3.14: Number of companies with a registered secured creditor

Secured creditor	All companies		Non-failures		Failures	
	No.	%	No.	%	No.	%
None	68	46.6	43	58.9	25	34.2
Bank	65	44.5	23	31.5	42	57.5
Another company	3	2.1	0	0.0	3	4.1
Building society	1	0.7	1	1.4	0	0.0
Local authority	5	3.4	5	6.8	0	0.0
Venture capital agency	2	1.4	1	1.4	1	1.4
Directors/members	2	1.4	0	0.0	2	2.7
Total	146	100.0	73	100.0	73	100.0

a floating charge on their assets and also in respect of who holds these floating charges. Some 65.8 per cent of all failed companies had a floating charge as against only 41.1 per cent of non-failed companies. Of the 48 failed companies with secured creditors, 42 or 87.5 per cent of these secured creditors were banks. For the non-failed companies with secured creditors the proportion with floating charges held by a bank is 76.7 per cent. None of the companies with floating charges held by Local Authorities failed. If Table 3.14 accurately reflects the major sources of finance utilised by the small company then the non-failed companies make greater use of other financial/public institutions than the failed companies.

Dependence upon bank finance may reflect the lack of any attempt to obtain finance from other sources or, alternatively, to the lack of success in obtaining funds elsewhere owing to the recognition of the risky nature of these enterprises. However, the banking community is not generally seen as willing to lend to companies that other financial sources regard as being too risky. Indeed, the introduction of the Loan Guarantee Scheme was justified on the reverse argument — that the lending policies of the banks are too conservative and that they are unwilling to extend or renew credit to ventures that have even a relatively small element of risk attached to them.

If this is the case then perhaps attention ought to be focused more upon the behaviour of the banks as secured creditors when dealing with small companies in financial difficulties than upon the companies themselves. The strong relationship between failure and secured bank creditors shown in Table 3.14 may therefore reflect the greater willingness of the banking community to call in the receiver when a company begins to experience financial difficulties. In this way the banks are able to make good their security before additional trading losses further reduce the company's asset base.

CONCLUSION

This chapter has drawn upon a sample of 146 companies to investigate the ownership, management characteristics and institutional factors which largely determine the financing and content of the financial statements of small manufacturing companies. The major objective has been to demonstrate that the small company is a vastly different creature from that found in the large quoted company sector. This implies that the large body of empirical work based upon the performance of quoted companies will be of limited relevance to the policy-maker or researcher interested in the performance of the small company. Thus, the present chapter provides a more appropriate context in which to evalute the empirical findings of later chapters concerned with the performance and prediction of failure in small companies.

The ownership and management structure of the vast majority of small companies appears to be closer to that of unincorporated enterprises such as sole traders or partnerships than to that of the large quoted company. Most of the companies in this study are controlled by two or three directors and their immediate families and have few non-director shareholders. The largest occupational grouping of the directors of small companies consisted of former craft/technical workers who had received their training in the same or similar industries to that in which their company was presently operating. The analysis also indicated that the second largest occupational grouping, the 'professional' director, was more commonly associated with failed companies.

These 'closely held' companies rarely experience any changes in the membership of their board of directors. There is little evidence to suggest that 'outsiders' with specific business or financial skills to offer, such as accountants or production and marketing managers, are co-opted onto the board of directors. Only a minority of directors appear to be directors of other small companies which suggests that the one small company is their major source of income and employment.

This unitary ownership and management structure has potentially serious consequences in terms of the production of the financial statements. Essentially, it means that the accuracy and reliability of the company's financial records, which form the basis of the empirical investigation into the financial performance of small companies used in later chapters, are generally incapable of being independently verified. This problem has long been recognised by the professional accountancy bodies and therefore the auditor is recommended to issue a 'small company qualified audit report' to alert interested parties to this problem. However, very few auditors actually issue such a qualification because the majority of small companies (86 per cent) have their accounts audited by small local firms of auditors who, for good economic/business reasons, prefer not to issue audit qualifications which may conceivably lose them a client.

Furthermore, the accounts of companies audited by local auditors are generally of a 'low quality' in that many of the Companies Acts and/or professional accounting standards requirements are ignored. For instance, companies audited by local firms of auditors were less likely to disclose their accounting policies and took longer to submit their accounts to Companies House than companies audited by large firms of auditors. Furthermore, failing companies, with a median submission lag of 12.7 months, also tended to delay submitting their accounts. This lack of sufficient and timely information clearly reduces the diagnostic usefulness of these financial statements.

Few of the companies studied actually issued any new share capital once the company had been established. Neither did any company 'capitalise' any of their retained earnings during the three-year period examined. Generally, most of the companies were highly dependent upon bank finance which was, in 87 per cent of cases, only advanced on the basis of loans secured on the company's productive assets.

NOTES

1. The average ages of the failed and non-failed companies were 16.34 and 17.25 years respectively. The resulting t-statistic for testing

for differences in two sample means was a mere 0.34 with 144 degrees of freedom. A Chi-square test (with 17 degrees of freedom) was used to determine whether the failed and non-failed samples differed significantly in terms of industrial composition at industrial order level. The resulting statistic of 20.96 indicated that no statistically significant differences existed between the two samples.

2. This is confirmed by a recent questionnaire survey of small-company directors by Page (1984). When asked 'What is the main advantage of running your business as a company rather than as a partnership or as an individual?' the responses most frequently mentioned were as follows:

(1) Limitation of liability
(2) Tax savings
(3) Ability to raise finance
(4) Ease of transfer of ownership
(5) The formal setting-out of the rights and duties of owners and managers

3. The use of personal guarantees that lenders often demand of directors may, in some cases, render limited liability something of a fiction. However, despite this possibility, nearly half of the directors in the Page (1984) study still regarded the limitation of liability as the biggest advantage accruing from company status. The reasons for this are clearly that, even if the director has given a personal guarantee, the worst scenario in the event of business failure for a director would be the loss of his/her home and business. The owner of an unincorporated business in a similar situation would be made personally bankrupt.

4. These figures exclude the executors of deceased shareholders unless they also held shares of their own.

5. For the purposes of this analysis, directors have been deemed to be members of the same family if they share a private address with another director or if they share the same surname. Obviously, this will underestimate the actual number of family connections because it excludes married daughters and other maternal kin.

6. The percentage of small company directors with some formal accounting/financial training is similar to those presented by Page (1984).

7. Page (1984) reports that only 27 per cent of the directors in his sample fall into this category. These differences are probably due to the fact that his sample contains (an unspecified) number of non-manufacturing companies.

8. For the purpose of this study, a firm of accountants has been classified as national/international if it appeared in the 'Top 20 Accountants by Fee Income', in *Accountancy*, Nov. 1983, p. 23. All other firms of accountants have been classified as 'local'.

9. Only eight companies changed their auditors over the three years covered by the present study. Of these eight companies, seven were failed companies. In all cases the auditors had expressed their willingness to remain in office.

10. Carsberg *et al.* (1985), produced evidence which indicated that

it was the accountants themselves, rather than the small company directors (who were generally blissfully unaware of the costs of compliance) that were most opposed to existing or additional disclosure requirements. The major reasons given by the accountants for opposing further disclosure requirements concerned the additional work-load involved.

11. P. Moiser (1985) makes much the same point.

12. Furthermore, the directors may, if other creditors have not already done so, secure these loans on the company's assets so that in the event of business failure they have some chance of rescuing some of their capital ahead of other creditors. In the present sample only two companies, both failures, had floating charges held by their directors and both were created within one year of failure!

4

Size and Firm Performance: Size, Profit and Growth in Small and Large Companies

INTRODUCTION

Throughout this book it is emphasised that the small firm is not simply a scaled-down version of a large firm. Because they are managed by their owners, because they represent an alternative to paid (salaried or wage) employment and because so many are, or could become over a very short period, close to failure small firms have different aspirations from large firms. Furthermore most small firms lack market power in both the product market and in the purchase of inputs and so are generally price takers. Hence, small firms are likely to respond differently from large firms to financial and non-financial stimuli such as taxation incentives and other opportunities for expansion. As a group small firm performance is likely to be more variable than that of a group of large firms.

Despite these clear differences of type between large and small firms the emphasis within both theoretical and empirical economics has been to view firm size as a continuum with small firms at one end of the spectrum and large firms at the other. Discussions on how firms move from the small to the large end of that spectrum have concentrated upon the role of scale economies at the plant level and organisational diseconomies at the enterprise level.

This chapter has two functions. Firstly, it selectively reviews the existing empirical research relating firm performance in terms of growth and profitability to size. It demonstrates that, with the significant exception of Wedervang's (1965) studies of the Norwegian economy and Boswell's (1972) qualitative analysis the emphasis has been on relatively large firms. Secondly, it provides new results from tests, identical to those conducted in the work on large firms, which are conducted on the small firm data base described in Chapter 2. It highlights the nature and extent of differences in the results obtained. Finally, towards the end of the chapter a discussion is conducted of the factors other than scale which distinguish small from large firms.

SIZE AND GROWTH IN LARGE FIRMS

Individual firm growth plays an important role in determining the characteristics and dynamism of any modern economy. For this reason the science of economics would have been expected to have had clearly defined theories on the relationship between firm growth and other firm attributes. Whilst theories do exist it would be difficult to describe them as either clearly defined or well developed.

There are at least three separate theoretical arguments relating growth to size. First, if all firms face identical U-shaped average cost curves, then a negative relationship between firm size and growth is to be expected. This is because large firms are assumed to be at or near their optimum size and would therefore have to grow only slightly, if at all, to reach peak efficiency. On the other hand smaller firms would be operating at a level well below the optimum size and would therefore have a large inducement to grow very quickly.

A second theory of the relationship between size and growth argues that the modern corporation is characterised by a divorce of ownership from control and this divorce is clearest amongst large firms. Larger firms are managed by professionals who generally have only a small equity stake but whose income is determined by the size of the company and by their position within the company. Hence such individuals, providing they can satisfy the shareholders by achieving a satisfactory rate of return will, personally, obtain higher incomes by choosing projects which increase corporate size rather than profits.

A third theory proposes that growth should be regarded as a statistical phenomenon resulting from the cumulative effects of the chance operation of a large number of forces each operating independently. The chances of growth/shrinkage of individual firms will depend on their profitability and upon other factors such as access to new markets and to finance. If the following three assumptions are made, then the probability of a firm growing at a given proportionate rate during any specified period is independent of the initial size of the firm:

(1) Growth in one period is independent of growth in another.
(2) The probability that a firm will have a particular growth rate is the same for all firms.
(3) No single period is so important so as to remain a dominant influence.

Gibrat (1931) argued that if growth and size were indeed to be independent there would need to be two necessary conditions.

(a) Firms of different size classes have the same average proportionate growth rate.
(b) The dispersion of growth rates about the common mean is the same for all size classes.

The bulk of the empirical literature concerned with the relationship between size and growth has restricted itself to determining whether these necessary conditions are satisfied for firms which remain in existence over a period of time.

In testing the first requirement of the Law of Proportionate Effect, one approach often adopted is to divide the size distribution of firms into a number of size/classes and then use a statistical test, such as the Welch-Aspin test[1], to determine if the average growth rates for the various size classes are equal. Studies by Hart (1962, 1965), Hymer and Pashigan (1962), Hay and Morris (1984), Boswell (1972), Singh and Whittington (1968), Eatwell (1969), Mansfield (1962), Rowthorn and Hymer (1971) and Droucopoulos (1982), show that the average rate of growth does not on the whole vary in any systematic way with the size of the firm. However, studies by Dunning and Pearce (1981), Samuels (1965), Singh and Whittington (1975) and Meeks and Whittington (1975) find a positive relationship between firm size and growth. Finally, studies by Aislabie and Keating (1976), Wedervang (1965) and Meeks and Whittington (1976) find a negative relationship between firm size and growth. To some extent this variability is a reflection of the different time periods, different countries, different industries and different size classes covered by the studies. Nevertheless the lack of consistency amongst the studies is also compatible with the view that there is, in fact, little systematic relation between size and growth.

However, given that the primary interest of this book is the very small end of the size distribution of firms, more attention should be given to those studies dealing with such firms. Wedervang (1965) and Aislabie and Keating (1976) find that smaller firms/plants tend to have a higher growth rate. Hay and Morris (1984) and Boswell (1972) find no systematic relation; whereas Shen (1965, 1968, 1970) tended to find that larger plants grew more quickly than smaller plants. This relationship between size and growth, even for smaller firms/plants therefore is highly ambiguous.

The second condition for the Law of Proportionate Effect to hold, namely that the size of firm and the variance of its growth rates are unrelated, has been tested by sub-dividing firms into different size classes and then using a statistical test such as the Chi-squared, to determine whether the variances in growth rates for the different size classes are equivalent.

A number of studies have concluded that the dispersion of growth rates is negatively related to increases in firm size. Hart's 1965 paper draws such a conclusion. However, in his 1962 paper, where he used profits as a surrogate for size, the results were so ambiguous as to leave no room for the drawing of firm conclusions. Hymer and Pashigan (1962) also found evidence of an inverse relationship. This conclusion was drawn by calculating the standard deviation of the growth rates of size classes of firms in ten industries when the size distribution for each industry was split into quartiles. The standard deviation increased in 23 out of a possible 30 cases when moving from a quartile containing larger firms to a quartile containing smaller firms. It should be noted that no tests of significance were used.

The study by Singh and Whittington (1968) supports the Hymer and Pashigan results. Their results are, however, confined to four industries and although there is a decline in dispersion of growth as size increases, the relationship is not monotonic. This finding is confirmed in their 1975 work. They note, however, that large firms do not experience as high a degree of uniformity in their growth rates as would be compatible with the often-proposed view that large firms are merely an aggregation of small firms and should, therefore, show a lower degree of dispersion in their growth rates. This tendency for a negative relationship to exist between size and dispersion of growth is further corroborated by the studies of Eatwell (1969) Aislabie and Keating (1976).

Another way of testing the Law of Proportionate Effect is to regress the log of closing size upon the log of opening size

$$\log S_{it+1} = a + b \log S_{it} + \log E_{it} \tag{4.1}$$

If b is found to be equal to 1 and the variance of the logged error term is constant this implies that the process of growth is purely stochastic and the Law of Proportionate Effect is verified, whereas if b is found to be greater (less) than unity the larger (smaller) grow faster.[2]

Equations of form 4.1 have been tested by Hart (1962), Samuels (1965), Singh and Whittington (1968, 1975) and Droucopolous (1982). The studies by Hart and Droucopolous suggest that b is not significantly different from one, whereas the other studies suggest that it has a value greater than one. However, Singh and Whittington find that a value of $b > 1$ need not necessarily hold when individual industries are considered. Furthermore, Chesher (1979) argues that the Law of Proportionate Effect need not be in operation even though the b's are close to unity if the disturbances are serially correlated.

A similar approach to testing equation 4.1 is to regress

$$\text{Var} \log S_{it+1} = b^2 \, \text{Var} \log S_{it} + E_{it}^2 \tag{4.2}$$

Equations of form 4.2 have been used by Hart and Prais (1956), Hart (1962, 1965) and Samuels (1965). Hart and Prais's work tends to suggest that the Law of Proportionate Effect does not hold and the b's tend to be less than 1 suggesting that small firms grow faster. The work by Hart suggests the Law holds whereas the work by Samuels suggests that the b's have a value greater than unity. Overall, the regression studies yield the tentative conclusion of there being little consistent relationship between growth and size.

The evidence presented above does not unambiguously reject the Law of Proportionate Effect nor does it lend it wholehearted support. The assumptions underpinning the law do not imply that the growth of firms occurs by chance, but rather that the incidence of factors which induce growth and decline in each period is unrelated to the initial size of the firm. Such assumptions are not implausible but for the Law of Proportionate Effect to hold, growth in one period cannot lead to growth in another. It is this last implausible assumption which provides the final test for the Law of Proportionate Effect. The problem has been investigated by Singh and Whittington (1968, 1975) and Droucopolous (1982) via the technique of regression analysis. Both studies used the following equation for testing purposes:

$$g_{it+1} = a + bg_{it} + E_{it} \qquad (4.3)$$

where g_{it} is the growth of the ith firm in period t. Droucopolous concludes that his few regressions with significant results suggest that the growth of firms in one period cannot be used to predict growth in the next. Singh and Whittington's (1968) regression results do show slight persistency in growth but when individual industries are considered these are found to be significant only for a single industry. In their later work Singh and Whittington (1975) believe their results:

indicate that there is a definite tendency for the relative growth rates of individual firms to persist: the 'b' coefficient is positive in almost all the individual industries and in all industries together, ... On the other hand since the values of R^2 are uniformly low (about 0.05), the past growth record of the firm cannot be regarded as a good predictor of its future growth. (p. 21)

In conclusion, the evidence currently available suggests that growth and initial size are probably unrelated, at least for relatively large firms, whereas the dispersion of growth rates decreases with size.

SIZE AND GROWTH IN SMALL NORTHERN ENGLAND COMPANIES

In this section a number of the tests discussed above are conducted upon data for small manufacturing companies, with a view to determining the extent to which the Law of Proportionate Effect applies *within* the small firm sector. In conducting these tests for small companies, however, several additional complications arise.

In large-firm studies the measure of asset size generally used is Net Assets, whereas in the small firm sector a measure of Total Assets may be more appropriate partly because a number of the companies included in the data set have negative Net Assets, and partly because the structure of the balance sheet of small companies means that current liabilities are significantly less important in large companies than in small.

The work undertaken on large companies used financial assets as the prime indicator of size, yet in defining whether or not a manufacturing business is, or is not, small the number of employees is the basis for most government definitions (Cross, 1983). In this section both the Net Assets and Total Assets measure of size will be used, but it can be seen from Table 4.1 that the three measures of size are not perfectly correlated with one another.

The table shows, for example, in 1971 that the correlation coefficient between Net Assets and employment for the 205 companies providing employment and financial data for that year, was 0.5771, whereas that between Total Assets and Net Assets was 0.9461. These relationships remain broadly similar for the selection of years for which data are provided, with a correlation coefficient of approximately 0.94 between Net and Total Assets. For all years the correlation coefficient between Total Assets and employment size is higher than that between Net Assets and employment size.

However, even this table fails to show the presence of extreme cases. These are shown in Tables 4.2 and 4.3. Table 4.2 shows that there was one company which in 1971 had more than 100 employees and yet in that year had negative Net

Table 4.1: Key measures of size: simple correlation coefficients

Financial size	Employment in			
	1971	1975	1978	1981
Net assets	0.5771	0.6652	0.5516	0.6511
	(0.9461)	(0.9270)	(0.9418)	(0.9469)
Total assets	0.7081	0.6793	0.6269	0.6974
N	205	315	331	221

Note: Significant at 95% level accordingly.

Assets. Furthermore, another company had Net Assets of less than £5,000 and yet had more than 50 employees. Similar extremes are apparent from an examination of Table 4.3. Here there is one company which in 1975 had negative Net Assets, but which had more than 50 employees, whilst three had Net Assets of more than £100,000 and yet had less than 10 employees.

A similar examination of the relationship between total assets and employment size showed that there were substantially fewer extreme values and suggests that these two measures are more consistent indicators of size amongst small companies than the Net Assets measure. Nevertheless, for the purposes of this analysis, all three measures of size will be used although the limitations of the Net Assets measure needs to be borne in mind.

Table 4.2: Net assets and employment in 1971

	Employment					
Net Assets	1-9	10-24	25-49	50-99	100+	Total
£						
Negative	4	2	0	0	1	7
£ 0 - 4,999	36	14	1	1	0	52
£ 5,000- 9,999	33	17	4	0	0	54
£ 10,000-24,999	17	37	8	2	0	64
£ 25,000-49,999	5	25	12	5	0	47
£ 50,000-99,999	0	3	7	5	2	17
£100,000+	0	0	2	7	4	13
Total	95	98	34	20	7	254

Table 4.3: Net assets and employment in 1975

	Employment					
Net Assets	1-9	10-24	25-49	50-99	100+	Total
£						
Negative	6	3	0	1	0	10
£ 0 - 4,999	24	7	3	0	0	34
£ 5,000- 9,999	37	8	1	0	0	46
£ 10,000-24,999	52	39	5	2	0	98
£ 25,000-49,999	12	46	17	0	1	76
£ 50,000-99,999	9	26	26	3	0	64
£100,000+	3	13	19	18	10	63
Total	143	142	71	24	11	391

It is also unclear from an examination of large-firm studies over what length of time Gibrat's Law is expected to hold. Some studies have examined changes over five-year periods whereas others have examined a twenty-year period. Broadly speaking the choice of period appears to have been dependent on the nature of the available data. Where only surviving firms are included in the analysis then perhaps the duration of the period makes little difference. However in the case of small firms, where approximately 50 per cent of new starters cease to trade within three years (Ganguly, 1985), the choice of period has to be sufficiently long to allow variations in growth rates to be identifiable, yet not so long as to ensure that only a small proportion of the small firms in existence at the start of the period survive until the end. A final complication is that when conducting analysis upon small firms the group will include significantly more young companies than a collection of large firms. These young firms are both more likely to fail than similar sized but older firms and are also more likely to experience rapid growth (Storey, 1985a). Separately identifying both an age and a size effect presents additional problems.

For these reasons it was decided to sub-divide the period 1970-80 into two. Data for 1970 were relatively poor and so the periods 1971-75 and 1975-80 were chosen. Whilst these do not coincide with points in the trade cycle, they are indicators of the relatively prosperous early 1970s and the major recession that the region experienced towards the end of the 1970s. A total of five separate size categories were chosen according to both the Net Assets and Total Assets criteria of size discussed above.

Table 4.4 shows that mean growth in Total Assets for surviving companies with Total Assets of less than £5,000 was 154 per cent per annum between 1971 and 1975. For the years 1975-80 annual growth rate of the smallest-sized companies which survived was 164 per cent. At the other extreme the largest-sized companies in this analysis, with Total Assets in excess of £50,000, showed an annual growth rate in Total Assets amongst surviving companies of 27 per cent in the 1971-75 period and 20 per cent in the 1975-80 period. The table demonstrates that the smallest-sized companies, with Total Assets of £5,000 or less, perform very differently from the other groups of small companies. The smallest companies have a mean growth rate amongst survivors of nearly five times that of any other size group in both the 1971-75 and 1975-80 period. Furthermore

Table 4.4: Annual % growth in total assets

Size (Total Assets)	1971-1975				1975-80				Failure Rate
	X̄	X^MED	σ	N	X̄	X^MED	σ	N	
Less than £5,000	154.2 (148.8)	95.4 (94.8)	178.7 (172.6)	28 (29)/(32)	164.3 (97.7)	22.8 (0)	555.1 (330.1)	22 (37)/(63)	40
£5,000-9,999	29.8 (29.1)	20.7 (15.3)	34.4 (33.4)	33 (34)/(39)	24.2 (18.8)	5.9 (0)	80.2 (62.3)	28 (36)/(66)	22
£10,000-24,999	36.2 (34.3)	14.9 (13.3)	51.8 (49.1)	73 (77)/(88)	37.5 (31.8)	19.0 (12.3)	63.8 (54.2)	79 (93)/(121)	15
£25,000-49,999	31.0 (29.9)	21.3 (19.8)	40.0 (38.6)	54 (56)/(68)	35.5 (33.1)	26.0 (23.2)	47.0 (43.8)	56 (60)/(86)	7
£50,000+	26.8 (26.3)	18.5 (15.2)	28.2 (27.7)	55 (56)/(66)	20.1 (19.5)	14.2 (14.0)	22.0 (21.3)	91 (94)/(139)	3

Notes: a. Firms with negative net assets are excluded

b. Figures in parentheses show values when failed companies are taken into account

c. In the final column for each time period the first figure in parentheses gives number of firms providing data in the start year and final year *plus* those which are known to have ceased trading between those dates. The second figure adds those companies which although known to be trading in the final year provided no financial data for that year.

this difference is not merely attributable to extreme values, since even the median growth rate (X^{MED}) of these very small surviving companies is virtually five times that of any other size group in the 1971-75 period.

It will be recalled from Chapter 2 that the data base has a significant under-representation of companies failing in the 1971-75 period, with this under-representation being reduced in the 1975-80 period. The results of including only surviving companies are shown in parentheses. The final column of Table 4.4 shows that 40 per cent of companies which in 1975 had Total Assets of less than £5,000 had failed by 1982, compared with only 3 per cent of those with Total Assets of more than £50,000. The effect upon calculated growth rates of including or excluding failed companies can be seen in the second row of data for each size band. Here a value of zero is given to each failing company so that the arithmetic mean growth rate of all companies (survivors *plus* non-survivors) can be seen to be 149 per cent in the 1971-75 period and 98 per cent in the 1975-80 period for companies with Total Assets of less than £5,000 in the appropriate base year. Even so this mean growth rate is virtually five times that of any other size group in the 1971-75 period and three times that for other size groups in the 1975-80 period, even though 40 per cent of companies in this size group in 1975 failed to survive to 1980.

Whilst it is clear that companies with Total Assets of less than £5,000 are significantly more likely both to grow more rapidly and to fail than the larger companies in the data set, no other relationship between size and growth is clear. The final column of the table, however, shows that failure rates decrease monotonically with size. Hence, except for the smallest size bands, there appears little clear evidence of growth being related to size, where this is measured in terms of net assets.

Table 4.4 also presents data on the variance of growth rates which studies of large firms have shown to be broadly decreasing with increasing firm size. An examination of the period 1971-75 shows the variance of growth rates to be highest in the smallest size category and lowest in the largest size category. The relationship was, however, not a monotonic one since the second smallest size category had the second smallest growth variance. During the 1975-80 period the variance of growth rates was consistently lower for larger companies, suggesting a result comparable to the large firm studies.

Table 4.4 used the criterion of Total Assets and in the context of small firm development this may be appropriate. However, the Net Assets measure is used in large firm studies and so results are presented in Table 4.5. They are broadly similar to those of Table 4.4. The table shows that during the 1971-75 period surviving companies in the smaller size category experienced substantially faster rates of growth in Net Assets than other sizes of small company. It also shows that, amongst survivors, growth rates appeared to be most rapid in the smallest companies and to decline continuously with size. During the 1975-80 period arithmetic mean growth rates amongst survivors were also highest amongst the smallest size group (but only 44 per cent per annum) and lowest amongst the largest size band (26 per cent). The three intermediate size groupings, however, shows little evidence of any relationship with mean growth rates.

It will be recalled that the presence of failed companies in the population is inadequately reflected in the observations for the 1971-75 period but rather better represented amongst those for 1975-80. Here further clear evidence of failure being linked to size is shown in the final column of Table 4.5, with 46 per cent of companies with Net Assets of less than £5,000 in 1975 failing to survive for five years, compared with only 7 per cent of those with Net Assets in excess of £50,000. The presence of differential failure rates is also demonstrated by comparing mean growth rates in the 1975-80 period. Once failures are taken into account the arithmetic mean growth in Net Assets of the smallest-sized companies is at 24 per cent actually the *lowest* of any size group.

An examination of the variance of growth rates shows that for surviving firms the variance of Net Asset growth rates declined with increasing size in the 1971-75 period. In the 1975-80 period whilst this relationship appears broadly true for surviving companies, it disappears when non-surviving companies are included.

It will be recalled that the Law of Proportionate Effect may be tested directly by an examination of the b coefficient in equation 4.1 reproduced below:

$$\log S_{it+1} = a + b \log S_{it} + \log E_{it} \qquad (4.1)$$

The results of this analysis are presented in Table 4.6. It takes

Table 4.5: Annual growth in net assets

Size £ (Net Assets)	1971-1975				1975-80				Failure Rate
	X	X^{MED}	σ	N	X	X^{MED}	σ	N	
Less than £ 5,000	108.6 (100.8)	32.9 (28.7)	210.0 (195.0)	52 (56)/(76)	44.0 (23.7)	19.6 (0)	72.3 (38.9)	7 (13)/ (19)	46
£ 5,000- 9,999	41.3 (39.0)	24.5 (20.4)	62.0 (58.6)	51 (54)/(66)	35.0 (24.3)	21.7 (8.9)	38.6 (27.0)	16 (23)/ (35)	30
£10,000-24,999	35.7 (34.6)	21.3 (14.8)	49.6 (48.4)	64 (66)/(79)	38.2 (34.0)	19.4 (15.7)	61.3 (53.7)	56 (64)/ (95)	13
£25,000-49,999	29.5 (28.8)	16.7 (17.1)	38.3 (37.4)	42 (43)/(55)	38.2 (32.1)	25.3 (17.4)	53.5 (45.0)	64 (76)/(100)	11
£50,000+	17.9 (17.2)	14.0 (8.8)	21.6 (20.8)	25 (26)/(30)	26.0 (24.1)	18.3 (17.3)	29.6 (27.4)	138 (149)/(201)	7

Notes: a. Figures in parentheses show values when failed companies are taken into account.

b. In the final column for each time period the first figure in parentheses gives the number of companies providing data in the start year and final year *plus* those which are known to have ceased trading between those dates. The second figure adds those companies, which although known to be trading in the final year providing no financial data for that year, to the first bracketed figure.

c. Failure rates are calculated by dividing known failure by known failures plus companies providing records in both final years. It does *not* include companies providing data in the base year but not the final year.

Table 4.6: Regression results: closing and opening size

Equation: $\log S_{it+1} = a + \log bS_{it} + \log E_{it}$

Industries		1971-75 a	b	R²	N	1975-80 a	b	R²	N
All Industries	Net Assets	+ 1.673 (21.1)	+ 0.811 (8.78)	0.628	265	+ 1.251 (5.785)	+ 0.904 (24.757)	0.668	308
	Total Assets	+ 1.472 (7.83)	+ 0.867 (25.61)	0.706	276	+ 1.353 (7.326)	+ 0.900 (31.284)	0.751	324
Mechanical Engineering	Net Assets	+ 1.621 (2.487)	+ 0.851 (7.215)	0.520	50	+ 2.013 (4.478)	+ 0.799 (10.749)	0.619	73
	Total Assets	+ 1.912 (3.472)	+ 0.819 (8.873)	0.602	54	+ 2.131 (4.673)	+ 0.798 (11.519)	0.648	74
Metal Goods	Net Assets	+ 2.591 (4.857)	+ 0.669 (5.657)	0.533	30	+ 0.507 (1.578)	+ 1.018 (19.529)	0.896	46
	Total Assets	+ 1.400 (2.585)	+ 0.911 (8.892)	0.738	30	− 0.342 (0.600)	+ 1.14 (11.394)	0.756	44
Timber & Furniture	Net Assets	+ 2.218 (3.312)	+ 0.734 (5.42)	0.503	31	+ 0.865 (1.533)	+ 0.949 (10.843)	0.776	36
	Total Assets	+ 1.161 (2.841)	+ 0.929 (13.09)	0.847	33	+ 1.394 (3.658)	+ 0.882 (15.894)	0.866	41
Paper & Printing	Net Assets	+ 2.146 (5.524)	+ 0.674 (8.053)	0.669	34	+ 0.538 (0.609)	+ 1.031 (6.204)	0.554	33
	Total Assets	+ 1.597 (3.824)	+ 0.799 (9.910)	0.754	34	+ 0.776 (1.089)	+ 1.013 (8.167)	0.669	35
Other Manufacturing	Net Assets	+ 1.263 (4.801)	+ 0.965 (16.115)	0.688	120	+ 1.916 (5.764)	+ 0.801 (14.239)	0.632	120
	Total Assets	+ 1.594 (5.397)	+ 0.833 (15.48)	0.661	125	+ 1.447 (4.204)	+ 0.885 (16.535)	0.681	130

the two time periods 1971-75 and 1975-80 and the two measures of size, viz. Net Assets and Total Assets. The values of R^2 obtained show that size in the opening year is strongly positively correlated with size in the final year. The b coefficient clearly demonstrates that smaller companies have faster rates of asset growth than larger small companies since the coefficients are consistently less than unity. Only for the Metal Goods and the Timber and Furniture sectors in the 1975-80 period does the b coefficient have a value of excess in unity, although there are a number of sectors where the b coefficient is not significantly different from unity at the 99 per cent level.

A second implication of the Law of Proportionate Effect is that growth rates of firms in time t are independent of their growth rates in time $t + 1$ so if size and growth are unrelated then growth in t and growth in $t + 1$ are unrelated. Our analysis thus far, however, has indicated that, subject to a number of caveats, the relationship between size and growth is weakly negative. It suggests that there may therefore be a weakly positive relationship in the persistency of growth rates over time.

This relationship is examined in Table 4.7, which shows growth in both Total Assets and Net Assets over the two time periods 1971-75 and 1975-80. The left-hand side shows the results for the linear model and the right-hand side shows the results for the log model. It is important to recognise that in constructing this table short-life companies are omitted. Hence there are a maximum of only 196 observations for the Total Assets measure of size for the linear model. By including only small firms that exist over the whole of the nine-year period the analysis is therefore restricted to, by definition, exceptional small firms.

Nevertheless the results show that, for the linear model, there appears to be no evidence of a persistency of growth rates over time. For the All Sector model both 'b' signs are non-significantly negative and the value of R^2 appears to be extremely low. No persistency of growth rates appears over time. Using the log model, however, the Total Assets measure of growth appears to demonstrate a significantly positive degree of persistency over time for the All Sector grouping. No such relationship is apparent for the All Sector model using the Net Assets measure. Furthermore, at the level of the individual sector models only the paper and printing sector, using the Net

Table 4.7: Regression results: persistency of growth 1971-1975 and 1975-1980

Sectors		$G_{75-80} = a + b\,G_{71-75} + E$				$\text{Log } G_{75-80} = a + b\,\text{Log } G_{71-75} + E$			
		a	b	R^2	N	a	b	R^2	N
All Sectors	Net Assets	26.104 (5.711)	− 0.028 (0.618)	0.002	191	2.061 (11.754)	+ 0.028 (0.57)	0.002	148
	Total Assets	36.488 (2.656)	− 0.145 (0.707)	0.003	196	2.209 (9.505)	+ 0.162 (2.310)*	0.031	166
Mechanical Engineering	Net Assets	32.336 (2.700)	− 0.069 (0.495)	0.006	41	1.625 (3.996)	+ 0.096 (0.828)	0.0216	33
	Total Assets	17.443 (4.622)	+ 0.046 (0.858)	0.018	43	2.181 (4.007)	+ 0.180 (1.075)	0.329	36
Metal Goods	Net Assets	19.371 (2.287)	− 0.071 (0.901)	0.037	23	2.445 (4.256)	− 0.144 (0.881)	0.049	17
	Total Assets	13.899 (3.627)	− 0.041 (0.622)	0.018	23	0.867 (1.058)	+ 0.420 (1.737)	0.144	20
Timber & Furniture	Net Assets	35.992 (1.940)	− 0.058 (0.585)	0.018	21	1.292 (1.435)	+ 0.239 (1.134)	0.114	12
	Total Assets	22.159 (2.37)	− 0.059 (0.283)	0.004	21	2.596 (2.122)	+ 0.026 (0.070)	0.0003	17
Paper & Printing	Net Assets	14.782 (3.785)	+ 0.136 (3.511)*	0.369	23	1.769 (6.392)	+ 0.116 (1.361)	0.104	18
	Total Assets	14.233 (3.576)	+ 0.297 (3.569)*	0.377	23	2.053 (3.087)	+ 0.317 (1.504)	0.124	18
Other Manufacturing	Net Assets	26.184 (3.511)	− 0.033 (0.335)	0.001	83	2.305 (8.792)	− 0.004 (0.056)	0.0005	68
	Total Assets	58.921 (1.938)	− 0.295 (0.742)	0.006	86	2.363 (8.195)	+ 0.131 (1.516)	0.031	75

Note: In this and subsequent tables in this chapter an asterisk indicates significance at the 95% confidence level.

Assets measure, shows a significant positive relationship.

It therefore appears from the evidence presented in this section that amongst small manufacturing companies a weakly negative relationship exists between size and growth. It appears to be broadly true that the smallest sizes of company grow faster than the larger (small) companies. The relationship is, however, relatively weak because once the smallest size of company is omitted from the analysis no general relationship is apparent. Amongst small companies there appears little evidence of persistency of growth rates over a nine-year period.

THE EFFECT OF AGE ON GROWTH

Most of the empirical work on large firms which has attempted to test the Law of Proportionate Effect had used simple regression techniques relating size and growth. It has been argued by a number of authors (e.g. Hull, 1985, Johnson, 1986) that age is likely to be a better explanation of growth in small firms rather than size. For example if there is a minimum efficient firm size in the ith industry then a newly established firm would be expected to grow quickly until that size is reached. After that, growth would be more likely to be limited by factors such as aggregate demand for the products of i.

The age of firms may therefore be regarded as a potentially important explanation of firm growth, an explanation which may in some circumstances be regarded as independent of size. To test the hypothesis, equations of the following form were specified:

$$G = a + b_1 S_t + b_2 A_t + E \qquad (4.4)$$
and
$$\log G = a + b_1 \log S_t + b_2 \log A_t + \log E \qquad (4.5)$$
where A_t = Age in year t
S_t = Asset size in year t
G_t = Change in asset size between t and $t + 1$

Tests of equations 4.4 and 4.5 were conducted but the impact of the age variable is most clearly seen in the log model with the results shown in Table 4.8. For the 1971-75 period its introduction shows that for the All Sector model both age and size

Table 4.8: Regression results: size, growth and age, log model   Equation: $\log G = a + b_1 \log S + b_2 \log A + \log E$

Industries		1971-75					1975-80				
		a	b_1	b_2	R^2	N	a	b_1	b_2	R^2	N
All Sectors	Net Assets	5.138 (16.944)	− 0.244 (3.731)*	− 0.365 (3.994)*	0.181	225	2.952 (2.53)	− 0.233 (0.218)	− 0.074 (0.083)	0.054	275
	Total Assets	4.449 (13.576)	− 0.066 (1.084)	− 0.485 (6.166)*	0.167	247	4.019 (12.854)	− 0.065 (1.25)	− 0.314 (5.044)*	0.114	290
Mechanical Engineering	Net Assets	4.926 (5.265)	− 0.123 (0.655)	− 0.463 (2.504)*	0.213	42	2.492 (6.355)	− 0.019 (0.286)	− 0.161 (2.003)*	0.084	62
	Total Assets	3.834 (3.573)	− 0.034 (0.194)	− 0.472 (2.36)*	0.107	50	4.052 (4.716)	+ 0.0178 (0.128)	− 0.573 (4.022)*	0.239	61
Metal Goods	Net Assets	6.049 (8.041)	− 0.44 (2.339)*	− 0.294 (1.166)	0.326	28	2.566 (4.232)	− 0.172 (1.546)	+ 0.122 (0.979)	0.068	39
	Total Assets	3.743 (4.675)	− 0.102 (0.611)	− 0.554 (2.646)*	0.218	29	2.683 (4.265)	+ 0.0796 (0.75)	− 0.287 (2.302)*	0.119	42
Timber & Furniture	Net Assets	6.281 (5.422)	− 0.309 (1.303)	− 0.501 (1.471)	0.233	24	3.501 (4.797)	− 0.163 (1.352)	− 0.081 (0.459)	0.109	29
	Total Assets	4.651 (4.364)	− 0.026 (0.148)	− 0.742 (3.072)*	0.278	29	4.561 (5.901)	− 0.178 (1.331)	− 0.239 (1.161)	0.204	32
Paper & Printing	Net Assets	5.644 (6.209)	− 0.511 (2.103)*	− 0.261 (0.834)	0.294	30	2.400 (4.633)	− 0.018 (0.174)	− 0.053 (0.55)	0.019	28
	Total Assets	5.481 (5.525)	− 0.496 (2.371)*	− 0.109 (0.471)	0.249	27	3.578 (3.409)	+ 0.078 (0.394)	− 0.308 (1.889)	0.117	30
Other Manufacturing	Net Assets	4.555 (9.98)	− 0.238 (2.601)*	− 0.186 (1.304)	0.112	101	3.366 (9.657)	− 0.189 (2.99)*	− 0.003 (0.043)	0.084	117
	Total Assets	4.639 (9.981)	− 0.115 (1.278)	− 0.454 (3.638)*	0.164	112	4.209 (7.887)	− 0.0966 (1.093)	− 0.295 (2.65)*	0.088	125

Note: Significant at 95% level accordingly.

coefficients are significantly negative for the Net Assets measure of size and that the introduction of age significantly increases the value of R^2 for the equation. For the Total Assets measure of size for the 1971-75 period, the introduction of the age variable adds significantly to the value of R^2 although age, rather than size now has a significant 't' coefficient. At a sectoral level the introduction of age significantly improves all the equations, with either age or size having significant 't' statistics for all sectors except the Net Assets measure of growth in the Timber and Furniture industry. Similar, though less spectacular, improvements are found by examining changes in the 1975-80 period. Here the introduction of the age variable leads to a substantial improvement in R^2 for the All Sectors Total Assets equation. At a sectoral level age or size have significant 't' statistics in most equations.

SIZE AND PROFITABILITY IN LARGE FIRMS

Economic theory accords profitability the central role in determining firm size. If profits increase with firm size then this provides an unambiguous incentive for further growth. If, however, profits decline with firm size the only incentive for growth is if these lower profits can be achieved with a higher degree of certainty.

Singh and Whittington (1968) argue that an analysis of profitability and size should be conducted at an industry level for four reasons. First, when considering the relationship between profitability and size the custom has been to use the rate of return on gross or net assets as the measure of profitability. As is to be expected the size distribution of firms considered in most studies shows positive skewness when industries in aggregate are analysed. However, as Whittington (1980) notes, such skewness is reduced considerably when individual industries are considered. Second, economies of scale and monopoly power exist to different degrees in different industries, so that the most profitable size of firm varies between industries. Third, the relative prosperity of different industries varies in different periods because of demand conditions which are independent of the size of the firms in the industry: so aggregating industries with varying degrees of prosperity could lead to a spurious relationship between size and profitability.

Fourth, the errors in measurement of rates of return arising out of different depreciation and asset valuation conventions are likely to be greater between industries than between firms in the same industry.

A number of early studies looked at the degree of correlation between size and profitability e.g. Dewing (1921), Crum (1934, 1939), and Summers (1932). These studies found considerable variation between industries which is hardly surprising given the variable presence of scale economies and monopoly power, and differing levels of demand. Given these factors and the significant differences of average size between industries, the results of multi-sector studies should be viewed with caution. When individual industry groups are analysed, any systematic relationship between mean class profitability and size frequently disappears — see Singh and Whittington (1968), Stekler (1963) and Summers (1932).

As with size and growth the relationship between profitability and size can be tested by linear regression analysis. Singh and Whittington considered the following functional forms for the regressing of profitability on size

$$P = a + b S + E \qquad (4.6)$$
$$P = a + b \log S + E \qquad (4.7)$$

where P is the rate of return on net assets and S is the opening size of companies. Equation 4.6 implies that absolute changes in the rate of return on net assets are linearly related to absolute changes in opening size. Singh and Whittington found only one industry out of four which they examined had a statistically significant value for the b coefficient. Furthermore, the degree of explanation of the rate of return by size was very low. Although most of the b coefficients were not statistically significant the vast majority had negative values suggesting that profitability tended to decline with size. Singh and Whittington then restricted their sample to include only growing and profitable companies. Such a restriction improved the significance of the equation in almost every case and the values for the b coefficients were almost all negative. A further test conducted by Singh and Whittington was to regress post-tax profitability on equity assets. The results tended to offer weaker confirmation of their earlier results.

Equation 4.7 presents the hypothesis that a given proportionate change in opening size causes the same absolute change in the rate of return for all sizes of firm. Singh and Whittington found the degree of explanation obtained by this formulation was higher than with equation 4.6 and the b coefficients were more significant. The logarithm of size seems to have provided a better explanation of profitability than the absolute value of size. This conclusion also held when the equation was tested on post-tax profitability on equity assets. Their correlation and regressions yielded the same result:

> that the average rate of profit is independent of the size of the firm if all companies are considered ..., however, ... the exclusion of non-growing and unprofitable firms gives rise to a weak, but statistically significant tendency for profitability to decline with size. (p. 128)

Singh and Whittington argue that changing the sample gives different results because non-growing and unprofitable firms tend to be smaller than average. They also note that the incidence of revaluations is higher in larger firms which may also partly explain the negative relation between size and profitability. In contrast to the Singh and Whittington results Stekler (1963) found a strong positive relation between size and profitability. However this difference in results is not as strong as it may at first appear as Stekler did not exclude unprofitable and non-growing firms.

In a more recent study Whittington (1980) argued that the functional form of equation 4.7 better reflects the non-skewness of profitability and skewness of size. He also argued that there may be advantages of using a measure of size other than Net Assets. Since Net Assets are usually the denominator of the dependent variable, using it also as the explanatory variable will mean that any measurement error of observation will lead to a downward bias in the estimate of the slope coefficient b. An erroneously observed high rate of return would therefore be associated with an erroneously observed low measure of size. To overcome these problems Whittington used three size measures (Net Assets, Gross Assets, Sales) and four measures of profitability (Rate of Return on Net Assets, Rate of Return on Gross Assets, Profitability Margin, Sales/Asset Ratio). The period covered in the analysis was 1960-74 and the sample was composed only of continuing firms. The semi-log form of equation 4.7 was used to show a clear negative relationship between the Rate of Return and Net Assets, although the proportion of the variance of rate of return explained by size was low. Whittington found a similar relationship when Gross Assets were substituted for Net Assets, but, when he substituted Sales, the value of the b coefficient dropped dramatically. Given the problem of measurement bias discussed above, Whittington concluded that the Sales results are likely to be the least biased and that there is relatively little association between profitability and size but what there is, is negative in direction.

The above results of Whittington were obtained when a number of industries were considered together. At a sectoral level he found considerable inter-industry variation, with the majority of slope coefficients being non-negative but not statistically significantly different from zero. The overall conclusion drawn by Whittington was:

> ... no important positive or negative relationships having been revealed, the results have drawn attention to the sensitivity of the results to the choice of size measure ... Bates (1965) and Newbould, Stray and Wilson (1977) have established that there is a strong positive association between alternative measures of firm size. This association does not mean that these measures can be used as substitutes for one another without introducing potentially misleading sources of bias in statistical estimates. (pp. 344-5)

Even if the average Rate of Return is slightly higher amongst smaller firms they may suffer from a higher dispersion of profitability around the mean. Indeed there are two *a priori* reasons why the dispersion of profitability might be expected to decline with size. First, large firms are usually more diversified. However, since a low dispersion of profits comes from a greater variety of activities which persistently earned different rates of return, this might lead to a greater inter-firm dispersion amongst large firms which were often somewhat arbitrarily classified as belonging to the same industry. Thus there may be a less systematic relationship between the dispersion of profitability and size at the industry level than when all firms are considered across industries (Whittington, 1980). Second, there may be several managerial reasons why large firms exhibit a lower dispersion of profitability since they are more likely to be managed by employees than by owners. Managers are assumed to be more risk averse than owners and to have a higher level of minimum competence. They are also more likely to benefit personally from choosing projects which yield corporate growth rather than necessarily high profitability. Subject to the achievement of a satisfactory level of profit managers are more likely to be more competent in choosing projects which have lower risks, but which are likely to yield lower rates of profits and higher corporate growth.

Singh and Whittington found there was a tendency for the degree of dispersion of profit rates to decline with the size of firms. This was the case for each industry group considered, and is corroborated by the work of Jones (1969) on the mechanical engineering industry. Whittington (1980) also found a significant decline in dispersion of profits as firm size increases. This latter work considered all industries together and used a regression rather than a correlation approach.

A further relationship of interest is that between the variability of an individual firm's profitability and its size. Whittington (1980) used the standard deviation from the firm's average profitability, and from a time trend for the period, as two measures of inter-temporal stability. In both instances he found that the variability of the individual firm's profitability through time decreases as the size of firm increases within the same broad industry group, as well as across all firms. However the proportion of variance explained is low, thus indicating that there are other important factors determining the stability of profits.

A related issue is the persistency of profits through time. Singh and Whittington (1968) examined the relationship between the average Rates of Return on Net Assets in the periods 1948-54 and 1954-60 for the populations of firms which continued over the whole twelve year period. They found that in every industry there was a fairly strong tendency for all firms to show a persistency of profits. The persistency of profits was greater than that found for growth.

To conclude, the empirical literature on average profitability and size suggests that if a relationship is to exist then it will be weakly negative. Although the large firms may suffer from lower average profits they at least have a lower dispersion in their profit rates. Concerning the stability of profit rates the evidence is somewhat ambiguous. Whittington's (1980) work suggests large firms have greater inter-temporal stability, Singh and Whittington's (1968) work suggests that all firms show an equal probability for persistency of profit.

SIZE AND PROFITABILITY IN SMALL NORTHERN ENGLAND COMPANIES

To test for an association between profitability and size amongst companies included in the present data set a number of formulations are possible.

First it is possible to identify a number of definitions of profitability which, although likely to be positively correlated with each other, are not necessarily coincident. A decision has to be made on whether pre-tax or post-tax profits are to be used, and the form of any deduction for distribution to the directors, interest charges, etc. It is also necessary to decide which size variable is the most appropriate by which to normalise total profits — i.e. Total Assets, Net Assets or perhaps Sales.

In general this analysis is seeking a measure of gross profitability to reflect the economic performance of the company in the market place. It therefore chooses the pre-tax level of profit before deductions, rather than taking account of differences in tax liability or the decision of directors on payments to themselves. As noted earlier, the justification for a measure of size with which to normalise absolute levels of profits is less clear and so pre-tax profit is normalised by both Total Assets and Net Assets.

A second familiar problem is the choice of time period over which to conduct the analysis. In the discussions over the relationship between growth and size the periods 1971-75 and 1975-80 were chosen and these are again used in this section. Finally it was also decided, either to include only companies which provided data for the base year and the final year, or all companies in the base year, giving a zero value to those which failed before the final year.

In deriving a contingency table of profitability and size several formulations are possible:

Option 1 takes profitability data for those companies, of a given size in the base year, which provided data in the base year and the final year, and for this group calculates the arithmetic mean and variance using only base year and final year data.

Option 2 estimates mean and variance for surviving companies using all years for which data were provided. However, both Option 1 and Option 2 risk bias since they include only companies trading over a five-or six-year period. Such companies are likely to be more profitable than those companies which fail over that period.

Option 3 recognises this potential bias and additionally includes companies which provide data in the base year but which had ceased to trade by the final year. The inclusion of these companies will not only reduce the profitability of the sample as a whole but, as was shown in the section on size and growth, will have a specific size effect since failures are highly concentrated in the smaller size bands. The use of Option 3 will therefore serve to reduce mean profitability of the smallest size groupings since failure rates are highest in this group.

Even Option 3 does not fully reflect the profitability of *all* small companies since short-life companies which begin trading *after* the base year are excluded because it would be impossible to classify them on a comparable size to base year companies. For example if 1975 is the base year then companies in existence in 1975, whether or not they survived until 1980, would be classified according to their size in 1975. It is, however, clearly inappropriate to include companies which started trading in 1976 to 1977 by classifying them according to the year in which they started trading (or any other year for that matter!)

Profitability and size: Option 1 method

The results shown in Table 4.9 (a) show that for the Total Assets measure of size there is clear evidence in both the 1971-75 period and the 1975-80 period that arithmetic mean profitability rises monotonically with size for companies in business throughout the period. For the smallest sized group of companies pre-tax profits divided by Total Assets was negative, even amongst companies that remained in business for a five-year period. On the other hand pre-tax profitability for companies

108

Table 4.9: The relationship of size and profitability: Option 1

(a) Total Assets Measure

Total Assets	% Profitability 1971-75			% Profitability 1975-80		
£	X̄	σ	N	X̄	σ	N
0- 4,999	2.5	23.1	29	−6.8	13.3	7
5,000- 9,999	4.4	7.2	37	−5.0	19.3	17
10,000-24,999	5.1	11.4	76	1.6	11.7	63
25,000-49,999	6.4	7.3	62	4.8	8.8	66
50,000-99,999	8.9	12.6	34	7.3	9.2	71
100,000+	10.4	7.5	31	9.2	10.5	96

(b) Net Assets Measure

Net Assets	% Profitability 1971-75			% Profitability 1975-80		
£	X̄	σ	N	X̄	σ	N
0- 4,999	24.8	78.4	59	17.2	87.0	20
5,000- 9,999	13.3	30.4	55	−20.5	82.7	24
10,000-24,999	10.2	24.5	69	7.6	20.7	84
25,000-49,999	17.2	24.0	47	12.8	14.4	59
50,000-99,999	13.6	27.2	16	14.8	14.2	52
100,000+	15.4	11.2	12	15.0	22.9	61

with Total Assets of more than £50,000 in the base year was between 7 and 10 per cent in both periods. When pre-tax profits are normalised by Net Assets in Table 4.9 (b) the relationship is much less clear.

An examination of pre-tax profits divided by Net Assets for the 1971-75 period shows no apparent relationship between profitability and size. Indeed the smallest companies in terms of Net Assets in 1971 appear to be the most profitable. Matters are somewhat clearer during the 1975-80 period. Here, although again the smallest size of company appears to be the most profitable, once this group is excluded profitability appears to increase with increasing size. The relatively poorer results obtained with the Net Assets measure is almost certainly attributable to the volatility of this measure of size amongst smaller companies, reflecting the importance of current liabilities in the asset structure. Within current liabilities the relatively greater importance of bank overdraft in small company balance sheets makes the use of Net Assets measure of size highly volatile.

An examination of the variance of profitability for different sized companies does not produce any clear results. Whilst in the 1971-75 period the variance with the smallest size group of companies is the highest, there is no evidence, when this group is excluded, that variance falls with increasing size. Indeed no discernible pattern is observable.

An examination of the variance of profitability with the Total Assets measure of size in the 1975-80 period also shows no consistent pattern and no pattern is observable for the Net Assets measure of size. Hence unlike the large firm studies our data for smaller companies show no evidence that the variance of profitability declines with size.

Option 2 Method

To determine the extent to which the results are biased by using only base year and final year data, Option 2 includes companies providing data not only in the base year and final year but also in *all* intermediate years. The results are shown in Table 4.10. The value for each company is therefore the arithmetic mean profitability of that company for each year between base and final year, with the overall mean for companies in the size group being the sum of these values divided by the number of companies in the size group in the base year.

The broad relationships observed in Table 4.9 remain unchanged in Table 4.10 with the addition of data for intermediate years. It remains broadly true that pre-tax profitability, when normalised by the Total Assets measure of size, is positively associated with size, but that the Net Assets measure of size does not show any clear relationship. The major change occurs in the 1971-75 period for the smallest size group of companies. Here when only 1971 and 1975 data are used for calculating mean profitability then 59 companies achieved +24.8 per cent profitability on Net Assets. However, when all years' data were included only 49 companies were included and their *annualised* profitability was −13.2 per cent. The effect of this was to improve significantly the relationship between size and profitability suggesting, as with the 1975-80 period, a positive relationship. In both cases the largest size firms had the highest mean profitability rates and the smallest size firms had the lowest profitability rates in the 1971-75 period and the second lowest for the 1975-80 period.

Table 4.10: The relationship of size and profitability: Option 2
(a) Total Assets Measure

Total Assets	% Profitability[a] 1971-75			% Profitability 1975-80		
£	X̄	σ	N	X̄	σ	N
0- 4,999	−1.0	20.7	26	−8.0	10.3	7
5,000- 9,999	3.3	5.4	36	−5.9	16.8	16
10,000-24,999	5.4	7.8	72	2.5	10.4	60
25,000-49,999	7.1	5.8	60	5.9	6.9	64
50,000-99,999	8.4	9.7	32	7.4	6.3	69
100,000+	10.5	5.7	31	8.9	7.7	93

(b) Net Assets Measure

Net Assets	% Profitability[b] 1971-75			% Profitability 1975-80		
£	X̄	σ	N	X̄	σ	N
0- 4,999	−13.2	81.7	49	6.9	35.7	15
5,000- 9,999	11.8	16.5	51	− 5.1	37.2	21
10,000-24,999	10.8	16.0	68	9.3	11.3	77
25,000-49,999	16.6	16.9	45	12.3	12.2	57
50,000-99,999	13.4	20.5	16	13.4	9.2	49
100,000+	16.8	6.3	12	14.3	15.2	60

Notes: a. Profitability = Pre-Tax Profit/Total Assets.
      b. Profitability = Pre-Tax Profit/Net Assets.

Option 3 Method

The Option 3 'Total Assets' results shown in Table 4.11 confirm those of Options 1 and 2. Here mean profitability increases with size and the variance of profitability shows no discernible general relationship with size. The Net Assets results indicate broadly similar trends.

The results presented in Tables 4.9, 4.10 and 4.11 show that unambiguous relationships between size and profitability do not exist with Options 1 and 2. However, when the third options measure is added it appears to be broadly true that the smaller firms tend to have lower mean profitability and a higher variability of profitability than the larger firms. Thus the result of the 'larger firm' studies — that the larger firms have a lower

Table 4.11: The relationship of size and profitability: Option 3

(a) Total Assets Measure

Total Assets	% Profitability[a] 1971-75			% Profitability 1975-80		
£	X̄	σ	N	X̄	σ	N
0- 4,999	−5.4	17.8	32	−2.9	3.8	13
5,000- 9,999	0.7	1.5	41	−1.1	5.8	30
10,000-24,999	1.0	2.2	84	0.4	6.1	92
25,000-49,999	1.7	1.4	66	0.6	2.6	94
50,000-99,999	1.6	3.5	39	1.4	1.5	91
100,000+	2.6	1.4	32	1.7	1.6	118

(b) Net Assets Measure

Net Assets	% Profitability[b] 1971-75			% Profitability 1975-80		
£	X̄	σ	N	X̄	σ	N
0- 4,999	−4.3	19.5	64	−0.6	9.1	39
5,000- 9,999	2.4	4.4	56	−7.1	38.3	53
10,000-24,999	2.6	4.4	76	−0.4	21.8	103
25,000-49,999	−0.9	2.8	52	2.0	2.8	78
50,000-99,999	3.2	4.9	18	2.2	4.0	64
100,000+	4.2	1.6	12	3.8	3.0	70

Notes: a. Profitability = Pre-Tax Profit/Total Assets.
b. Profitability = Pre-Tax Profit/Net Assets.

variability of profitability at the cost of lower average profits — is not confirmed by the results presented here.

Studies of large firms used regression techniques to test for a relationship between size and profitability. As noted earlier two forms of equation were favoured, both of which were estimated at the industry level and at the aggregate level.

$$P = a + b S + E \qquad (4.8)$$
and
$$P = a + b \log_e S + E \qquad (4.9)$$

In replicating this analysis separate tabulations are provided for the two time periods 1971-75 and 1975-80 and for the two measures of size, i.e. Total Assets and Net Assets. Using the simple linear model the results for the Total Assets measure are shown in Table 4.12. In part (a) of the table the coefficients apply to the 1971-75 period and in part (b) they apply to the

1975-80 period. The right hand side of the table presents co-efficients derived from data only on profitable firms whilst the left hand side presents coefficients derived from data on all firms.

From the earlier analysis it is to be expected that the b coefficient for the Total Assets measure of size will be significantly and positively associated with profits, confirming that larger firms, defined in terms of Total Assets, are more profitable, so that for each £10,000 increase in size profitability rates rose by approximately 2.8 per cent. At a sectoral level in the 1971-75 period three sectors also show significantly positive b coefficients, e.g. Mechanical Engineering, Timber and Furniture and the Other Manufacturing sector. The b coefficients for Mechanical Engineering and for Other Manufacturing are similar to that for the all Manufacturing but that for Timber and Furniture is more than double those for the other sectors indicating that increasing size has a substantially greater effect on profitability in this sector.

Using the Total Assets measure of size and profitability for the 1975-80 period shows that when all sectors are aggregated the b coefficient on size is positive, although it has a lower value than for the 1971-75 period. At the sectoral level, however, only the Metal Goods sector has a significant 't' statistic at the 95 per cent level, but all sectoral coefficients are positive.

When only profitable firms are included in the analysis broadly similar results are obtained. In the 1971-75 period the All Industries grouping has a significantly positive b coefficient which, as would be expected, has a lower slope and a higher intercept. At the sectoral level only Timber and Other Manufacturing have significantly positive coefficients. However, in the 1975-80 period none of the b coefficient is significantly positive.

The exclusion of unprofitable firms therefore appears somewhat to weaken the observed relationship between profitability and size, in terms of Total Assets in both time periods. Furthermore the relationship of size and profitability appears weaker in the 1975-80 period with an All Industries b coefficient of only 0.0008 compared with 0.0028 for the earlier period.[3]

Finally Table 4.13 provides results for the logarithmic model for the two time periods for both the Net Assets and Total Assets measure of size. The table confirms earlier results with the linear model that when the Net Assets measure of size is

113

Table 4.12: Profitability and size: linear regression results (Total Assets Measure)
(a) 1971-75

	All cases				Profitable firms only			
	a	b	R^2	N	a	b	R^2	N
All Industries	4.467 (6.789)	+0.0028 (3.983)*	0.0586	257	6.873 (14.298)	+0.0019 (3.811) *	0.0614	224
Mechanical Engineering	5.838 (5.131)	+0.0023 (2.147)*	0.0876	50	7.353 (6.519)	+0.0018 (1.788)	0.071	44
Metal Goods	6.729 (3.843)	+0.0018 (0.639)*	0.016	27	7.125 (4.014)	+0.0017 (0.571)	0.013	26
Timber & Furniture	2.913 (2.229)	+0.0067 (3.856)*	0.339	31	3.371 (2.565)	+0.0063 (3.672)*	0.325	30
Paper & Print	3.939 (2.334)	+0.0018 (0.517)	0.009	31	7.076 (4.639)	-0.0001 (0.044)	0.00009	24
Other Manufacturing	3.672 (3.14)	+0.0028 (2.515)*	0.0517	118	7.24 (10.45)	+0.0016 (2.524)*	0.061	100

(b) 1975-80

	All cases				Profitable firms only			
	a	b	R^2	N	a	b	R^2	N
All Industries	4.479 (7.152)	+0.0008 (3.205)*	0.0323	329	8.135 (18.525)	+0.0003 (1.60)	0.010	253
Mechanical Engineering	7.648 (7.714)	+0.0008 (1.748)	0.043	90	8.969 (9.04)	+0.0005 (1.276)	0.0261	63
Metal Goods	2.911 (2.241)	+0.0014 (2.516)*	0.128	45	6.091 (5.928)	+0.0009 (1.999)	0.102	37
Timber & Furniture	1.157 (0.631)	+0.0009 (1.746)*	0.074	40	7.074 (5.102)	+0.00012 (0.343)	0.005	28
Paper & Print	3.927 (2.645)	+0.0018 (0.710)*	0.0165	32	6.891 (6.632)	−0.0003 (0.135)	0.0008	26
Other Manufacturing	4.141 (3.369)	+0.0008 (1.557)*	0.0198	122	8.979 (12.243)	+0.00005 (0.174)	0.0003	99

Note: *Significant at 95% level accordingly.

Table 4.13: Profitability and size: log model
(a) Net Assets Measure

	1971-75				1975-80			
	a	b	R^2	N	a	b	R^2	N
All Industries	1.988 (6.062)	+0.0883 (1.369)	0.009	207	2.724 (8.958)	−0.0286 (0.569)	0.0012	257
Mechanical Engineering	4.126 (3.504)	−0.279 (1.329)	0.044	40	1.854 (2.834)	+0.106 (1.010)	0.0164	63
Metal Goods	2.414 (3.136)	−0.015 (0.086)	0.0003	24	2.685 (3.799)	−0.053 (0.436)	0.005	38
Timber & Furniture	−0.051 (0.053)	+0.437 (2.298)*	0.169	28	3.685 (3.374)	−0.181 (1.097)	0.0442	28
Paper & Print	1.548 (1.328)	+0.141 (0.582)	0.151	24	1.512 (1.965)	+0.144 (1.006)	0.044	24
Other Manufacturing	2.205 (4.874)	+0.0686 (0.749)	0.0063	91	3.233 (6.363)	−0.087 (1.027)	0.0102	104

(b) Total Assets Measure

	1971-75				1975-80			
	a	b	R^2	N	a	b	R^2	N
All Industries	0.253 (0.776)	+0.252 (4.361)*	0.0789	224	0.925 (3.061)	+0.143 (3.121)*	0.037	253
Mechanical Engineering	-0.453 (0.419)	+0.357 (1.988)*	0.086	44	0.588 (0.773)	+0.207 (1.832)	0.052	63
Metal Goods	1.193 (1.551)	+0.0922 (0.619)	0.157	26	0.323 (0.414)	+0.201 (1.657)	0.0727	37
Timber & Furniture	-0.357 (0.397)	+0.311 (2.021)	0.127	30	0.765 (0.907)	+0.124 (1.053)	0.041	28
Paper & Print	-0.25 (0.228)	+0.348 (1.701)	0.116	24	1.064 (1.353)	+0.126 (0.931)	0.0348	26
Other Manufacturing	0.297 (0.647)	+0.259 (3.175)	0.093	100	1.355 (2.698)	+0.0926 (1.226)	0.015	99

Note: *Significant at 95% level accordingly.

used only companies in the Timber and Furniture sector in the 1971-75 period show a positive relationship between size and profitability. For the Total Assets measure of size, profitability and size are positively related at an aggregate level for both time periods, although this relationship appears rather weaker in the 1975-80 period than in the earlier.

THE ROLE OF AGE OF COMPANY

In examining the relationship of growth and size in small firms it was argued that age could be an important factor which was affecting growth independent of size. A similar argument can be presented for the effect of age upon profitability. For example, it would be expected that since most young companies claim to expand on the basis of retained profits (Storey, 1982) that younger companies would be more profitable than similar-sized older companies. Thus if there is a minimum efficient size of firm in industry i then a recently established firm in that industry will need to generate high profits in order to achieve sufficient growth to generate scale economies.

To test these hypotheses linear and log models of the following form were specified.

$$P = a + b_1 S + b_2 A + E \qquad (4.10)$$
$$\log P = a + b_1 \log S + b_2 \log A + E \qquad (4.11)$$

The results derived for equation 4.10 are shown in Table 4.14. It includes results for both the Net Assets and Total Assets measures of size, and shows no support whatsoever for the view that the age of a small company is an important factor, independent of size, in explaining variations in profitability. Neither at the All Sector level nor for any individual sector does the age variable have a significant 't' statistic or add more than marginally to the explanatory power of the equation. The size variable, however, continues to be significant in the same equations as in Table 4.12.

On the other hand when the log model is used the age variable (in Table 4.15) appears to exert some effect upon profitability that is independent of size and in the direction predicted. For the 1971-75 period, All Sectors, the age variable is

118

Table 4.14: Regression results: profitability; size and age, linear model $P = a + b_1 S + b_2 A + E$

Industries		1971-75					1975-80				
		a	b_1	b_2	R^2	N	a	b_1	b_2	R^2	N
All Sectors	Net Assets	5.745 (1.916)	+0.007 (1.506)	−0.0004 (0.208)	0.0096	241	10.697 (6.391)	+0.002 (2.308)*	−0.098 (1.376)	0.020	284
	Total Assets	4.524 (6.398)	+0.0028 (3.675)*	−0.0015 (0.274)	0.051	'257	4.549 (5.48)	+0.0009 (3.002)*	−0.0062 (0.168)	0.032	310
Mechanical Engineering	Net Assets	17.943 (3.894)	+0.002 (0.549)	−0.2947 (1.641)	0.027	44	16.172 (8.351)	+0.0017 (1.702)	−0.194 (1.971)	0.073	69
	Total Assets	5.015 (3.168)	+0.0023 (2.157)*	+0.035 (0.352)	0.108	49	8.494 (7.147)	+0.001 (2.053)*	−0.069 (1.146)	0.063	67
Metal Goods	Net Assets	16.864 (3.093)	+0.0001 (0.012)	−0.257 (0.572)	0.013	27	0.909 (0.129)	+0.0051 (1.158)	+0.042 (0.139)	0.043	38
	Total Assets	7.226 (3.091)	+0.0027 (0.822)	−0.113 (0.608)	0.039	27	2.311 (1.382)	+0.0015 (2.362)*	+0.028 (0.364)	0.138	44
Timber & Furniture	Net Assets	4.6274 (0.995)	+0.028 (2.492)	+0.117 (0.555)	0.252	27	6.307 (1.552)	+0.003 (1.838)	−0.0899 (0.674)	0.106	32
	Total Assets	3.286 (1.668)	+0.0073 (3.545)*	−0.051 (0.552)	0.357	27	0.792 (0.304)	+0.0008 (1.173)	+0.032 (0.34)	0.072	37
Paper & Print	Net Assets	11.433 (3.216)	+0.0089 (0.980)	−0.266 (1.49)	0.084	28	−0.0696 (0.017)	+0.010 (1.114)	+0.103 (0.757)	0.087	29
	Total Assets	5.12 (1.914)	+0.0027 (0.622)	−0.070 (0.534)	0.017	29	2.206 (1.141)	+0.0019 (0.674)	+0.054 (0.822)	0.052	31
Other Manufacturing	Net Assets	−1.561 (0.260)	+0.011 (1.306)	−0.0004 (0.012)	0.015	115	12.710 (4.56)	0.0011 (0.608)	−0.0879 (0.675)	0.005	116
	Total Assets	3.997 (3.277)	+0.0026 (2.224)*	−0.0010 (0.149)	0.039	125	3.700 (2.26)	+0.0008 (1.279)	−0.034 (0.434)	0.021	131

Note: *Significant at 95% level accordingly.

Table 4.15: Regression results: profitability; size and age, log model $\log P = a + b_1 \log S + b_2 \log A + \log E$

Industries		1971-75					1975-80				
		a	b_1	b_2	R^2	N	a	b_1	b_2	R^2	N
All Sectors	Net Assets	1.634 (5.082)	+0.213 (3.289)*	-0.154 (1.89)	0.055	199	1.714 (6.42)	+0.179 (3.831)*	-0.156 (2.961)*	0.069	235
	Total Assets	0.839 (2.757)	+0.194 (3.545)*	-0.073 (1.081)	0.056	213	0.957 (3.122)	+0.159 (3.176)*	-0.059 (1.028)	0.040	247
Mechanical Engineering	Net Assets	2.948 (2.586)	-0.0179 (0.078)	-0.174 (0.704)	0.021	37	1.657 (2.64)	+0.235 (2.12)*	-0.266 (2.179)*	0.106	57
	Total Assets	1.094 (0.931)	+0.164 (0.867)	-0.143 (0.633)	0.026	40	0.595 (0.799)	+0.238 (1.951)	-0.082 (0.662)	0.066	58
Metal Goods	Net Assets	2.44 (3.133)	+0.052 (0.262)	-0.189 (0.741)	0.026	24	1.040 (1.571)	+0.222 (1.962)*	-0.076 (0.656)	0.114	33
	Total Assets	1.292 (1.551)	0.171 (0.957)	-0.294 (1.408)	0.087	25	0.339 (0.422)	+0.205 (1.577)	-0.027 (0.191)	0.072	36
Timber & Furniture	Net Assets	0.382 (0.415)	+0.376 (2.00)*	-0.0035 (0.014)	0.176	25	2.211 (2.511)	+0.044 (0.297)	-0.054 (0.28)	0.005	24
	Total Assets	-1.407 (1.389)	+0.455 (2.684)*	+0.078 (0.377)	0.27	26	0.950 (1.05)	+0.169 (1.06)	-0.173 (0.674)	0.047	26
Paper & Print	Net Assets	0.602 (0.538)	+0.482 (2.065)*	-0.316 (0.923)	0.183	22	0.803 (0.987)	0.323 (1.929)	-0.112 (0.881)	0.164	22
	Total Assets	0.765 (0.808)	+0.209 (1.136)	-0.048 (0.171)	0.069	22	0.983 (1.18)	+0.124 (0.784)	+0.022 (0.198)	0.045	24
Other Manufacturing	Net Assets	1.564 (3.191)	+0.219 (2.357)*	-0.109 (0.969)	0.062	91	1.93 (4.46)	+0.175 (2.241)*	-0.191 (2.106)*	0.065	99
	Total Assets	0.876 (2.243)	+0.192 (2.767)	-0.035 (0.410)	0.270	101	1.341 (2.561)	+0.119 (1.417)	-0.069 (0.727)	0.020	103

Note: *Significant at 95% level accordingly.

significantly negative at the 90 per cent level for the Net Assets measure, although it is not significant for any of the individual sectors. For the Total Assets equations the All Sectors age coefficient is non-significantly negative — a result which is repeated for all the individual sectors. When the 1975-80 period is examined the results are clearer with the age variable having a significantly negative coefficient and size having a significantly positive coefficient in the Net Assets equation for the All Sector model. Even so, these two variables only explain approximately 7 per cent of the variance of profitability across the whole sample, suggesting that bias could be introduced by the non-inclusion of relevant variables. At the sectoral level the age and size variables have significant 't' statistics both in the Mechanical Engineering Industry and in the Other Manufacturing sectors, whilst size is significant in the Metal Goods industry. The results for the Total Assets measure of size are less encouraging, with size continuing to exert a positive and significant influence on the All Sectors model but for no individual sectors. The age coefficients have negative signs both for the All Sectors model and for four out of the five individual sectors. Nevertheless it is not statistically significant from zero in any single equation.

The generally better results obtained in Table 4.15 compared with Table 4.14 could be attributed either to the choice of a log model *per se* or the inclusion within Table 4.15 only of profitable companies. To assess the relative impacts of these influences, Table 4.16 applies the linear model only to profitable companies. Comparing Table 4.14 with Table 4.16 shows that the removal of approximately 40 loss making companies has relatively little impact in the 1971-75 period. Neither size nor age provides a significant explanation of variations in the Net Assets measures of profitability, whereas size does provide a significantly positive coefficient in the Total Assets equation both for the All Sector model and for the Timber and Furniture sector. In this it parallels the results in Table 4.14.

In the 1975-80 period however the exclusion of between 40 and 50 loss-making firms makes the results much closer to those obtained in Table 4.15. For the All Sector Net Assets equation the size coefficient is significantly negative, although this is not repeated for any of the individual sectoral equations. However, unlike the results of the log model in Table 4.15, the size coefficient is significant at the 90 per cent but not at the 95 per cent

Table 4.16: Regression results: profitability; size and age, linear model: profitable companies only

$$P = a + b_1 S + b_2 A + E$$

Industries		1971-75					1975-80				
		a	b_1	b_2	R^2	N	a	b_1	b_2	R^2	N
All Sectors	Net Assets	15.728 (14.052)	+0.0016 (0.994)	-0.0087 (1.113)	0.0118	211	16.129 (14.026)	+0.0012 (1.819)	-0.122 (2.465)*	0.028	241
	Total Assets	7.419 (14.354)	+0.0015 (3.206)*	-0.002 (0.835)	0.049	217	8.298 (14.607)	+0.0003 (1.575)	-0.0088 (0.356)	0.010	253
Mechanical Engineering	Net Assets	22.428 (4.724)	+0.0014 (0.399)	-0.38 (1.33)	0.048	38	17.554 (9.591)	-0.0012 (1.259)	-0.162 (1.674)	0.0522	60
	Total Assets	8.063 (5.064)	+0.0018 (1.814)	-0.047 (0.50)	0.080	41	9.174 (7.904)	+0.0007 (1.38)	-0.027 (0.425)	0.033	61
Metal Goods	Net Assets	18.027 (3.233)	-0.0023 (0.198)	-0.0586 (0.115)	0.0029	24	11.993 (4.969)	+0.002 (1.935)	-0.117 (1.196)	0.126	33
	Total Assets	7.256 (3.050)	+0.0016 (0.496)	+0.002 (0.010)	0.011	25	6.324 (4.786)	+0.0009 (2.096)	-0.027 (0.478)	0.117	36
Timber & Furniture	Net Assets	6.831 (1.592)	+0.0235 (2.225)	+0.149 (0.773)	0.252	25	13.053 (4.098)	+0.0014 (1.657)	-0.072 (0.652)	0.051	24
	Total Assets	3.493 (1.783)	+0.0067 (3.197)*	-0.029 (0.315)	0.331	26	7.631 (3.883)	+0.0002 (0.361)	-0.021 (0.300)	0.006	26
Paper & Print	Net Assets	11.457 (3.252)	-0.0009 (0.092)	+0.0095 (0.045)	0.0004	22	8.313 (3.969)	+0.0009 (0.198)	+0.082 (1.216)	0.086	22
	Total Assets	7.103 (2.974)	-0.002 (0.489)	+0.064 (0.451)	0.0142	22	5.346 (4.384)	-0.0011 (0.613)	+0.081 (2.012)*	0.162	24
Other Manufacturing	Net Assets	16.02 (10.68)	+0.0016 (0.873)	-0.0085 (1.198)	0.0248	102	18.442 (8.075)	0.0004 (0.332)	-0.145 (1.388)	0.0197	102
	Total Assets	7.986 (11.305)	+0.0012 (1.946)	-0.003 (0.896)	0.045	103	8.807 (9.019)	+0.000004 (0.014)	+0.015 (0.342)	0.001	106

Note: *Significant at 95% level accordingly.

level in the Net Assets equation. The Total Assets Equation for the 1975-80 period produces a somewhat strange result since the age coefficient is non-significantly negative both for the All Sector model and for all the individual sectors except for Paper and Printing where a significantly *positive* coefficient is derived. This is due to the presence of a highly profitable but old company and explains why, when the log model is applied in Table 4.20, the effect of this 'extreme' case is reduced.

Persistence of Profitability

It is also possible to examine the extent to which profitability persists from one period to the next. Again the two periods examined are 1971-75 and 1975-80, with two measures of profits using both a log and a linear relationship of the form.

$$\pi_t = a + b \, \pi_{t-1} \tag{4.12}$$
and
$$\log \pi_t = a + b \log \pi_{t-1} \tag{4.13}$$

The results are shown in Table 4.17. The table shows that for those firms providing data for the whole of the period 1971-80 there was clear evidence of persistence of profitability over the two periods, i.e. those small firms making high profits in the 1971-75 period continued to earn high profits in the 1975-80 period. This result occurs with both profitability measures and both the linear and log models. At a sector level, using the linear model, the positive relationship appears for the Total Assets measure of profitability in the Mechanical Engineering sector and Other Manufacturing. The significantly positive b coefficient is derived for the Net Assets equations for the Mechanical Engineering sector. The logarithmic specification also yields significant b coefficients but at a sectoral level only the b coefficient from Other Manufacturing equations is significant.

The clearest evidence of the persistence of profitability over time is shown in Table 4.18 which examines profitable firms only using a linear model. These equations show that approximately 20 per cent of the variation in profitability in 1975-80 can be explained by profitability levels in the earlier period. At a sectoral level the relationship is found to be robust in the

123

Table 4.17: Persistency of profitability; 1971-1975 and 1975-1980, regression results

Sectors		$\pi_{75\text{-}80} = a + b\pi_{71\text{-}75} + E$				$\log \pi_{75\text{-}80} = a + b \log \pi_{71\text{-}75} + \log E$			
		a	b	R^2	N	a	b	R^2	N
All Sectors	Net Assets	7.958 (6.601)	+0.105 (2.14)*	0.029	157	1.655 (7.066)	+0.277 (3.134)*	0.076	122
	Total Assets	0.503 (0.480)	+0.591 (5.582)*	0.151	177	1.304 (6.497)	+0.285 (2.993)*	0.065	131
Mechanical Engineering	Net Assets	5.649 (2.559)	+0.568 (5.233)*	0.453	35	1.495 (2.319)	+0.364 (1.532)	0.075	31
	Total Assets	3.433 (2.515)	+0.660 (5.069)*	0.409	39	1.247 (2.208)	+0.419 (1.67)	0.091	30
Metal Goods	Net Assets	8.514 (2.175)	−0.199 (0.939)	0.052	18	2.409 (3.826)	−0.175 (0.66)	0.038	13
	Total Assets	1.203 (0.44)	+0.222 (0.618)	0.018	22	1.928 (3.15)	−0.314 (0.921)	0.061	15
Timber & Furniture	Net Assets	3.587 (0.749)	+0.165 (0.763)	0.033	19	1.844 (3.207)	+0.148 (0.687)	0.041	13
	Total Assets	1.386 (0.577)	+0.351 (1.546)	0.123	19	1.255 (2.353)	+0.128 (0.471)	0.016	15
Paper & Print	Net Assets	0.102 (0.0025)	+0.269 (0.910)	0.046	19	1.578 (3.205)	+0.243 (1.215)	0.156	10
	Total Assets	1.041 (0.529)	+0.271 (1.203)	0.078	19	1.669 (3.954)	+0.013 (0.058)	0.0003	11
Other Manufacturing	Net Assets	9.689 (5.687)	+0.048 (0.857)	0.011	66	1.405 (4.183)	+0.401 (3.233)*	0.164	55
	Total Assets	−1.134 (0.570)	+0.702 (3.62)*	0.147	78	1.085 (3.778)	+0.422 (3.182)*	0.148	60

Note: *Significant at 95% level accordingly.

Table 4.18: Persistency of profitability; 1971-1975 and 1975-1980 regression results: Profitable firms only

		$\pi_{75-80} = a + b\, \pi_{71-75}$			
		a	b	R^2	N
All Sectors	Net Assets	8.48 (7.273)	+0.306 (5.332) *	0.192	122
	Total Assets	4.783 (6.074)	+0.413 (5.752)*	0.204	131
Mechanical Engineering	Net Assets	7.262 (2.832)	+0.517 (4.316)*	0.391	31
	Total Assets	5.205 (2.576)	+0.587 (3.265)*	0.276	30
Metal Goods	Net Assets	11.285 (3.96)	−0.091 (0.646)	0.036	13
	Total Assets	7.049 (3.196)	−0.131 (0.476)	0.017	15
Timber & Furniture	Net Assets	6.819 (1.795)	+0.281 (1.742)	0.216	13
	Total Assets	4.55 (2.323)	+0.239 (1.354)	0.124	15
Paper & Print	Net Assets	8.999 (2.442)	+0.057 (0.255)	0.008	10
	Total Assets	6.471 (3.429)	−0.0188 (0.101)	0.001	11
Other Manufacturing	Net Aseets	8.027 (5.176)	+0.349 (4.375)*	0.265	55
	Total Assets	3.95 (3.549)	+0.507 (5.153)*	0.314	60

Note: *Significant at 95% level accordingly.

Mechanical Engineering and Other Manufacturing industries.

Our conclusions therefore are similar to those of Singh and Whittington who show that rates of profit persist over time, particularly, in our case, for firms making positive levels of profit in the base year. Profitability appears to be more persistent than growth over the same time period.

It would, however, be unwise to assume that this result indicated stability of profitability of firms over time. In fact the reverse is the case since the year-to-year volatility of profit rates is considerable. This is shown in Table 4.19 where profit rates of all companies in 1975 are grouped. Thus in 1975 there were 54 companies or 20 per cent of all companies which had negative profits. The profit rates of all companies over the five years after

Table 4.19: Variability of profitability

Profit Rate in 1975	Number of companies in 1975		Companies remaining in 1975 profit group for:							
			0 or 1 year		2 years		3 years		4 or more years	
	No.	%	No.	%	No.	%	No.	%	No.	%
Negative	54	20	33	61	9	17	8	15	4	7
0 – 4.9%	45	17	31	69	7	16	3	7	4	9
5 – 9.9%	50	19	36	72	9	18	5	10	0	0
10 – 19.0%	66	24	36	55	12	18	9	14	9	13
>20%	55	20	39	70	8	14	3	5	5	9
Total	270	100	175	65	45	17	28	10	22	8

1975 were then examined to see the number of years in which they remained within the same profitability range. Overall 65 per cent of companies remained in their 1975 profitability range for only one year out of the next five and only 8 per cent of companies remained in the same profit range for four or more years.

Several possible explanations for this apparent volatility are possible. Firstly it may be a sectoral effect with certain industries being very volatile, but further analysis showed that this volatility was found in all industries. Secondly, it could be due to the presence of failed companies. Thus a firm which provided only a single year's data after 1975 would be included in the 65 per cent figure. It might also be argued that such firms would probably be earning low rates of profit in 1975 and that high volatility would be characteristic of companies making low or negative profits. As Table 4.19 shows, however, there is no evidence that companies making low or negative profits are more likely either to be more or less volatile than the sample as a whole. Finally it could be argued that 1975 was not a typical year but analyses conducted for other years (not reproduced here) illustrate a similar pattern.

The broad pattern of persistence of profitability over a long period of time amongst surviving small companies therefore has to be taken in conjunction with considerable year-to-year fluctuations in profitability. There is no evidence that these fluctuations depend upon the absolute level of profitability of the companies.

CONCLUSION

This chapter has examined the relationship between size and the performance of firms of different sizes, with performance being defined in terms of profitability and growth. It restates the results of the major existing empirical work on this matter, but argues that these cannot necessarily be generalised to the type of very small firms which are examined in this volume.

The large firm study results are shown on the left-hand side of Table 4.20. Very broadly this shows that growth rates are unrelated to size whilst profitability falls with increasing size. The dispersions of both performance measures are found to fall with increasing size.

127

The results obtained in this chapter on these relationships for smaller firms are complicated on three grounds. Firstly, an appropriate measure of size has to be constructed and so use is made *both* of Net Assets and Total Assets, with the latter being the technically preferred measure. Secondly, the choice of time periods over which these relations are expected to hold needs to be made. It cannot be too long since the high rates of failure amongst small companies mean that any relationships so derived would reflect surviving rather than all small companies. Alternatively the period chosen cannot be too short since this would risk any relationships having had insufficient time to become established. In this chapter periods of five or six years were chosen. Finally, explicit account of the importance of small failed companies is taken by providing tabulated data with and without failures.

The results of our studies are shown on the right hand side of Table 4.20. It will be recalled that using the contingency table approach it was shown that growth rates were lowest in the largest companies and highest in the smallest companies. This relationship was particularly apparent when only surviving companies were included and for the 1971-75 period. However, when failed companies were included and particularly when the smallest size group was eliminated then any relationship became less clear. The use of regression techniques, using survivors and all size bands, showed broadly negative signs for the linear model and significantly negative signs for the log model. Finally, a coefficient of less than unity was obtained when the log of closing size was regressed on the log of opening size, suggesting that smaller firms were growing faster.

To some degree however, rapid growth amongst the smallest

Table 4.20: Comparison of results of small and large firm studies

		Size of firm	
		Large firm studies	Small firm study
Growth rates	Mean	Unrelated	Weakly negative
	Dispersion	Negative	Unrelated
Profit rates	Mean	Negative	Positive
	Dispersion	Negative	Weakly negative

Note: Significant at 95% level accordingly.

group of firms may be attributable to their relative youth. Hence, when age is specifically included as a variable in the regression equations it has a significantly negative coefficient, whilst size also appears to continue to exert a negative effect. In summary therefore the relationship of size to growth is likely to be negative amongst small firms, but is strongly influenced by young firms which tend to be small and the relationship is far from consistently apparent throughout the analysis. It is for this reason that the summary Table 4.20 describes the relationship as weakly negative.

The large firm studies showed that the dispersion of growth rates fell with increasing size, partly because larger companies were more likely to be managed by professionals who, due to their risk aversion, would be less likely than owners to choose risky projects with high growth potential. Secondly, the larger number of projects undertaken by large companies will inevitably result in a reduced variance across the corporate group for any given time period.

Amongst small firms in this study evidence of a relationship between the variance of growth rates and initial size was unclear. It was shown that amongst very small firms high dispersion mirrored high mean growth rates, but that once this group was eliminated there was no evidence of any association between size and the variance of growth rates. This is somewhat reassuring since the firms in this sample are exclusively owner-managed and do not have a wide product base. Hence it would be difficult to attribute either of the explanations given above, for the variance of growth to decline with size amongst large firms, to this collection of small firms.

The remainder of Table 4.20 shows that, in contrast to the large firm studies, profitability increases with size, with the larger firms in this sample showing higher rates of profit than smaller firms. These results are relatively clear whether or not failed firms are included in the sample, whether the measure of pre-tax profitability is normalised by Net or Total Assets and even when loss-making firms are excluded. The relationship is clear at almost all sectoral levels. This result should of course not be a surprise since it suggests the presence of a L-shaped Long Run Average Cost (LRAC) with there being cost advantages of firms reaching a minimum efficient size. Nevertheless it always remains reassuring to obtain such results!

Table 4.20 also shows that the variance of profitability rates is not clearly related to initial size, once the smallest cases have been removed. Nevertheless the general pattern may be weakly negative which is a cause for concern since neither the ownership nor the diverse markets/projects argument is likely to apply to this collection of firms. Most of these firms are likely to have a single product, and many are likely to have only a single customer or at most a handful of customers, and in this respect the relatively large firms in this study are unlikely to differ significantly from those at the small end. It is not easy to provide an alternative explanation, for small firms, of why the variance of profitability should decline with size; it merely needs to be clearly stated that the large firm explanations are inadequate in this case.

In short, Table 4.20 clearly demonstrates that a small firm is not simply a scaled-down version of a large firm. Indeed it could even be argued that it is unwise to undertake comparisons of this type because they ignore the importance of factors such as age which have a significant effect on small firm performance and little impact on large firm performance. This chapter has shown that, *ceteris paribus*, young firms are both more profitable and grow faster than older firms. To ignore the age factor is to lose an important dimension of understanding.

Finally it is also important to emphasize the volatile nature of the performance of small firms. We note that, over time, profitability appears to be more persistent than asset growth, and yet the year-to-year variations appear massive. It is our view that only with this understanding of small firm performance is it possible to discuss adequately the questions of public policy raised in the next chapter.

NOTES

1. If the variances of the different sub-groups are not equal, the Welch-Aspin test for equality of means is more appropriate than the more familiar Student's t-test. (See Aspin and Welch, 1949).

2. For a mathematical proof of this reasoning see Chesher (1979).

3. Using the Net Assets measure of size there is no evidence of any relationship between size and profitability, either at the aggregate level or for any sector, with the exception of the Timber and Furniture industry.

5

Public Policy: Profits, Jobs and Picking the Winners

INTRODUCTION

The previous chapter discussed the relationship of size to the performance indicators of growth and profitability. It concluded that amongst small firms the very small tended to grow slightly faster but were less profitable than larger small firms. It also showed that younger small firms grew faster and were more profitable than similar sized but older firms.

The purpose of this chapter is to investigate the link between financial performance and employment growth. This has major policy implications for, as will be demonstrated, the prime thrust of current public policy towards small businesses in many advanced countries has been to reduce the operating costs of small firms on the assumption that this will lead to increased profits, which in turn leads to additional workers being employed.

The validity of these assumptions will now be investigated. The chapter begins by briefly outlining the major items in the package of measures introduced or currently under discussion by the Conservative administration to help small businesses in the United Kingdom. The relationship between employment change and profitability is tested on the sample of 636 companies, and it is concluded that attempts to raise gross trading profits are likely to have very modest effects upon employment. On the other hand policies targeted towards potentially successful, growing firms are more likely to create significant numbers of jobs. The final section of the chapter is concerned with identifying the characteristics of highly successful companies which could become the focus of this policy.

UK PUBLIC POLICY TO ASSIST SMALL FIRMS

Most developed countries now have a package of policies designed to assist small firms, primarily on the grounds that the small firms sector is thought to be an important vehicle both for new employment creation and for technical change. Reservations about both those hypotheses were expressed earlier in Chapter 1 so this chapter will be devoted to whether current policies will achieve the employment objectives.

In the United Kingdom several ministerial statements have been made on the role of public policy in promoting small business. For example in its '*Burdens on Business*' (HMSO, 1985) Government reports the views of small businessmen on the perceived impact on their firms of the administrative and legislative requirements of central and local government.

The report concludes that a reduction in red tape would yield benefits for jobs in the following way:

> *... reductions in compliances costs would be likely to feed through into profits and prices; the end result being a higher level of employment in the whole economy* (para 2.5.3).

It appears that Government has similar views on the mechanism for other aspects of small firm policy since it views the reduction in business burdens for small firms as 'one element in the Government's wider strategy for enterprise and employment'.

Figure 5.1 shows that in the United Kingdom six broad groups of initiatives designed to promote the growth of the small firm sector have been implemented. Some are clearly designed to raise the rates at which new businesses are formed, such as the Enterprise Allowance Scheme, under which unemployed workers who start their own businesses no longer have to forgo their unemployment pay and are paid a fixed sum of £40 per week.

The Government also gives enthusiastic support to Enterprise Agencies (Trusts in Scotland) which are a partnership between the public and private sectors in which information and advice is provided locally to new and small businesses. The Manpower Services Commission also finances Educational Institutions to provide training courses for individuals wishing to start their own business and, in the longer run, the Government

Figure 5.1: Small business assistance in Britain

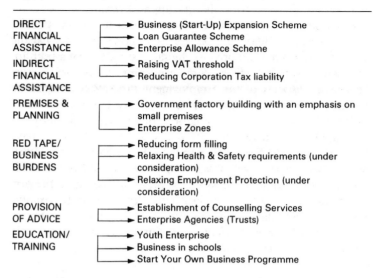

DIRECT FINANCIAL ASSISTANCE
- Business (Start-Up) Expansion Scheme
- Loan Guarantee Scheme
- Enterprise Allowance Scheme

INDIRECT FINANCIAL ASSISTANCE
- Raising VAT threshold
- Reducing Corporation Tax liability

PREMISES & PLANNING
- Government factory building with an emphasis on small premises
- Enterprise Zones

RED TAPE/ BUSINESS BURDENS
- Reducing form filling
- Relaxing Health & Safety requirements (under consideration)
- Relaxing Employment Protection (under consideration)

PROVISION OF ADVICE
- Establishment of Counselling Services
- Enterprise Agencies (Trusts)

EDUCATION/ TRAINING
- Youth Enterprise
- Business in schools
- Start Your Own Business Programme

is keen to promote a greater knowledge of businesses and self employment amongst schoolchildren. It gives a high priority to including business awareness and understanding directly within the school curriculum.

The remainder of the initiatives identified in Figure 5.1 are targeted primarily at existing small businesses. The Business Expansion Scheme provides tax relief to individuals investing directly in bona fide small businesses. When the scheme began, it was called the Business Start-Up Scheme, at which time only new businesses were eligible for support, but the risk of investing in start-ups was judged to be so high that little investment funding was forthcoming. The scheme was then widened to include established small businesses, and the name changed. Under the Loan Guarantee Scheme the Government guarantees 70 per cent (originally 80 per cent) of a loan issued by an eligible bank, where the loan would not have been made under normal banking criteria. In return the borrower has to pay an interest premium on the loan and the scheme itself is supposed to be self-financing.

Direct and indirect financial assistance programmes were a feature of the first phase of small firm policy in the UK between 1979 and 1982. Since then no major new financial initiatives have been introduced and, instead, policy seems to have been increasingly directed towards relaxing and removing the 'constraints' on new and small firms. Active consideration is being given to relaxing Health and Safety legislation so that very small firms would not have to provide the same standards of safety for their workers as large firms. Similar exemptions are being considered for aspects of the Employment Protection Legislation dealing with unfair dismissal and maternity leave, and relaxations in a number of regulatory 'burdens', particularly in planning legislation, are likely.

Currently small firms policy in the UK appears to stem from certain fundamental yet possibly conflicting propositions. The first is that the small business sector would thrive if government regulations were reduced. In particular it is argued that many government regulations which are tolerable for large firms, impose a disproportionately large burden on smaller firms. Hence, small firms should be exempted from having to complete a number of administrative forms, paying some taxes and having to meet some aspects of current Health and Safety and Employment Protection legislation etc.

A second proposition is that small firms are at a disadvantage compared to large firms and that public policy should correct for that disadvantage. This leads to policies such as the Loan Guarantee Scheme which is designed to offset the higher risk to the financial institutions of lending to small firms. The view that small firms are disadvantaged is also a justification for the establishment of business advice and information services. These are justified on the grounds that small firms have to deal with a similar range of problems to large firms, yet cannot have 'in-house' access to the latter's professional specialist knowledge. Furthermore, at one time, the provision of public factories suitable for small firms was also justified on the grounds of the difficulties which small firms experienced in obtaining premises. However, it has recently become clear that the construction of small units can be profitably undertaken by the private sector.

The third proposition justifying the package of assistance and advice offered to small firms is that in the United Kingdom there is a need to place greater emphasis upon business and particularly small business. This ideology justifies the restructuring of the school curriculum to include business, influencing undergraduates' choice of career patterns, major television, poster and other advertising campaigns designed to encourage individuals to start businesses and more subliminal press and media reporting of successful entrepreneurs.

Finally, the Government, in establishing both the Enterprise Allowance Scheme and in funding the provision of 'Start Your Own Business' courses, is attempting to bring small business or self employment to the attention of those who perhaps had never considered this option.

Almost all the initiatives outlined in Figure 5.1 involve a public cost, paid either by central or local government[1] and in this sense, the operations of small businesses are being subsidised. The element of subsidy is clear in the Loan Guarantee Scheme which is not self financing. It is equally clear in the case of the Business Expansion Scheme where publicly subsidised tax relief is given to those investing in small firms — the prime beneficiaries of which are those paying tax at high marginal rates. Nevertheless, the subsidy is also apparent in other items of policy. For example, public provision of information and advice services, which are free or at below cost to the entrepreneur, means that the latter no longer has to devote so much time to collecting information. That time may then be spent on other productive activities.

The optimal level of public financial assistance available to small businesses depends on questions of both allocative efficiency and distributive justice. The key point is that the initiatives outlined in Figure 5.1 impose an initial (first-round) cost upon the taxpayer, and the extent to which this is desirable either in terms of efficiency or equity can only be examined within the formal welfare economics framework. We are unaware of any such studies having yet been undertaken.

It is now necessary to bring together the two elements of our argument. We stated that one inferred objective of small firm policy was to create employment, perhaps through stimulating technical change. We have also noted that policy initiatives have been directed primarily to reducing the cost schedule facing small firms, whereas policy has not been directed towards increasing the *demand* for the products of small firms. For example, unlike the USA there has been no quota system in public sector contracts under which a certain proportion of the order has to be placed with small firms. From this we must infer that the politicians' 'black box' model of small firm policy operates as in Figure 5.2.

135

Figure 5.2: Job creation in small firms

PUBLIC SUBSIDY ⟹ | SMALL FIRM | ⟹ NEW JOBS

In the most bald terms, there appears to be an assumption that by the payment of a public subsidy of some form, the costs of a small business will be reduced. Given that the demand side remains unchanged, it is to be expected that profits will rise and that those increased profits will lead the firm to increase the size of its workforce in the way outlined in DTI (1985).

AN EXAMINATION OF SMALL BUSINESS SUBSIDIES

There are several reasons why public subsidies of the type described above may not result in increased employment amongst recipient firms. As a framework for examining the relationship between subsidies and employment in small firms, we have tried to sketch in some of the elements within the small firm box in Figure 5.2. This is shown in Figure 5.3. It takes the reduced costs which a subsidy provides and then examines the nature of the leakages and feedbacks which could occur between the provision of the subsidy and any additional employment creation. The public subsidy is injected on the left-hand side of Figure 5.3, in the form of reducing the firms' costs below that which they would have been without the subsidy. The subsidy is injected into the black box and the thick horizontal line within the box shows how the flow of this subsidy can ultimately result in an increased demand for labour. However, the subsidy effect can also leak away in several ways and these are shown as vertical lines emerging from the black box. The purpose of constructing the box in this way is to enable us to test, once the accounting information system begins, the magnitude of these leakages.

Starting at the far left-hand side, it is clear that any public subsidy may never appear in the accounts or be reflected in the performance of the small firm. As we have noted in Chapter 3 small company accounts are widely recognised as being less reliable than those of large companies because of the lack of an independent verification of the figures provided. Small company audit guidelines clearly recognise the possibility that not all

Figure 5.3: The impact of small business subsidies

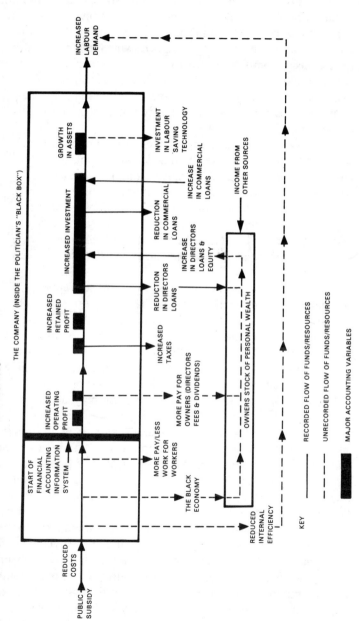

the transactions of the company (particularly cash sales) have been entered in the books. Hence it is quite possible that, prior to the start of the accounting system shown in Figure 5.3, leakages may take place into the black economy. Equally it is possible that some of the subsidy may leak away in the form of reduced internal efficiency of the firm which may feel that it no longer has to compete as effectively as previously. Ironically this could actually lead to more labour being employed in order to maintain output at its previous levels but, presumably, the payment of subsidies to small firms is not designed to increase employment by this route.

This outcome may seem unlikely in competitive markets where most small firms are found. However, there is some circumstantial evidence that it exists amongst smaller, and particularly new firms. Casual observation suggests that new businesses which start with a collection of two-year rent-free periods in factories, or other forms of temporary subsidy never adjust to the reality that they experience once the subsidy is removed. In these cases, failure follows quickly after the subsidy is removed.

It is now assumed that the effect of the subsidy appears in the company accounts in the form of increased operating profits, i.e., to the right of the thick vertical line in Figure 5.3. The thick horizontal blocks indicate that it is possible to quantify each of the leakages to the right of the start of the accounting information system. Hence if, prior to the subsidy, the firm was making a satisfactory level of profit and the subsidy is a 'windfall' gain then the owners of the company may decide to pay themselves higher fees and dividends or they may decide that, from their point of view, the company is already at an optimum size. More leisure and/or consumption are, in these circumstances, likely outcomes from the provision of a public subsidy. A second form of leakage is that if the subsidy results in increased operating profits some will necessarily disappear in the form of taxation.

Once a retained profit figure is obtained, subsequent leakages are also likely to take place. It must be remembered that small companies are generally financed largely from loan capital provided either from personal sources or from the banks. If the company experiences an increase in profitability owing to the receipt of a subsidy, the owner may wish to reduce his/her dependence upon this source of finance rather than use it for reinvestment purposes. Two potential, major sources of leakages from retained profits are, therefore, the reduction in directors' loans and the reduction in commercial loans, reflecting the risk aversion of small businessmen and the fact that much of their capital (human and financial) is tied up in the business.

Figure 5.3 also makes it clear that increased investment within the firm may be financed either by increases in directors' loans and/or commercial loans. The former, however, could be financed indirectly by the public subsidy working through the black (unrecorded) economy, so as to increase the wealth of directors enabling them to provide the additional (formal) loans. A proportion of the increased retained profits, however, may result in an investment in plant and machinery. Clearly, this will result in Asset Growth of the business but whether that leads to an increased demand for labour depends on whether or not the investment is labour-displacing.

Figure 5.3 makes it clear that, in principle, the provision of a subsidy could result in increased employment in the small firm but that there are, in practice, a large number of ways in which the subsidy could leak away and feed back. It is then an essentially empirical question whether, in practice, these leakages are of importance. Figure 5.3 shows that once the Accounting Information System begins, it is possible to quantify the losses through leakages and enable an estimate to be made of their importance.

PROFITABILITY AND EMPLOYMENT IN SMALL FIRMS

From an examination of Figure 5.3 the following two hypotheses may be tested:

(1) Government policy chooses only to influence trading profit, yet an important determinant of employment growth in small companies is retained profit, where the difference in an accounting sense, can be explained by Directors' Fees, Dividends, Interest, Tax payments and any extraordinary items.

(2) Two small companies may have a similar performance as measured by average trading profits but one may choose to use the surplus to reduce external borrowing and

increase Directors' Fees, whereas the other may retain the profit within the business and employ more workers.

The implications of this are that Government provides incentives for corporate retention in the form of raising earned income for company directors whilst reducing corporate income tax; the alternative is for Government to reduce its emphasis upon 'across the board' policies, the benefits of which either leak away before they appear in the accounts of the small company or which are 'consumed' by small-company directors.

Testing the Hypotheses: 1974-78 Data

To test these hypotheses we have selected the 1974-78 period during which complete financial and employment data were available for 225 out of our sample of 636 companies. The full sample was subdivided between those which increased their employment between 1974 and 1978 which were defined as 'Expanders' and those which had stable or contracting employment which were defined as 'Others'.

Table 5.1 shows the ten accounting items which were selected for investigation and Table 5.2 shows the industrial composition of the sample both for the 1974-78 period and for the subsequent selection of companies in the 1978-81 period. It can be seen that the sample contains a wide range of industries and, after conducting a Chi-squared test, there appears to be no significant sectoral difference between the Expanders and Others. The inclusion of only firms which provided employment and financial data for both 1974 and 1978 means that many short-life companies are excluded. To this extent it represents a

Table 5.1: Accounting items

---

(1) Gross Trading Profit
(2) Directors' Fees and Dividends
(3) Interest Payments
(4) Taxation (includes Deferred Tax)
(5) Retained Profit for Year
(6) Equity (Share Capital and Reserves)
(7) Directors' Loans
(8) Other Loans and Overdrafts
(9) Tangible Fixed Assets
(10) Net Working Capital (Stocks and W-I-P + Debtors—Creditors)

Table 5.2: Industrial composition of the sample 1974–78 and 1978–81

1968 SIC Orders		Expanders		Others		Total	
		1974–78	1978–81	1974–78	1978–81	1974–78	1978–81
III	Food, Drink & Tobacco	11	4	8	6	19	10
VI	Metal Manufacture	4	0	3	5	7	5
VII	Mechanical Engineering	28	17	22	28	50	45
VIII	Instrument Engineering	3	4	2	3	5	7
IX	Electrical Engineering	5	1	4	7	9	8
X	Ship and Marine Engineering	2	1	4	3	6	4
XI	Vehicles	4	0	2	5	6	5
XII	Metal Goods NES	19	11	15	25	34	36
XV	Clothing and Footwear	3	0	4	7	7	7
XVI	Bricks, Pottery etc	1	2	4	2	5	4
XVII	Timber, Furniture etc	6	8	21	14	27	22
XVIII	Paper, Printing & Publishing	10	15	18	10	28	25
XIX	Rubber, Toys, Misc. etc	4	3	7	5	11	8
	Non-manufacturing & others	4	6	2	9	6	15
		104	72	116	129	220	201

Note: 1974–78 : X^2 with 13 d.f. = 16.37
1978–81 : X^2 with 13 d.f. = 25.04

test of the potential impact *amongst longer life small companies* of public subsidies designed to raise small company profitability. It does not take into account the impact of entry.

Mean and standard deviations are shown in Table 5.3 for the ten accounting variables, normalised by Total Assets for both the Expanders and the Others. It is clear that Average Gross Trading Profit ÷ Total Assets for firms which expanded employment is not significantly different from the Others. Average Gross Trading Profit was 33.26 per cent for the Expanders and 30.71 per cent for the Others. Indeed, the only variable where the absolute levels differed between the Expanders and Others was Retained Profits and, consequently, Average Tax Payments. Retained Profits at 6.01 per cent for the Expanders were almost double the 3.3 per cent for the Others.

141

Table 5.3: Employment and profits : 1974–1978

Variable	N	Expanders X̄	σ	N	Others X̄	σ	t-value
Ave Gross Trading Profit	103	33.26	15.4	122	30.71	16.7	−1.19
Δ " " "		23.55	21.8		7.93	26.8	−4.85**
Ave Directors' Fees	103	19.03	14.6	122	20.91	15.9	0.83
Δ " "		11.78	12.7		7.24	16.0	−2.37*
Ave Interest Payments	103	0.72	0.15	122	0.55	0.15	−0.82
Δ " "		0.79	1.9		0.17	1.4	−2.77**
Ave Tax Payments	103	3.56	3.1	122	2.26	2.4	−3.48**
Δ " "		2.49	6.2		−0.40	5.3	−3.75**
Ave Retained Profit	103	6.01	3.9	122	3.30	4.1	−5.08**
Δ " "		5.53	10.6		−0.31	12.4	−3.81**
Ave Equity	103	33.02	16.9	122	37.31	20.7	1.64
Δ "		27.63	18.9		13.83	21.3	−5.15**
Ave Directors' Loans	103	13.69	15.4	122	14.84	16.8	−0.54
Δ " "		3.49	13.1		2.13	17.6	−0.68
Ave Other Loans	103	13.45	12.3	122	11.23	12.0	−1.37
Δ " "		12.01	17.9		4.91	16.0	−3.12**
Ave Fixed Assets	103	32.79	18.8	122	29.37	15.6	−1.45
Δ " "		29.18	25.7		11.62	19.0	−5.74**
Ave Net Working Capital	103	26.03	19.2	122	27.55	17.0	0.62
Δ " " "		17.78	21.6		10.21	21.8	−2.61**

Notes: a. Δ — Change in Profits, etc, divided by Total Assets.
b. In this and subsequent tables in this chapter a single asterisk means significant at the 95% level and a double asterisk at the 99% level in a 2-tail test.
t-tests for differences in means
variables all scaled by Average Total Assets (1974–78)

Table 5.3, however, also shows that the firms which expanded their employment between 1974 and 1978 were those which experienced an *increase* in profitability, rather than a high absolute level of profitability. It shows that there were significant differences between the Expanders and Others. Thus, the Expanders had a 23 per cent increase in Gross Trading Profit compared with 7.93 per cent for the Others. For Retained Profit the Expanders experienced a 5.53 per cent increase, whereas the Others experienced a 0.3 per cent decline. Other characteristics of the Expanders were that they underwent a major increase in Equity, an increase in Directors' Loans and had major increases in Fixed Assets. They also increased the pay of the Directors faster than did the Others.

These differences could be caused by differences in the sizes of the firms at the start date. To test this effect, data are presented in Table 5.4 on the size of each variable in 1974. The

Table 5.4: Initial values : 1974–1978

Variable	Expanders		Others		
	X̄	σ	X̄	σ	t-value
Trading Profit	23.24	13.6	27.46	19.2	1.92
Directors' Fees	13.71	11.4	17.74	16.2	2.18*
Interest Payments	0.39	1.3	0.51	1.6	0.63
Tax Payments	2.47	3.5	2.19	3.4	0.61
Retained Profit For Year	3.97	4.8	3.83	6.6	0.18
Equity	20.58	15.8	30.65	20.2	4.22**
Directors' Loans	11.89	13.1	14.51	18.0	1.36
Other Loans	8.17	10.6	9.67	13.8	0.92
Net Working Capital	18.27	15.7	23.51	20.1	2.19*
Fixed Assets	19.71	12.7	24.02	14.1	2.42*

Notes: Expanders (103) and Others (122)
t-tests for differences between mean initial values (1974) scaled by Average Total Assets

table shows that in 1974 only four variables differed significantly between the Expanders and the Others. These were that the Expanders in 1974 paid the Directors less than the Others, had lower Equity, Net Working Capital and lower Fixed Assets. These all point to the fact that the Expanders were smaller and probably younger.

Tables 5.3 and 5.4 have, therefore, shown that companies which expand their employment (Expanders) have a number of accounting ratios which are significantly different from those companies which did not increase their employment (Others). For the period 1974-78 it appears that Expanders are better distinguished from Others according to their level of Retained Profit ratios rather than the level of Trading Profit ratios. In Table 5.5 all companies, both Expanders and Others, are correlated with employment change. The table shows both the simple correlation coefficient for the absolute levels of ten accounting ratios and changes in employment and the correlation coefficient for *changes* in these accounting ratios with changes in employment.

It is striking that the absolute level of Retained Profit provides the strongest correlation with employment change of all ten absolute variables having a simple correlation coefficient of $r = 0.389$ which is significant at the 99 per cent level. The other absolute variable significant at the 99 per cent level is Average Trading Profit, with $r = 0.164$.

Table 5.5: Correlation coefficients between % Δ in employment and accounting variables scaled by Average Total Assets : 1974–1978

Variable	Coefficient	Sig.
Ave Trading Profit	0.164	0.007**
Δ " "	0.404	0.000**
Ave Directors' Fees	0.028	0.340
Δ " "	0.255	0.000**
Ave Interest	0.055	0.210
Δ "	0.127	0.030
Ave Tax	0.135	0.022*
Δ "	0.223	0.000**
Ave Retained Profit	0.389	0.000**
Δ " "	0.332	0.000**
Ave Fixed Assets	0.105	0.059
Δ " "	0.365	0.000**
Ave Directors' Loans	−0.034	0.306
Δ " "	0.045	0.252
Ave Other Loans	0.057	0.201
Δ " "	0.144	0.016*
Ave Working Capital	−0.056	0.204
Δ " "	0.150	0.013*
Ave Equity	−0.083	0.110
Δ "	0.399	0.000**

Table 5.5 also presents correlation coefficients between changes in employment and *changes* in the ten accounting ratios. It shows that these are, with the exception of changes in Directors' Loans, significantly positively associated with change in employment. The strongest correlation (r = 0.404) is between *changes* in Trading Profit and changes in employment, and this is higher than for *changes* in Retained Profit (r = 0.332).

This would appear to offer some support to the Government view that attempting to increase the rate of Trading Profit will induce additional employment creation. However, it is somewhat disconcerting that the *level* of Trading Profit is less strongly associated with employment increase, and this may suggest that whilst a steep change in employment may be induced by increasing Trading Profit, subsequent increases are decreasingly effective. Instead, only by acting upon the Retained Profit ratios can further increases in employment be generated.

To assess the relative impacts of changes in Trading Profit and Retained Profit upon employment change, Table 5.6 was

Table 5.6: Regression analysis : employment change, age and profitability 1974-78

	C	Age	Δ RP	Δ TP	R̄²	N
All cases						
Δ E =	0.0561	−0.003	+0.767		0.101	211
	(1.32)	(2.141)*	(4.307)**			
Δ E =	−0.029	−0.0017		+0.429	0.155	211
	(0.66)	(1.123)		(5.769)**		
Others						
Δ E =	−0.318	+0.0025	+0.436		0.085	115
	(7.208)	(1.795)	(2.561)*			
Δ E =	−0.351	+0.0031		+0.317	0.123	115
	(8.008)	(2.187)*		(3.40)**		
Expanders						
Δ E =	0.377	−0.005	+0.516		0.152	96
	(8.794)	(2.894)**	(2.661)**			
Δ E =	0.349	−0.0005		+0.142	0.087	96
	(7.009)	(0.242)		(2.067)*		

Note: Only firms with more than five employees included.

constructed. It presents simple regression coefficients but two additional factors are introduced. First, companies with less than five employees in 1974 are excluded since it was felt that a substantial percentage increase in employment in these companies could bias the results. This is also true for the results of Table 5.5. Hence the total sample size is reduced to 211 companies. Second, we noted earlier that there appeared to be some evidence that companies which were expanding employment tended to be smaller and perhaps younger.

Table 5.6, therefore, includes a specific age variable with the equation where age is defined as the number of years before 1974 when the company was incorporated:[2] Table 5.6 shows that age and changes in Retained Profit explain only 10 per cent of the variance in change in employment between 1974 and 1978 for 211 small companies. However, both variables have significant 't' statistics at the 95 per cent level with increases in retained profit and youth being positively associated with employment increases. As would have been expected from Table 5.4, changes in Trading Profit and age explain a higher proportion of the variance in employment change (15.5%).

The second part of Table 5.6 deals only with 115 non-expanding companies (Others). It shows that the changes in Retained Profits and age variable explain approximately the same level of variation as in the 'all cases' equation (8.5%) and that again changes in Retained Profit have a significant 't' statistic. The major contrast with the 'all cases' results, however, is that the age variable has a positive sign. The positive sign is repeated in the equation including changes in Trading Profits and, in this case, the 't' statistic is significant at the 95 per cent level. This suggests that amongst companies that are experiencing either stability or a decline in employment those whose Trading or Retained Profits are declining or growing less rapidly experience the fastest rate of employment decline. On the other hand, it suggests that age has a stabilising effect upon employment change, with the older firms, when experiencing either small increases or declines in profitability, being significantly less likely to shed labour than younger firms. For the non-expanders changes in Trading Profit explain a higher proportion of employment change than changes in Retained Profit.

The third part of Table 5.6 contains the regression coefficients for the 96 companies which expanded and had more than 5 workers in 1974. It shows that for the Expanders changes in Retained Profit and changes in Trading Profit are both significant factors in explaining changes in employment, but that the changes in Retained Profit and age equation explains 15 per cent of the variance in employment change compared with only 8.7 per cent for the Trading Profit and age equation. Note that amongst Expanders age is negatively associated with increased employment, suggesting that younger firms expand faster than older firms for a given change in profitability. It also suggests that for the group it is changes in Retained Profit rather than in Trading Profit that are more strongly associated with employment change.

Testing the Hypotheses: 1978-1981 Data

It is important to determine the extent to which the above results are sensitive to the particular time period chosen. It could be argued that the period 1974-78 was both one of relative prosperity and one in which there was only limited public policy towards small firms, and that the results are, therefore, irrelevant to current conditions. As noted earlier, the most recent employment data available are for 1981 and so we shall, in this section, repeat the above tests for companies providing financial and employment data for the period 1978-81.

Table 5.7 presents data on differences in the mean and standard deviations for 201 companies which were either Expanders or Others. This table is comparable to Table 5.3 for the 1974-78 period. The first point to note is that whereas 45 per cent of the sample expanded their employment during the 1974-78 period, only 36 per cent did so in the 1978-81 period. With this exception, the similarities between the two tables are much clearer than the contrasts. At the 99 per cent significant level, the only absolute accounting ratio which distinguishes the Expanders from the Others is Retained Profit, although Trading Profit and Interest Payments are significant at the 95 per cent level. Hence the importance of the absolute level of Retained Profit in distinguishing between Expanders and Others is apparent for both the 1974-78 and 1978-81 periods.

An examination of changes in the accounting ratios in Table 5.7 shows the results are broadly similar to those obtained for the 1974-78 period in Table 5.3. It shows that expanding companies have significantly more rapid increases in Trading Profit and Equity (at the 99 per cent level) than other companies. At the 95 per cent significance level changes in Directors' Fees,

Table 5.7: Employment and profits : 1978–1981

Variable	N	Expanders		N	Others		t-value
		X̄	σ		X̄	σ	
Ave (AP) Gross Trading Profit	72	31.95	14.8	129	27.55	16.0	−1.97*
Δ " " "		8.77	19.0		0.17	17.4	−3.17**
Ave (AD) Directors' Fees	72	18.37	13.3	129	17.87	14.4	−0.25
Δ " "		6.85	12.2		2.93	9.4	−2.37*
Ave (AI) Interest Payments	72	0.52	2.0	129	1.22	2.0	2.36*
Δ " "		0.14	2.3		0.64	2.0	1.55
Ave (AT) Tax Payments	72	2.15	3.3	129	1.28	2.7	−1.92
Δ " "		−0.96	5.3		−1.50	5.1	−0.70
Ave (AR) Retained Profit	72	6.17	5.5	129	3.98	5.0	−2.81**
Δ " "		0.63	10.1		−2.35	9.9	−2.02*
Ave (AS) Equity	72	33.55	16.9	129	36.06	17.6	0.99
Δ "		13.19	14.9		7.85	12.8	−2.56**
Ave (ADL) Directors' Loans	72	11.36	14.3	129	10.36	13.1	−0.49
Δ " "		0.34	9.3		0.61	9.2	0.20
Ave (AOL) Other Loans	72	13.04	12.7	129	15.54	13.5	1.31
Δ " "		3.58	12.3		3.08	11.1	−0.28
Ave (AF) Fixed Assets	72	34.55	17.0	129	34.66	16.8	0.04
Δ " "		11.94	15.5		6.82	12.5	−2.40*
Ave (AW) NWC	72	23.95	17.9	129	26.65	15.7	1.07
Δ "		4.23	16.9		2.27	14.8	−0.83

Notes: t-tests for differences in means.
Variables all scaled by Average Total Assets (1978–81)

Retained Profit and Fixed Assets are different for expanding and for other companies. In many respects these parallel results obtained in Table 5.3 where we noted that *changes* in Trading Profit were more important than *changes* in Retained Profit in distinguishing between expanding and non-expanding companies. On the other hand, the *absolute* level of Trading Profit was poorer at distinguishing between expanders and non-expanders than Retained Profit.

It will be recalled from Table 5.4 that potentially part of the explanation for any differences between Expanders and Others was attributed to different mean initial values of the two groups. It was shown that the expanders were generally smaller, having lower levels of Equity, Directors' Fees, Fixed Assets and Net Working Capital. However, from Table 5.8 there appears to be no difference in the initial values of any of the 10 accounting variables of the two groups in 1978 apart from Interest and Equity.

Table 5.9 shows the simple correlation coefficients between both the absolute levels and the changes in the ten accounting ratios and the changes in employment in the 1978-81 period. The absolute level of Trading Profit ($r = 0.215$) and Retained Profit ($r = 0.282$) were the only accounting ratios which were significantly correlated with employment change at the 99 per cent level, with the correlation being stronger for Retained Profit than for Trading Profit. This result exactly parallels that for the 1974-78 period. An examination of *changes* in these

Table 5.8: Initial values : 1978–1981

Variables	Expanders		Others		
	X̄	σ	X̄	σ	t-value
Trading Profit	27.3	14.9	27.2	17.7	−0.02
Directors' Fees	15.0	11.9	16.3	14.7	0.67
Interest Payments	4.3	1.3	0.9	1.4	2.38*
Tax Payments	2.3	3.1	1.8	3.5	−1.18
Retained Profit for year	5.9	5.8	5.2	6.0	−0.57
Equity	26.9	15.0	31.8	16.3	2.15*
Directors' Loans	11.0	13.5	9.8	13.0	−0.62
Other Loans	11.1	12.3	13.6	12.8	1.36
NWC	21.3	15.5	24.8	15.9	1.53
Fixed Assets	28.3	16.4	30.7	16.4	0.97

Notes: t-tests for differences between mean initial values (1978) scaled by Average Total Assets

Table 5.9: Correlation coefficients between % Δ in employment and accounting variables scaled by Average Total Assets : 1978–1981

Variables	Coefficient	Sig.
Ave Trading Profit	0.215	0.001*
Δ " "	0.288	0.000*
Ave Directors' Fees	0.094	0.092
Δ " "	0.219	0.001*
Ave Interest	−0.095	0.090
Δ "	−0.057	0.213
Ave Tax	0.148	0.018*
Δ "	0.038	0.297
Ave Retained Profit	0.282	0.000**
Δ " "	0.237	0.000**
Ave Fixed Assets	−0.096	0.089
Δ " "	0.200	0.461
Ave Directors' Loans	0.0141	0.420
Δ " "	0.066	0.176
Ave Other Loans	−0.151	0.017*
Δ " "	0.007	0.461
Ave Working Capital	0.047	0.255
Δ " "	0.148	0.018*
Ave Equity	0.130	0.427
Δ "	0.301	0.000**

accounting ratios over the period means that, at the 99 per cent level, changes in Trading Profit (r = 0.288), Directors' Fees (r = 0.219), Retained Profit (r = 0.237) and Equity (r = 0.301) are all positively correlated with changes in employment. These results broadly parallel those for the 1974-78 period when changes in Trading Profit were more strongly correlated with changes in Retained Profit, with matters being reversed for the absolute values of the variables.

Finally, Table 5.10 presents the regression results for the 1978-81 period. Again, the results obtained are broadly similar to those in Table 5.6 for the 1974-78 period. All three parts of the table take all companies which had more than five employees in 1978. The first part takes the complete sample of 213 companies and shows the age coefficient is not significant and that changes in Trading Profit and age explain only 7 per cent of the variance in employment change. Changes in Retained Profit and age explain only 4.6 per cent of the variance, but in both equations the change in profitability variable has a significant 't' statistic.

The results for the non-expanders (Others) are shown in the

149

Table 5.10: Regression analysis : employment change, age and profitability 1978-81

	C	Age	Δ RP	Δ TP	R^2	N
All Cases						
Δ E =	−0.139	−0.002	+0.785		0.046	213
	(2.156)	(0.649)	(3.125)**			
Δ E =	−0.182	−0.0009		+0.696	0.073	213
	(2.832)	(0.394)		(4.030)**		
Others						
Δ E =	−0.492	+0.0018	+0.314		0.014	135
	(6.251)	(0.616)	(1.182)			
Δ E =	−0.504	+0.002		+0.338	0.021	135
	(6.493)	(0.746)		(1.552)		
Expanders						
Δ E =	0.291	−0.004	+0.711		0.092	78
	(9.328)	(1.712)	(2.611)**			
Δ E =	0.350	−0.003		+0.702	0.074	78
	(6.861)	(1.653)		(1.788)		

second part of the table. Here neither age nor either of the changes in profitability measures is significant and the values of R^2 are not significantly different from zero. It is a matter of considerable concern that during this period *neither* of the changes in profitability indices is associated with employment change amongst those companies with a stable or contracting labour force. This is of particular concern when it is recalled that 135 out of the 213 companies (64 per cent) were in this category. Section 3 of the table, which presents coefficients for regression equations on companies expanding their labour forces, is somewhat better than for the non-expanders. Overall, however, changes in profitability, even amongst this group of expanding companies, explain significantly less of the variance in employment change than during the 1974-78 period. The equation in this part of Table 5.10 shows that changes in Retained Profit and age explain 9.2 per cent of the variance in employment, compared with 7.4 per cent being explained by age and changes in Trading Profit. Again, this parallels the results for Table 5.6 which show that changes in Retained Profit are, when taking account of age, more powerful than changes in Trading Profit in explaining employment change amongst the small companies which increase their labour force.

SYNTHESIS

This chapter has argued that a major thrust of Government policy towards existing small business has been to reduce their costs of operation and by so doing to increase their rate of profitability. This increase in profitability is expected to result in more jobs being created in those firms than would have been the case without the initiative.

Government has, however, chosen to influence the level of Trading Profit in small companies rather than the level of Retained Profit. It has not attempted to increase the incentives for profit retention and indeed may have increased the likelihood of leakages by reducing the rates of personal income tax paid by high income earners. Nevertheless, if a policy of raising Trading Profit in small firms is to be effective in terms of increasing employment, then a strong association between Trading Profit, or changes in Trading Profit, and employment changes would be expected.

We found only modest evidence of such an association. It does not appear to be the case that those companies with the highest trading profits are necessarily those which are increasing employment most rapidly. Neither does it appear that those companies which have increased their trading profitability most rapidly have generated the most rapid increase in employment.

In general, the association between profitability and employment is weak but it does appear that the companies which grow in employment are those which have higher Retained Profit rather than higher Trading Profit. This suggests that a public policy which increases the Trading Profits of small companies may simply result in higher 'leakages' in the form of decreasing external borrowing and higher Directors' Fees, especially where this is combined with a policy to reduce the marginal tax rates for high income earners. It does not suggest that much of this will necessarily filter through into increased employment in the small firm sector.

These results have two possible implications. The first is that if changes in Retained Profit are more strongly associated with employment change than changes in Trading Profit, then policies which encourage profit retention deserve attention. In particular the ability of directors to remove profits from the business either directly through dividends or Directors' Fees or indirectly through Loan Accounts could be reviewed. The second is an abandonment of 'across the board' policies to help small firms and much greater emphasis upon picking the winners. It is to a discussion of this concept that the remainder of the chapter is devoted.

THE IMPORTANCE OF 'WINNERS'

All the major studies of employment change in small businesses in the UK have pointed to the diversity of performance of the sector. It is a characteristic that of those new firms starting in businesses perhaps half will cease to trade within three years and the vast majority of those which remain in business will have ceased to exhibit any increase in employment once they are more than three or four years old. Employment creation therefore takes place in relatively few small firms yet it is these firms that offer the key to the creation of new jobs.

This is illustrated in Table 5.11 which shows employment in 1978 in surviving wholly new manufacturing firms in Northern England, where new is defined as established after 1965. Note that the table is not restricted to companies but also includes sole proprietorships, partnerships, etc. From our records (Storey, 1985a) we were able to identify a total of 1145 new businesses started after 1965, only 774 of which had survived until 1978.[3] At that time there were eight firms employing more than 100 workers and a further 39 firms employing between 50 and 100 workers. In total these 47 firms employed 4,005 workers or 33.8 per cent of all workers employed in manufacturing businesses established in the region since 1965. *In the broadest terms one-third of the jobs are found in less than 4 per cent of those businesses which start to trade.*

THE ARGUMENTS AGAINST SELECTIVITY

If one-third of jobs in new firms in a region are created by a handful of such firms it may appear to be an attractive strategy to concentrate very limited public resources into ensuring that this group of firms grows rather faster. Clearly a small proportionate change in their rate of employment growth will, in terms of numbers of jobs created, make a relatively large contribution to job creation.

Some powerful arguments, however, have been presented

Table 5.11: Employment in 1978 in surviving openings of wholly new manufacturing firms Tyne & Wear, Durham and Cleveland

Employment size in 1978	Number of firms	% of survivors	Employment in 1978						% of total 1978 employment in new firms in each size group
			Males		Females				
			FT	PT	FT	PT	Total		
1-9	429	55.4	1,296	55	289	222	1,862		15.7
10-24	217	28.1	2,324	49	645	279	3,297		27.8
25-49	81	10.5	1,865	57	568	203	2,693		22.7
50-99	39	5.0	1,477	11	942	199	2,629		22.2
100+	8	1.0	1,162	—	200	14	1,376		11.6
Total	774	100.0	8,124	172	2,644	917	11,857		100.0

Note: FT — Full time.
    PT — Part time.

against such a strategy. First, since these firms are growing rapidly they therefore have few problems and public assistance is irrelevant. Second, the public sector has a poor record at 'picking winners' — or even avoiding losers — so that even if the policy is desirable it is impractical. Third, public resources would be more effectively used in attempting to increase the total number of businesses which are started since an increase in the number of businesses started will presumably lead to an increase in the number of winners. Finally arguments against selectivity are sometimes raised on the grounds of equity, in the sense that it is unfair to direct public resources to a small group to the exclusion of the majority.

The first argument that because firms are growing rapidly they do not require assistance of the type which can be provided by the public sector, is not supported by survey evidence. Studies of new businesses in Britain by Storey (1985b) and by Geiser (1981) for the Federal Republic of Germany both report that those businesses which were growing fastest encountered the *most* problems. Such results are, of course, only to be expected, since if the firm is growing it is likely to require new premises and additional labour. In both these matters the public sector could help. Growing firms will also be more hungry for information on new markets and opportunities than firms more interested in consolidation. Growing firms are also more likely to be attempting to extend their borrowing. In all these circumstances the public sector, in the UK, could be of assistance. Clearly some entrepreneurs may be unwilling, from a philosophical viewpoint, to take advantage of such assistance (and almost certainly even fewer will be willing to acknowledge that it made a difference to their business). Nevertheless it is clear that if public assistance, in whatever form, can lower the barriers over which the fast-growth entrepreneur has to climb then this is a potentially importance advance.

With the exception of the matter of equity the remaining arguments against selectivity hinge on the practicability of the strategy, and it is to determining whether there are any clearly identifiable differences between fast growth and non-fast growth companies that the remainder of the chapter is devoted.

Bearing in mind their importance, it is surprising that small fast growth companies have, with the exception of work by Hutchinson and Ray (1986) and Birley (1985), been the subject of relatively limited study in the UK.

THE CHARACTERISTICS OF RAPIDLY GROWING NEW MANUFACTURING COMPANIES IN NORTHERN ENGLAND

A fast growth new company is defined as one which has more than 50 employees within five years of incorporation, and all other companies are defined as non-fast growers.

From the sample of 636 companies it was possible to obtain employment and financial data on 24^4 companies which could be classified as fast growth. For these companies qualitative information of the type discussed in Chapter 3 was also collected.

General characteristics

Having derived the sample of fast growth companies this section compares their characteristics with those of non-fast growth companies. Table 5.12 shows the extent to which in terms of employment the fast growth companies expand their labour forces faster than the non-fast growth companies. However, much of this is because they are larger from their second year of trading. Thus in their second year of life the arithmetic mean employment in the fast growers was more than four times as high as the arithmetic mean employment of the non-fast growers and their median employment was three times as high. By their fifth year the arithmetic mean employment of the fast growers was more than six times as high and the median employment nearly six times as high. In terms of employment the median employment growth amongst fast growers was more than double that for non-fast growers. Alternatively we can see that the median non-fast growth company has ceased to grow in employment by its fourth year of life, whereas the fast growth company is still expanding by 10 per cent per annum.

The sectoral composition of the fast growth and non-fast growth companies is shown in Table 5.13. It shows that fast growth companies are concentrated in the so-called 'Other Manufacturing' sector in trades such as rubber, plastics, toys, musical instruments etc. Although this sector contains only about 5 per cent of the independent companies in Northern England it provides 25 per cent of the fast growth companies. A second sector that contains a disproportionately high number of fast growth companies is Textiles. The sector contains only 2

155

Table 5.12: Employment growth by age of company

	Non-fast Growers			Fast Growers		
	X̄	X^MED	N	X̄	X^MED	N
Year 2	10.1	8.0	88	44.9	24.5	10
Year 3	12.2	10.0		70.7	34.0	
Year 4	12.3	11.0		89.8	55.5	
Year 5	14.6	11.0		97.5	61.0	

Note: Only 10 fast growers and 88 non-fast growers provided employment for all the years. To include companies providing data for only occasional years leads to difficulties in estimating whether differences in values are due to the presence of different companies.

Table 5.13: Industrial sector composition of companies

	Non-fast Growth Number of companies	%	Fast Growth Number of companies	%
Other Manufacturing	32	5	6	25
Mechanical Engineering	124	20	5	21
Textiles	7	2	4	17
Timber & Furniture	76	12	3	13
Food & Drink	37	6	2	8
Paper & Print	62	10	1	4
Instrument Engineering	18	3	1	4
Shipbuilding & Allied	14	2	1	4
Metal Goods not elsewhere specified	85	14	1	4
Other Sectors	171	27	0	0
Total	626	100	24	100

per cent of all independent manufacturing companies in the region yet provides 17 per cent of fast growth companies. The Mechanical Engineering and Timber and Furniture sectors provide an 'expected' number of fast growth companies i.e. about one-third of all independent companies in the region and one-third of all fast growth companies are in these sectors.

It is also important to notice that there are many sectors which do not have any fast growth companies and that in those sectors are 27 per cent of all independent companies. Notable by their absence are, for example, Electrical Engineering (High Tech), Clothing, Chemicals, Metal Manufacturing, Bricks, Pottery, Glass, Cement etc. and Vehicles.

The date of incorporation of the fast growth companies is also very significant. Recalling that only fast growth companies

156

incorporated after 1965 which reached 50 employees within five years of incorporation were included, Table 5.14 shows that 50 per cent were formed before 1970, compared with only 32 per cent of the non-fast growth companies.

The relative absence of fast growth companies being formed in the mid to late 1970s might be because recently incorporated companies have had insufficient time to reach the 50 employee level. This, however, is unlikely to be a major factor since, as we showed earlier, the *median* fast growth company reaches 50 employees within three years of incorporation. A more likely explanation is that there has been a genuine reduction in the number of fast growth companies established in the less prosperous period from 1974-5 onwards — even though there were many more companies actually incorporated in those years. This suggests that policies to create more firms may not necessarily lead to an increase in the number of winners. Indeed the evidence provided in this table suggests that the absolute number of winners has declined. We would, however, warn against the drawing of strong conclusions on this matter since the absence of new fast-growing firms could also reflect the slowness with which firms enter the sampling frame.

Finally the failure rates of the fast growth company are substantially lower than those of the non-fast growth company. Out of the 24 fast growth companies included, only eight are known to have failed and only four failed within ten years of incorporation. This is a failure rate of 17 per cent in a decade and significantly less than the failure rate of 40 per cent for the sample as a whole over the same period.

Financial characteristics

Fast growth companies are selected on the basis of their employment growth. This section examines the financial characteristics of fast growing employment companies, and asks whether they also exhibit fast growth in terms of assets, whether they are more profitable and whether they differ from non-fast (employment) growers in terms of key financial ratios.

To assist this analysis four tables are presented:

(1) Balance sheet structure of fast and non-fast growth companies two years after incorporation (Table 5.15).

157

Table 5.14: Date of incorporation of companies (Frequencies and cumulative per cent)

		1965-66	1967-8	1969-70	1971-2	1973-4	1975-6	1976-7	1978-9	Total
Fast Growers	Number	3	5	4	5	4	2	1	0	24
	Cumulative %	13	33	50	71	88	96	100	100	
Non-fast Growers	Number	36	29	39	59	65	71	23	3	325
	Cumulative %	11	20	32	50	70	92	99	100	

(2)   Balance sheet structure of fast and non-fast growth companies five years after incorporation (Table 5.16).

(3)   Profitability of fast and non-fast growth companies two, three, four and five years after incorporation (Table 5.17).

(4)   Other key financial ratios for fast and non-fast growth companies, two, three, four and five years after incorporation (Table 5.18).

Tables 5.15 and 5.16 show the balance sheet structure of fast and non-fast growth companies two and five years after incorporation. Data for one year after incorporation are not used because of the relatively few firms providing data at that time. However two years after start-up it is clear that the mean and median values of all major balance sheet items are substantially higher for fast growers than for non-fast growers. It will be recalled from Table 5.12 that median employment of the fast growers two years after start-up was approximately three times that of the non-fast growers. Table 5.15 shows that a similar relationship exists in terms of asset size. The median value of Total Assets of a fast grower is almost three times that of a non-fast grower and more than three times that of a non-fast grower when the Net Assets measure of size is used.

An examination of the balance sheet structure of companies

Table 5.15: Balance sheet structure 2 years from incorporation

	Non-fast Growers			Fast Growers		
	X̄	X^MED	N	X̄	X^MED	N
	£	£		£	£	
Total Fixed Assets	15,810	6,900	223	105,990	29,800	17
Stock and WIP	10,780	3,600	223	10,820	6,600	17
Current Assets	35,940	16,500	223	275,560	43,600	17
Total Assets	51,750	24,400	223	381,550	69,600	17
Bank Overdrafts & Loans	7,530	1,700	223	56,860	7,300	17
Current Liabilities	28,570	13,300	223	214,180	55,400	17
Share Capital						
and Reserves	11,190	3,300	223	90,890	16,400	17
Directors' Loans	6,310	3,000	223	−1,310	7,300	17
Deferred Taxation	1,911	0	223	36,641	0	17
Total Borrowing	3,770	300	223	41,150	3,300	17
Net Assets	23,180	10,300	223	167,370	34,300	17

Table 5.16: Balance sheet structure 5 years from incorporation

	Non-fast Growers			Fast Growers		
	X̄	X^MED	N	X̄	X^MED	N
	£	£		£	£	
Total Fixed Assets	29,990	13,400	163	232,850	53,950	21
Stocks and WIP	18,050	6,000	163	478,000	28,800	21
Current Assets	63,580	26,800	163	787,280	104,700	21
Total Assets	93,570	48,400	163	1,020,130	158,600	21
Bank Overdrafts & Loans	10,070	3,200	163	189,840	30,400	21
Current Liabilities	49,110	22,600	163	445,230	102,800	21
Share Capital and Reserves	25,440	8,000	163	389,170	40,800	21
Directors' Loans	8,160	4,600	163	8,230	4,200	21
Deferred Taxation	4,790	0	163	21,550	100	21
Total Borrowing	6,070	400	163	155,950	4,700	21
Net Assets	44,460	21,400	163	574,900	62,200	21

Table 5.17: % Profitability

	Non-fast Growers				Fast Growers			
	X̄	X^MED	σ	N	X̄	X^MED	σ	N
2 years				125				14
(i)	54.0	42.3	74.4		41.3	33.5	39.5	
(ii)	8.3	8.1	18.8		13.0	17.5	21.4	
(iii)	6.1	5.4	16.4		8.9	14.1	19.2	
3 years				125				14
(i)	44.0	36.2	46.3		40.1	35.0	24.5	
(ii)	2.7	5.3	23.9		10.8	14.8	25.4	
(iii)	1.1	4.4	22.3		6.6	9.7	22.7	
4 years				125				14
(i)	42.5	35.1	46.2		29.4	30.5	19.5	
(ii)	5.5	6.4	18.3		12.7	10.5	15.6	
(iii)	4.7	4.4	21.6		9.3	9.6	13.3	
5 years				125				14
(i)	42.4	36.4	44.1		16.0	18.7	25.6	
(ii)	5.5	5.5	14.5		−2.2	5.0	23.9	
(iii)	4.4	4.7	12.5		−2.9	5.6	19.7	

Notes: Profitability definitions

(i) = $\dfrac{\text{Pre-tax Profit}}{\text{Total Assets}}$ (before Directors' Fee and Depreciation)

(ii) = $\dfrac{\text{Pre-tax Profit}}{\text{Total Assets}}$

(iii) = $\dfrac{\text{Net Profit}}{\text{Total Assets}}$ (after extraordinary items, Tax and Dividends) after five years (in Table 5.16) shows that whilst the fast growers continue to be substantially larger than the non-fast growers the differential does not appear to have increased. For example the median size in terms of both Total Assets and Net Assets of fast growers is approximately three times that of a non-fast grower i.e. similar to the median differences after two years. The median fast growers' overdrafts plus loans increased by a factor of four, whereas the increase in most other items was nearer to two, except for fast growers' Directors' Loans which actually fell in absolute terms.

Table 5.17 shows rates of profitability for the first five years of life of the sample of new manufacturing companies. It defines three measures of profit and shows that for both Pre-tax Profit and Net Profit measures fast growers have a substantially higher mean and median rate of profit than non-fast growers for the second, third and fourth years of life. It is therefore somewhat surprising to find that profitability of the fast growers plunge in year 5. The negative mean value is primarily attributable to the massive losses of a single firm although even the median value for the fast growers in year 5 is almost identical to that of the non-fast growers.

Using the Gross Profit Margin measure it is clear that the mean and median for the non-fast growers are consistently *higher* than those of the fast growers for *all* years.

Finally there appears to be no trend in profitability amongst young companies. Mean and median profitability rates for non-fast growers appear broadly similar in years 3 and 5. For the fast growers there appears to be, if anything, a decline in profitability over time although this is almost entirely determined by the freak results obtained for year 5.

This all suggests that the companies which grow fast in terms of employment do not have higher gross profit margins, but do have higher retained profit, in their first five years of life thus supporting the statements made earlier in this chapter. It also demonstrates that fast growing companies, defined in terms of employment growth, are not necessarily exhibiting proportionally higher asset growth than non-fast growers.

We can also provide a more detailed Balance Sheet for fast and non-fast growth companies for their second and fifth years after incorporation (Tables 5.18 and 5.19). This shows that although retained profits are higher and employment growth faster for fast growth companies, the major

161

Table 5.18: Balance sheet analysis: comparison of fast-growing companies with non-fast growing companies: 2 years after incorporation

		Fast Growers (14)	Non-fast Growers (131)
	Fixed Assets:		
1. (a)	Net Tangible Assets (i.e. NBV of Land & Building + NBV of Plant & Machinery + NBV of Motor Vehicles.)	(22.2)	(29.0)
2. (b)	Intangible Assets:	(4.9)	(0.8)
	Current Assets:	(72.9)	(70.2)
3. (a)	Stock & Work in Progress	(29.7)	(21.1)
4. (b)	Debtors & Prepayments	(42.7)	(41.9)
5. (c)	Other Current Assets	(0.03)	(1.0)
6. (d)	Investments:	(0.0)	(0.3)
7. (e)	Cash & Bank Deposit Accounts	(0.4)	(6.0)
	Total Assets:	(100.0)	(100.0)
	Current Liabilities		
8. (a)	Short Term Loans & Bank Overdraft	(15.1)	(13.2)
9. (b)	Creditors & Accruals	(38.2)	(36.6)
10. (c)	Other Current Liabilities	(0.08)	(2.0)
11. (d)	Current Taxation	(0.6)	(2.0)
	Total Current Liabilities	(54.0)	(53.8)
Net Assets Financed By:			
12. (a)	Share Capital & Reserves:	(24.6)	(22.9)
13. (b)	Directors' Loan Accounts:	(−0.3)	(14.0)
14. (c)	Deferred Taxation:	(10.3)	(3.4)
15. (d)	Long Term Loans (Hire Purchase + Mortgage & Other Loans + Govt. Loans)	(11.4)	(5.9)
	Net Assets:	(46.0)	(46.2)

reason for asset growth being no more rapid than for non-fast growers is that such monies are used partly to increase stock and work in progress and partly to reduce the value of creditors' and directors' loans. It is apparent that cash balances remain essentially unchanged and overdraft facilities are not greatly extended.

In Part Two of this book key single financial ratios or combinations of ratios are used to identify the characteristics of failure. We now examine whether any of these single ratios appears very different between fast growers and non-fast growers. We also examine whether these ratios change over the

Table 5.19: Balance sheet analysis: comparison of fast-growing companies with non-fast growing companies: 5 years after the incorporation

		Fast Growers (14)	Non-fast Growers (131)
	Fixed Assets:		
1. (a)	Net Tangible Assets (i.e. NBV of Land & Building + NBV of Plant & Machinery + NBV of Motor Vehicles.)	(20.7)	(29.4)
2. (b)	Intangible Assets:	(1.4)	(0.5)
	Current Assets:	(79.3)	(70.1)
3. (a)	Stock & Work in Progress	(45.8)	(21.0)
4. (b)	Debtors & Prepayments	(31.8)	(41.1)
5. (c)	Other Current Assets	(0.0)	(0.2)
6. (d)	Investments:	(0.0)	(1.9)
7. (e)	Cash & Bank Deposit Accounts	(0.3)	(5.7)
	Total Assets:	(100.0)	(100.0)
	Current Liabilities		
8. (a)	Short Term Loans & Bank Overdraft	(17.4)	(21.9)
9. (b)	Creditors & Accruals	(28.1)	(37.8)
10. (c)	Other Current Liabilities	(0.0)	(1.0)
11. (d)	Current Taxation	(0.1)	(2.4)
	Total Current Liabilities	(45.6)	(52.7)
	Net Assets Financed By:		
12. (a)	Share Capital & Reserves:	(37.1)	(27.2)
13. (b)	Directors' Loan Accounts:	(0.5)	(8.4)
14. (c)	Deferred Taxation:	(1.8)	(5.2)
15. (d)	Long Term Loans (Hire Purchase + Mortgage & Other Loans + Govt. Loans)	(15.0)	(6.5)
	Net Assets:	(54.4)	(47.3)

first two to five years of a company's lifespan.

Table 5.20 presents data for six key ratios for the second to the fifth year of a company's lifespan, distinguishing between the fast growing and the non-fast growing companies. The conclusions which may be drawn from the table are that for any single ratio and for any year are there *no* statistically significant differences between either the means or medians of the fast growers and the non-fast growers. It suggests that fast growers, for example, are *not* more liquid or more solvent or less highly geared than non-fast growers. There is no evidence, either for fast growers or non-fast growers, of these ratios showing sig-

163

Table 5.20: Key financial ratios

		Non-fast Growers (N = 125)			Fast Growers (N = 14)		
		X̄	X^MED	σ	X̄	X^MED	σ
Year 2							
(i)	Current Ratio	1.75	1.30	1.48	1.17	1.21	0.30
(ii)	Quick Ratio	1.37	0.94	1.37	0.86	0.84	0.31
(iii)	Gearing Ratio 1	0.21	0.17	0.24	0.20	0.19	0.16
(iv)	Gearing Ratio 2	0.47	0.41	0.35	0.29	0.27	0.13
(v)	Solvency Ratio	0.91	0.48	3.6	0.38	0.24	1.09
(vi)	Equity Ratio	0.35	0.48	3.6	0.67	0.56	0.62
Year 3							
(i)	Current Ratio	1.70	1.29	1.66	1.30	1.14	0.45
(ii)	Quick Ratio	1.30	1.00	1.50	0.94	0.84	0.48
(iii)	Gearing Ratio 1	0.24	0.18	0.30	0.21	0.20	0.11
(iv)	Gearing Ratio 2	0.47	0.40	0.40	0.28	0.28	0.10
(v)	Solvency Ratio	0.73	0.49	5.02	0.50	0.26	0.97
(vi)	Equity Ratio	0.86	0.49	1.98	0.59	0.54	0.18
Year 4							
(i)	Current Ratio	1.78	1.33	2.31	1.25	1.23	0.29
(ii)	Quick Ratio	1.36	0.98	1.92	0.86	0.85	0.29
(iii)	Gearing Ratio 1	0.23	0.16	0.29	0.22	0.22	0.12
(iv)	Gearing Ratio 2	0.44	0.37	0.37	0.28	0.28	0.15
(v)	Solvency Ratio	1.20	0.49	10.70	0.56	0.42	0.67
(vi)	Equity Ratio	−0.67	0.42	7.99	0.75	0.66	0.57
Year 5							
(i)	Current Ratio	1.80	1.34	1.95	1.18	1.80	0.33
(ii)	Quick Ratio	1.37	0.98	1.83	0.79	0.82	0.22
(iii)	Gearing Ratio 1	0.23	0.17	0.39	0.26	0.26	0.17
(iv)	Gearing Ratio 2	0.42	0.35	0.43	0.29	0.34	0.20
(v)	Solvency Ratio	2.10	0.57	20.20	0.30	0.24	0.81
(vi)	Equity Ratio	0.59	0.56	0.84	0.75	0.66	0.56

Notes: (i) = $\dfrac{\text{Current Assets}}{\text{Current Liabilities}}$

(ii) = $\dfrac{\text{Current Assets} - \text{Stock}}{\text{Current Liabilities}}$

(iii) = $\dfrac{\text{Total Borrowing}}{\text{Total Assets}}$

(iv) = $\dfrac{\text{Total Borrowing} + \text{Directors' Loans}}{\text{Total Assets}}$

(v) = $\dfrac{\text{Net Working Capital}}{\text{Total Assets}}$

(vi) = $\dfrac{\text{Share Capital \& Reserves}}{\text{Net Assets}}$

nificant changes over the first five years of a company's life.

The major difference between fast growers and non-fast growers is that there is vastly greater variability amongst the non-fast growers than amongst the fast growers. This is evident from an examination of the standard deviations of the two groups. In particular the solvency ratio appears to exhibit particularly high variability.

We believe this demonstrates that univariate ratio analysis is unlikely to be a useful tool for distinguishing fast growers from non-fast growers, but this should not be a matter for concern, since, as we show, the fast growers are very different from the non-fast growers from their second year of operation.

Non-financial characteristics

It was noted above that whilst we have characterised companies which reached 50 employees within five years of incorporation as fast growers this, to some extent, is not wholly accurate. These companies, in fact grow no faster, as a group, in terms of assets than other *surviving* new businesses. In terms of assets the fast growers merely started from a higher base i.e. they were initially relatively large in terms of assets. Nevertheless for the sake of consistency we shall continue to refer to them as fast growers.

In this section we examine some 'qualitative' characteristics of fast growth and non-fast growth companies which can be identified from publicly available data and which were discussed in Chapter 3.

In all cases the 24 fast growth companies are compared with 142 non-fast growth companies for which qualitative data were available.[5] Only just over half of these companies had been incorporated after 1965, and exactly half had failed by 1983.

Throughout this section it will be demonstrated that the directors of the fast growing companies are *very different* from those of the non-fast growth companies. It will be shown that the fast growth companies are owned by professional directors rather than being family firms or 'one man bands'. The directors of fast growth companies had 4.5 other directorships compared with 0.9 other directorships for non-fast growth companies. In fact 71 per cent of the directors of non-fast growth companies claim to have no other directorships compared with only 21 per cent of directors of fast growth companies.

Each company director is required to classify himself according to occupation and this can be useful as an indication of previous occupational background. We have broadly distinguished between directors who refer to themselves as having a production background (e.g. Production Manager, Engineer, Fitter, etc.) or whether they classify themselves as a Professional (e.g. Company Director, Accountant, etc.).

In each non-fast growth company an average of 1.4 directors referred to a production background compared with only 0.6 directors in the fast growth companies. Alternatively 75 per cent of non-fast growth companies had at least one director with a production background compared with only 33 per cent for fast growth companies.

On the other hand 2.25 directors per fast growth company called themselves directors and 0.13 called themselves financial professionals compared with only 0.7 and 0.06 respectively for non-fast growth companies. Again 79 per cent of fast growth companies had one or more directors who were directors of other companies and 8 per cent had directors who were financial professionals. This compared with 38 per cent and 5 per cent respectively for the non-fast growth companies.

The converse of the presence of professional directors in fast growth companies is the role of families in non-fast growth companies. Amongst the fast growers only 25 per cent of companies were husband and wife teams whereas amongst the non-fast growers 53 per cent of companies had a husband and wife on the board of directors. In the majority of cases the wife's occupation was given as housewife and there is *no* case where the wife is the director of another company. The family connections amongst non-fast growth companies are also apparent from a study of the presence of blood relatives on the board: sons, daughters, etc. For example in 69.3 per cent of non-fast growth companies there was at least one blood relation amongst the directors, compared with only 16.7 per cent amongst the fast growth companies.

These results contrast to those in Chapter 3 where it was shown that professional directors were *more* likely to be the director of a failed company than individuals without any other company interests, and who had primarily a technical background. In no way, of course, are these results incompatible since they highlight that the directors of highly successful companies may also have a number of other companies within their ownership portfolio which perform less well.

From the above it is clear that the directors of fast growth companies have a much stronger professional background than directors of non-fast growth companies. It should therefore not be surprising to find that the accounts are more professionally presented, the information is more clearly specified, and that the auditors' qualifications are fewer. The information is, however, less timely. For example 70 per cent of fast growth companies having land and buildings had an explicit accounting policy for this item, compared with 36 per cent of non-fast growth companies. 75 per cent of fast growth companies had explicit accounting policies for plant and machinery and 79 per cent had policies for stock and work in progress. This compared with 49 per cent and 71 per cent respectively for non-fast growth companies.

Bearing in mind that half of the non-fast growers failed compared with only one-third of the fast growers, it is not surprising that auditors' qualifications were more apparent in the accounts of the former than the latter group. Only 8 per cent of the accounts of fast growers were subject to any form of auditors' qualification in the most recent two years of accounts compared with 14.3 per cent of the non-fast growers.

However the information available on fast growth companies is generally less recent. For example in the last year's data available for 68 per cent of non-fast growing companies there was a lag of six months or less between the ending of the financial year in which accounts were provided and the date of the auditors' report. However only 57 per cent of fast growing companies reported within six months. This slower reporting of fast growth companies was also found to occur in other years.

This is further illustrated in the lag between the ending of the financial year and the date at which the accounts are lodged with Companies House. For non-fast growth companies 50 per cent lodged within eight months whereas only 33 per cent of fast growers lodged in that time. In our view, these additional delays merely reflect the greater size and sophistication demanded by the directors of fast growth companies.

Although the fast growers generally have highly professional directors requiring high standards from their auditors only four out of 24 engage accountants in the United Kingdom Top 20 by Fee Income (*Accountancy*, November 1983). Of the remaining

20, all have different, primarily local, accountants with the exception of two mechanical engineering companies who had the same auditor and another two in different sectors who also had the same auditor.

Finally, from the viewpoint of accountancy practices it is interesting to note that changes in auditors are relatively infrequent — although more frequent amongst fast growers than amongst non-fast growers. Only 7.1 per cent of non-fast growers had changed auditors over a three-year period compared with 20.9 per cent of the fast growers. Where changes take place they broadly tend to be amongst fast growth companies presumably reflecting their need for more sophisticated accounting services as they grow larger.

Fast growth companies: a synthesis

Comparisons between fast growing (in terms of employment) and non-fast growing young independent Northern manufacturing companies yielded the following differences.

- Fast growing companies are concentrated in the rubber, plastics, toys sectors. They were also found in textiles, mechanical engineering and timber and furniture.
- There were *fewer* fast growth firms established in the post 1974 period than in the mid to late 1960s.
- the median fast growth company is three times larger in terms of assets and employment than the non-fast growth company by its *second* year of life.
- After its second year whilst it continues to grow in terms of employment it grows *no* faster in terms of assets than the non-fast growth company.
- The fast growth company in its first five years of life has *lower* gross profit margins but higher retained profits than the non-fast growth company.
- The fast growth companies were owned by directors, who were already directors of other companies. The non-fast growth companies were more likely to be family or one-man-band firms.
- Fast growth companies therefore tend to start much larger and be much more professionally managed than the non-fast growth firms.

168

— Few of either the fast growth or the non-fast growth companies use the large accountancy practices as auditors. Furthermore very few companies in either group change their accountants although changes are more frequent amongst the fast growers, and towards the larger practices.

CONCLUSION

This chapter has undertaken a selective review of UK government policy towards small firms. It has shown that during the 1979-82 period emphasis was placed on the introduction of new schemes of financial assistance but that since that time there has been a shift in policy. In particular a movement has been observed towards policies designed both to raise the rate of new firm formation and to reduce the perceived obstacles to business expansion. For example, considerable publicity has been given to the availability of free business advice. There is currently active consideration being given to reducing health and safety provisions within small companies, to the abolition of Wages Councils and to attempts to reduce the role of government and 'red tape'.

The concern of this chapter has been to speculate on whether such 'across the board' assistance to all small firms is likely to be effective in terms of new job creation. We conclude that the evidence suggests this is unlikely. In the most simple terms it appears that, based upon an observation of the performance of small manufacturing companies, much of the increased competitiveness which such companies may experience through cost reduction will not be used to employ more workers. Instead it is more likely to leak away and be used to supplement the income of the owners of the business or in reducing company external borrowing requirements.

It may be possible to reduce such leakages by providing appropriate financial incentives for small companies to retain and reinvest more of their profits, but sophisticated taxation schemes in the small business sector have often opened up a number of opportunities for avoidance, and been vigorously exploited.

Instead the chapter presents a reasoned justification for a selective, rather than an 'across the board' policy. Rather than directing the taxpayers' resources to all small firms, many of whom will not increase their employment levels after receipt of assistance, a case is presented for directing significant assistance towards those few small businesses which have the capacity, determination and managerial talent to grow in profitability and employment.

It has to be emphasised that employment growth in small businesses is concentrated in very few firms — the fastest growing 4 per cent of new firms create one-third of the jobs — but it has always been argued either that such firms did not need help or that they could not be identified. Previous work by Storey (1985b) has shown that fast growing firms are those where public assistance can make a major impact, but the present chapter has also begun the process of identifying the characteristics of these fast growing companies.

Defining a fast growth company as one reaching 50 employees within five years of incorporation, this chapter has shown that such companies are, by their second year of life, at least three times as large in terms of assets and employment as the average company. Secondly they have lower trading profits but higher net profits supporting the view that the crucial element is a willingness to retain profits for reinvestment. Finally these fast growth companies have professional directors with other corporate interests rather than being 'one man bands'.

It is *not* suggested that it is possible to devise an identi-kit picture of a successful company which is likely to create significant numbers of new jobs but it is clear that such companies are very different from the 'norm' from the second year of their life.

Whilst it is true that the failure rate amongst fast growth companies is significantly below that for the sample of companies as a whole, some of the characteristics of fast growth companies are also those of a disproportionately high number of failures. In particular it was noted that the presence of 'professional' directors is associated *both* with high growth and high failure rate companies. As we noted in the chapter this probably reflects the portfolio of companies of the professional director but it should act as a warning to anyone misguided enough to believe there are any 'golden rules' to picking fast growth companies.

NOTES

1. It was estimated by Mr. Nicholas Ridley, Financial Secretary to the Treasury, in a speech on 27 April 1983 that the full year revenue costs of central government assistance to small businesses was £500 m. No details of the basis of that calculation were given, nor were the components itemised (*British Business*, 6 May 1983).

2. We recognise that this is an imperfect measure of corporate age for two reasons. First, companies can trade either as sole proprietorships or partnerships for many years before becoming incorporated, so that some older businesses may be included in the younger age group. On the other hand some companies are incorporated but do not begin to trade for several years.

3. It must again be emphasised that there is an under-representation of short-life firms in the data base.

4. Fourteen of these companies have not been included in previous analysis since they were not included in the 1978 data base from which our sample of 636 companies was derived in Chapter 2. It is not until 1981 that they appear in the establishment data base.

5. In Chapter 3 there were a total of 146 companies supplying qualitative information. Four of these were found to be 'fast growth' companies and so were transferred to the fast growth group.

Part Two

The Small Company: Failure Prediction

6

Univariate Ratio Analysis

INTRODUCTION

In a small business the threat of failure is always close at hand. It may manifest itself in the form of an interview with the bank manager, a final invoice from a major creditor or a letter from a solicitor acting on behalf of one director. At a more aggregate level our comparisons between the performances of small and large firms, within the first half of this book, have always had to take account of the massive differences in the failure rates of the two types of businesses as shown in Chapter 1. We have also recognised the presence of different motivations and aspirations amongst small business entrepreneurs in Chapter 3. Finally, we also highlighted in Chapter 5 the highly variable performance, even of surviving small businesses.

Despite the clear differences in motivation, the key factor which distinguishes small from large firms is their differential failure rates. A study purporting to be about small firms is incomplete, and hence biased, if it is not at least partly a study of failures.

The term 'business failure' is both an emotive issue and a thorny definitional problem. As we noted in Chapter 2 it was difficult to agree a definition of failure which was both theoretically acceptable and would enable us to determine both those companies which had failed and the year in which such failures occurred.

In the context of this study we have chosen to regard a company as failed when it ceased trading and when it has no likelihood of restarting. There is no suggestion that the term 'failure' carries a pejorative connotation but it should be clear that small business failures, overall, do result in a substantial misallocation of societal resources.

In Part II of this book, we attempt to obtain a clearer, yet practical, understanding of small business failure by applying the type of business failure prediction models extensively undertaken for the large firm sector. Again the objective is partly the clear practical benefits of being able to predict small business failure but also to highlight the respects in which models for small and large firms differ.

The present chapter uses univariate ratio analysis, comparing the performances of failed and non-failed small companies according to single financial ratios. However it could be argued that failure is a multi-dimensional concept which is unlikely to be fully reflected in a single ratio. Hence in Chapter 7 the technique of multiple discriminant analysis (MDA) is used to examine whether selected combinations of ratios provide better predictions. Whilst MDA enables predictions to be made of which firms are classified as 'failures' and as 'non-failures' the technique is unhelpful in determining the unique explanatory power of individual ratios, and so in Chapter 8 the techniques of Probit, Logit and Factor Analysis are considered.

The data used in Chapters 6-8 are the adjusted or unadjusted Profit and Loss and Balance Sheet items of small company accounts but, as was shown in Chapters 2 and 3, UK companies are also required to disclose other 'qualitative' information which may be relevant to performance prediction. In Chapter 9 this qualitative information is used for failure prediction.

We now review some studies which have used univariate ratio and/or profile analysis as a tool for predicting corporate failure. Those ratios which have been shown to be useful in these studies are then used for predicting small firm failure amongst Northern England manufacturing companies. Despite the development of more sophisticated failure prediction models, practitioners and agencies dealing with small firms still seem to favour the use of financial ratio analysis in a univariate framework in order to assess the financial status of small firms. Given this preference amongst practitioners for the simple techniques, this chapter will examine the merits of the approach.

The chapter has three prime objectives: first, to evaluate and appraise the potential of ratio analysis via the visual inspection of profiles to identify the characteristics of failed and non-failed small manufacturing companies; second, to identify whether these ratios are stable over time; and third, to examine whether the conclusions drawn from univariate analysis lead to improved accuracy in multivariate models. It does not attempt to use univariate analysis for direct failure prediction since it will become clear that no individual ratio, nor any easily derivable statistic drawn from that ratio, adequately distinguishes between small failed and non-failed companies.

RATIO ANALYSIS: A BRIEF REVIEW

Financial ratio analysis has traditionally concerned itself with the study of financial statements at a point in time (cross-section) and with the trends in these relationships over time (time-series). If the purpose is failure prediction, then for both types of analysis a ratio for a specific company will need to be compared to a level of the ratio which best discriminates between failed and non-failed companies.

In deciding what type of information best distinguishes failed from non-failed companies the following questions require consideration. First, is there a model of success/failure to guide the selection of appropriate financial information? Second, are the potential types of discriminating information equally consistent across industries, across time and across different sizes of company? Third, what are the 'correct' criteria for selecting discriminating variables and the level of variables to be used as discriminating values? Finally, should the criterion be one of minimising total cost of error, or should the 'ease' of use by the final users also be taken into account?

Although every textbook on financial statement analysis contains sections on financial ratio analysis, they often fail to consider many of the above questions on whether financial ratio analysis is appropriate for discriminating between failed and non-failed companies. The discussion typically concentrates on the detailed definition of ratios. This section will consider these matters but will also examine the assumptions needed for ratio analysis to be a successful tool for the prediction of failure.

Whittington (1980) argues that the basic assumption for ratio analysis to be useful is that of proportionality, i.e. a proportionate relationship exists (or ought to exist) between the two variables whose ratio is calculated. This has to exist if the

177

common use of ratio analysis of comparing a company's 'ratios' to a standard for the ratios is to be useful as a guide to performance.

Whittington points out that two of the conditions necessary for proportionality to hold are likely to be violated in practice and this has implications for the cross-section and time series use of financial ratios. First, there may be a constant term in the relationship between the two variables which make up a ratio. For example, if the profit/sales ratio is being considered, an element of a company's profit may be unrelated to the sales element, so that the profit-to-sales ratio may inadequately describe the relationship between profits and sales. Second, the functional form of the relationship may be non-linear. Thus, a company facing decreasing returns to scale, or which was facing a saturated market might not be expected to yield a constant increment to profit for each pound added to sales. If either of the above conditions is thought to hold then regression techniques would be more appropriate than ratio analysis, providing the form of the equation can be fully specified. Recent work by McDonald and Morris (1984), however, found that ratio analysis performed satisfactorily in capturing the relationships between financial variables.

Using ratio analysis it is possible to focus on two important areas, company survival and company performance. Whilst the two areas are clearly interdependent, for expositional clarity they will be discussed separately.

Solvency of a company is critical to its survival and, although long-term insolvency is equivalent to company failure, it is short-term insolvency which precipitates the event. (Long-term insolvency or negative net worth is defined as an excess of total liabilities over total assets. In contrast, short-term insolvency is defined as an excess of current liabilities over current assets.)

Two short term solvency ratios in common use are the current ratio and the quick ratio.

$$\text{Current ratio} = \frac{\text{Current Assets}}{\text{Current Liabilities}}$$

$$\text{Quick ratio} = \frac{\text{Cash \& Short-term Marketing Securities \& Accounts Receivable}}{\text{Current Liabilities}}$$

Lee (1981) suggests that these ratios should not be less than two and one respectively. Despite their persistence in the literature, both ratios are theoretically unattractive because of their ambiguity and because they are subject to 'window-dressing'. For example, they could conceal high levels of current assets due to management inefficiency. Hence the 'benchmark' of two is difficult to justify. Working capital ratios are not subject to the same criticism, but Walter (1957) criticised all such ratios on the grounds that they did not specifically reflect cashflow. Subsequently, Beaver (1966) was able to demonstrate that cash flow to total debt performed better than the current ratio as a test of solvency. These criticisms led to the development of the 'defensive interval' measure (Quick Assets/Daily Operating Costs) which is an estimate of the number of days that existing levels of cash and debtors could finance the projected daily operating expenditures of the company.

Long-term solvency depends on the ability of the company to meet *all* its liabilities. Two ratios in common use are the Capital Gearing ratio and the Income Gearing ratio.

Capital Gearing = Net Total Debt/Total Debts or Total Assets

Income Gearing = Interest Payments/Profit Before Interest & Tax

The capital gearing ratio reflects the extent to which the company is financed by outside sources. The advantage of the income gearing ratio is that both operating income and annual interest can be recent values whereas the capital gearing ratio may be overstated because total assets are stated at historic values. Finally, ratios such as cashflow to total debt combine to some extent the two concepts of short-term and long-term solvency.

The general financial performance of a company may be assessed in two ways. Reference may be made first to its ability to generate income and second to the value of its shares. For unquoted companies, the analysis is restricted to the former approach.

One overall measure of financial performance is the Return on Capital employed. However, there are numerous definitions of income and capital employed so that a variety of ratios are in common use, one of which is:

$$\text{Return on Equity} = \frac{\text{Net Income Available to Common Shareholders}}{\text{Shareholders' Equity}}$$

Studies of the behaviour of financial ratios in company failure have taken place for the last 50 years, (Ramsey and Foster, 1931). However, attention will be restricted to the best known work utilising ratio analysis, which is Beaver's 1966 article.

Beaver analysed on a univariate ratio basis the financial statements of a matched sample of 79 failed and 79 non-failed companies (drawn from Moody's Industrial Manual) to determine the usefulness of such information for failure prediction. His approach was primarily concerned with the arithmetic mean values of the ratios, and was derived from a theory of a cash flow model. Beaver visualised the firm as a 'reservoir of liquid assets which is supplied by inflows and drained by outflows ... the solvency of the firm can be defined in terms of the probability that the reservoir will be exhausted'. (pp. 79-80)

From this Beaver derived four propositions:

(1) The larger the reservoir, the smaller the probability of failure
(2) The larger the net liquid asset flow from the operation (i.e. cash flow), the smaller the probability of failure
(3) The larger the fund expenditures for operations, the greater the probability of failure
(4) The larger the amount of debt held, the greater the probability of failure (p. 80).

From the above propositions, Beaver postulated that the mean value of six financial ratios would differ significantly between failed and non-failed companies as presented in Table 6.1.

Beaver argued that, *ceteris paribus*, each of the ratios would distinguish failed from non-failed companies up to five years prior to failure. Failure was defined as the inability of a company to pay its bills as they mature which includes bankruptcy, bond default, overdrawn bank account and non-payment of preference dividend. The companies were large US industrial public companies that failed between 1954 and 1964. Classification by size and industry in their most recent balance sheet

Table 6.1: Prediction of the mean values of failed and non-failed firms

	Ratios	Predicted[a]
1.	Cashflow/Total Assets	Non-failed > Failed
2.	Net Income/Total Assets	Non-failed > Failed
3.	Total Debt/Total Assets	Failed > Non-failed
4.	Working Capital/Total Assets	Non-failed > Failed
5.	Current Ratio	Non-failed > Failed
6.	No Credit Interval	Non-failed > Failed

Source: Beaver (1966).
Note: a. Non-failed > Failed means a prediction that the mean value of the non-failed will be greater than that of the failed firms.

indicated asset-sizes ranging from $0.6m-$45m with an average of $6m. The failed companies were paired with non-failed companies in the same industry with similar asset-size. Data for up to five years were collected: one year prior referred to the most recent financial statements within six months of the date of failure.

Beaver used three types of analysis, a comparison of mean values, a dichotomous classification test and an analysis of likelihood ratios, to determine the empirical validity of the predictions/propositions in Table 6.1.

A comparison of mean values of the ratios indicated persistent differences between failed and non-failed companies for each year prior to failure, which were consistent with the above proposition. He also showed that for several ratios there was evidence of progressive deterioration amongst failed firms as failure approached.

Beaver's dichotomous classification test was designed to rank the ratios which 'best' discriminated between failed and non-failed companies. The data were arranged in ascending order and the array for each ratio visually inspected to find the optimal cut-off point which minimised the number of incorrect predictions. The results indicated that some ratios were better predictors than others and all the ratios predicted non-failure better than failure. The efficiency of the dichotomous classification test was validated against a hold-out sample. The best performing ratio was the cash flow to total debt. The overall error rate for the hold-out sample was 13 per cent one year prior to failure and 22 per cent five years prior to failure.

The analysis of likelihood ratios overcame two limitations of the dichotomous classification test in that it considered both the probability of failure or non-failure and the asymmetrical loss functions of Type 1 and Type 2 errors.[1] Histograms were prepared to select the likelihood ratios. These showed that the distribution of non-failed companies was stable over time, whereas the distribution for the failed companies moved away from that of the non-failed companies as the date of failure approached. In addition to determining the degree of overlap and hence the predictive power of the ratio, the analysis showed that the distributions were heavily skewed. The present study supports the Beaver research findings by showing that the distributions of the ratios are, generally, skewed due to the presence of extreme values. In order to diminish the effect of the extreme values, this study will present data on medians, and on upper and lower quartiles of the ratios for failed and non-failed companies. This is intended to provide more representative values for the ratios so as to assist comparisons between failed and non-failed companies.

Although differences may exist between the means, medians and quartiles of ratios the merits of each ratio in distinguishing between failed and non-failed companies cannot be assessed without the additional knowledge of the overlap between the distributions. Hence the extent of the overlap of distributions for selected ratios is also provided.

Beaver concluded that reported financial data and financial ratios can predict company failure up to five years prior to the event. The most effective predictor was found to be the ratio of cash flow to total debt followed by net income to total assets. Turnover ratios were poor predictors and among the worst predictors was the current ratio. In a later study, Beaver (1968) analysed the components of various liquidity measures. Failed companies were found to have lower cash ratios and higher debtor ratios. As they operate in different directions, their inclusion in the current and quick ratios obscures relevant information — therefore cash ratios predict better.

Using more powerful statistical techniques than his predecessors, Beaver obtained a fairly high predictive ability with financial ratios. However, his approach attracted a number of criticisms. First, his method of selecting variables was deficient. By choosing ratios partly on the basis of popularity in the literature, some of the more 'important' ratios may have been excluded. Furthermore, the popular ratios, as objects of attention by analysts and management, are susceptible to 'window-dressing'. Second, the classification of companies took place on a univariate basis. This provided the potential for conflicting results when different companies were misclassified with different ratios. Altman (1968) argues that the financial status of a company is essentially multidimensional and, consequently, introduced the use of multiple discriminant analysis. This method of corporate failure prediction is developed in Chapter 7. Third, as Beaver noted, one of the problems with a paired sample design is that it can exclude important predictor variables.

Fourth, Beaver did not consider the usefulness of financial ratios to decision-makers and particularly how they would use the ratios in a practical context. It is the joint effect of the discriminating power of ratios and their use by decision-makers that determines the quality of the predictions. Because this chapter is primarily a replication of Beaver's work on a small firm data base, all of the above criticisms except the third will apply to the empirical work on small companies presented here. However, before discussing the empirical replication of Beaver's work, a brief review of the work which explicitly considered the fourth criticism would seem prudent.

In a study by Kennedy (1975), bankers were given six items of information: industry class, asset size, and four financial ratios, for each of twelve companies. For each item of information they were asked for their judgement of the probability that the comany would fail during the next year.

A sample of twelve (six failed, six non-failed) companies was selected from Beaver's sample of 79 pairs. The four ratios were the tangible equity to debt ratio (shareholders' equity minus intangible assets divided by current plus long-term liabilities), the current ratio, the inventory turnover ratio and the quick ratio. Only four ratios were used because of the order effect in a sequence of Bayesian probability revisions. The order effect can be a primacy or a recency effect. A primacy effect is one where information which occurs early in a sequence influences probability revisions more than later information. The recency effect refers to the finding that later information influences revisions more than earlier information. To control for an order effect with the four ratios, all possible permutations were used. To control for the influence of correlated ratios on the revision of probabilities the companies' ratios were randomly ordered.

Kennedy found that certain ratios seemed more useful than others. Even the useful ratios (equity to debt ratio) seemed to have a grey area within which the bankers could find little diagnostic value. Kennedy also found that the bankers gave more weighting to non-financial information than financial information for their credit-rating decision.

He concluded that different ratios were not used in an equally efficient manner and this clearly has significance for the results of Beaver. Even if certain ratios do clearly discriminate between failed and non-failed companies, they may not be useful in predicting failure if they are poorly understood or mistrusted by bankers/creditors. This problem would not apply if the bankers were presented with a black-box discriminating tool for which they only had to supply values for certain ratios.

As well as determining the efficiency of use of ratios by decision-makers, Libby (1975) presented evidence of a relationship between individual versus composite performance and expected versus actual performance. In addition, he analysed the consistency of interpretation of the ratios by loan officers over time and between loan officers.

A three group experiment was designed to test for the various types of consistency. Two sub-groups of 16 small bank and 27 large bank loan officers were used to check for consistency between loan officers. The sub-group of 27 large bank officers was split to check for time consistency. One half of the sub-group checked 30 companies and another 40 companies with each fourth company randomly repeated in a weekly sitting (total number of companies = 70). The other half of the sub-group checked 30 companies in one week and the other 40 companies in another.

Utilising principal component analysis, Libby identified five independent sources of variation within a 14-variable set. The five dimensions and five ratios derived from the rotated factor matrix are set out below:

	Dimension	Ratio
(1)	Profitability	Net income/total assets
(2)	Activity	Current assets/sales
(3)	Liquidity	Current assets/current liabilities
(4)	Asset balance	Current assets/total assets
(5)	Cash balance	Cash/total assets

The bank loan officers were asked to predict both 'failure' and 'non-failure'. To set the prior probabilities they were told that half the companies failed within three years. The results showed the predictive accuracy (74 per cent) of the loan officers was superior to random assignment. The results of further tests showed no significant difference between loan officers in interpreting the data and no time inconsistency. However, Libby found that a consensus judgement, where a company was classified as failed or non-failed depending on the majority decision, achieved an accuracy of 81.7 per cent. Libby concluded that the ratio information was correctly utilised by the loan officers. Also, he showed that factor analysis can be an important first step in failure analysis. Identifying independent sources of variation reduces the number of variables, removes superfluity and highlights the prominent characteristics of the data set.

Altman (1982) suggested the results may be overstated because, in practice, loan officers would not know the prior probabilities of the sample. However, perhaps the major limitation of the study was that the officers did not have to choose the information they would need to predict failure. Whilst Kennedy's study suggested that different ratios may not be used equally efficiently, so questioning Beaver's type of work, Libby suggests that if companies get into trouble then most loan officers act in a reasonably consistent manner. For any one company the final outcome should not therefore depend on who are the creditors and this should ease the prediction problem. On the other hand Kennedy suggests that two companies could be achieving roughly the same level of economic performance but suffer different fates at the hands of the creditors if they differ on key financial variables. According to Kennedy the decision to withdraw credit from a company seems to depend on certain key variables and these variables must be determined if failure prediction is to be accurate.

Zimmer (1980) extended Libby's work by considering the predictions of loan officers in a more realistic and practical context. This involved loan officers making annual predictions of failure based on a time-series of ratios.

Each of 30 loan officers from two Australian banks was provided with financial profiles of 42 real but disguised industrial companies listed on the Sydney Stock Exchange between 1961 and 1977. Half of the companies experienced failure within one year of the most recent financial statement. The subjects were

185

requested to identify which companies experienced failure and indicate their confidence in each prediction. Five ratios which captured the principal components of a company's financial statement were provided for each of the three years prior to the prediction.

The officers were told that half the companies failed. The results indicate that only two officers did not perform better than random accuracy. This result is consistent with Libby's results but not Casey's (1980), who conducted similar work. The inconsistency is explained by the fact that Casey did not specify the prior probability of failure facing the subjects, i.e. that a company stood a 50/50 chance of being a failure. Most of the prediction errors made by Casey's subjects were attributable to them predicting failed companies as non-failed. This is consistent with the fact that the actual rate of company failure is quite low. Therefore, the conclusion seems to be that the majority of loan officers only predict failure/non-failure at a rate better than chance if sample priors are given.

Apart from the fail/not fail decision the loan officers were asked to indicate the degree of confidence they had in their decisions. Zimmer postulated that if ratios are of use then the percentage of firms correctly predicted should increase with the degree of confidence the loan officers had in their predictions. Zimmer found that his postulate was correct. He also noted that predictive accuracy was not associated with time devoted to the exercise, formal qualifications or years of lending experience. Zimmer also found the loan officers to be fairly consistent as a group. In general the Zimmer paper supports the earlier findings of Libby that whilst different ratios may not be used efficiently, at least they all seemed to be used consistently. This suggests that, if the key variable used to determine future failures is related to past data which show a high degree of separation between failed and non-failed companies, and if future decision-makers are as consistent as shown by the above studies, then the Beaver type of analysis could enable accurate predictions to be made. Of course this assumes that decision-makers use financial ratios in a univariate manner or that their subjective weighting function can be determined.

Ratio analysis developed as a means of analysing financial performance both over time and between companies, but its use is constrained by the limitations of annual financial statements as a medium for communicating relevant and accurate information. Unfortunately financial statements are designed to meet the needs of several different user types leading to compromised requirements for accuracy.

The level of accuracy of financial statements particularly for the small company sector has been criticised for several reasons. First, despite the recent trend towards standardisation, financial statements are based upon conventions that rely heavily on arbitrary judgements and opinions. Methods of depreciation and stock valuations are two key examples. Second, the basis of historical cost accounting prevents the statements from reflecting the effects of inflation. Third, there is a tendency by many accountants to practise 'excess' conservatism. Fourth, there are problems of classifying items under appropriate headings by nature and in terms of liquidity. This is a serious problem as it makes it more difficult to derive accurate indicators of solvency and profitability and can cause inconsistent comparisons to be made between companies. Fifth, UK legislation exempts disclosure of annual turnover and other useful data for small companies, so reducing the scope of the analysis. Finally, annual financial statements only provide a static analysis of company performance, with no account being taken of seasonal fluctuations, window-dressing and other year-end bias.

Apart from the specific problems of financial statements and of applying ratio analysis to small companies there are other more general problems. First, if ratios are to be compared to a standard in order to judge performance, then the assumption of proportionality has to be met. Second, if ratios are to be used in prediction, then it is not necessarily sufficient to show that past failed and non-failed companies had different values for certain ratios. A fully convincing case is made only if it can be shown that the decision makers actually used this information in reaching their decision.

The evidence tends to suggest that agents do not use all ratios equally efficiently and, therefore, care should be taken in interpreting ex-post discrimination results as being equivalent to prediction results. Furthermore, existing work has concentrated on agents defining companies as failed or non-failed rather than dating failure. In a practical situation the dating of failure would be quite important, as the perceived time between prediction and predicted event will determine the optimal set of actions. Our review, however, suggests that whilst different ratios were not used equally efficiently, they were at least reasonably consistent. This indicates that failure prediction should be possible because the agents who might precipitate eventual failure do so in a consistent manner. Furthermore, the evidence suggests that loan officers have a better performance when acting as a committee, which in turn suggests that UK failure prediction models might well benefit from a study of the factors considered as relevant by UK decision makers. This highlights the need to know what information loan officers/creditors use and why they choose it.

SAMPLE DESIGN

The failed and non-failed companies analysed here are taken from the primary sample, the characteristics of which were described in Chapter 2. There, it will be recalled, the judgements over the time at which the company failed were set out. It was emphasised that, in some cases, it was extremely difficult to decide the date at which failure took place. However all companies which failed were classified according to the calendar year in which we believed it ceased to trade.

Since the date of failure can be unclear this presents problems of defining the concept of 'years prior to failure'. Such problems multiply when financial data, from which the ratios are derived, apply to financial years the end month of which varies considerably.

Faced with these difficulties the following decisions were made. Assume a company is known to have ceased trading in December 1980. In this case year $t = 1980$. If the last *full* year's financial accounts include the period after 1 July 1980 then these accounts are deemed also to refer to year t. If, however, the last *full* year's accounts only include the part of the year up until 30 June 1980 then these are deemed to refer to year $t - 1$. Thus a company which failed in December 1980, and where the last submitted accounts are for the period April 1979 to March 1980, is deemed to fail in year t and have its last submitted accounts referring to year $t - 1$. According to this definition no company which fails before 1st July in any year t can also have accounts for year t.[2] *In order to utilise the financial data for year* t *for companies failing in year* t, *this year's data are designated as arising from one year prior to failure.*

A second characteristic of small companies noted in Chapter

2 is that many have a relatively short trading life, and in many cases either provide data only for a few of the years in which they trade, or provide incomplete information during those years. This is a major difference between large and smaller firms and provides additional problems in conducting univariate ratio analysis. To overcome these problems it has been decided to examine three profile types, since each, taken independently, fails to reflect the diversity of the small company sector.

Profile Type I

The non-submission of data by failing companies in year t means it is very difficult to compare failed and non-failed companies in the year immediately prior to failure. Hence Profile Type I takes all companies failing in year t, and compares their ratios in year $t-1$ with those of all non-failed companies in year t providing information in year $t-1$. This comparison is set out in mathematical notation below.

	Failed		Non-failed
$\bar{r}_f^t \quad = \quad \dfrac{\sum\limits_{f=1}^{F} r_f^{t-1}}{F}$		$\bar{r}_n^t \quad = \quad \dfrac{\sum\limits_{n=1}^{N} r_n^{t-1}}{N}$	

$\bar{r}_f^t$ = Arithmetic mean ratio for year t for failed firms

$\bar{r}_n^t$ = Arithmetic mean ratio for year t for non-failed firms

F = Total number of failed firms in year t

N = Total number of non-failed firms in year t

r_f^{t-1} = Ratio in year $t-1$ for the f*th* failed firms

r_n^{t-1} = Ratio in year $t-1$ for n*th* non-failed firms

The number of failed and non-failed companies included in this profile analysis are as follows:

Year	1975	1976	1977	1978	1979	1980	1981
Failed	5	2	6	5	9	7	6
Non-failed	269	282	297	325	326	319	279

189

The table therefore shows that there were seven companies which failed in 1980, i.e. year t and for which financial data were provided for year $t-1$. We must re-emphasise again however, that in the text this is referred to as *two* years prior to failure for the reasons noted above. These seven cases are then compared with 319 non-failed companies which were trading in 1980 (year t) and which provided data for 1979 (year $t-1$).

It should be noted that the companies are classified according to whether or not they failed in a given year. It does not mean that they *never* failed as there are a number of cases of firms which are known to have ceased trading after 1983 yet which are included in the non-failed categories in the above table. However all firms classified as non-failed did not fail before 1983.

Profile type II

The major problem with Profile Type I is that for any given year there are only a maximum of nine failures and in one year there were only two failures. In order to increase the relevant sample size the data were pooled, so that where firms ceased to trade in year t, financial ratios R1—R7 shown in Table 6.2 were computed for years $t-1$, $t-2$, $t-3$ and $t-4$. Ratios were not computed for year t because of the relatively few firms which supplied data for that year. In calculating Profile Type II two points need to be recognised. Firstly, a failure, for example, in 1975 is treated in an identical manner to a failure in 1980 even though these occurred at different points in the trade cycle and under very different macro-economic conditions. Secondly, the number of companies included in the data set varies considerably. For example, only 41 companies that provided data two years prior to failure also supplied data five years prior. The presence of short-life companies within the data set means that the numbers and characteristics of companies supplying data from year to year vary considerably. In order to facilitate a comparison, the non-failed companies are selected as having not failed in the years 1977-80 with five years' prior data being compared with 1977 and two years' prior data being compared with 1980. Thus we compare the financial ratios of 98 failed companies five years prior to their failure with the 1977 ratios of 325 companies which either never failed or did not fail until

1983. The full comparison is set out below.[3]

Years prior to failure	5	4	3	2
Year for non-failed co's	(1977)	(1978)	(1979)	(1980)
Failed (number of cases)	98	95	75	41
Non-failed (number of cases)	297	325	326	319

Having a larger sample of failed companies (four and five years prior to failure) provides the opportunity to make an effective comparison between the levels and distributions of the ratios for failed and non-failed companies.

Profile type III

The major limitation of Profile Type II is in its method of construction since there are different companies included each year. From this it is impossible to tell whether, even if the mean value of a ratio declines in the years prior to failure, this is attributable to a real decline in companies providing the data or the entry into the data set of new companies with lower values or the exit of companies with higher values. There is clearly a need to eliminate entry and exit in order to determine whether, within a group of small companies providing data continuously over a four-year period, any profile deterioration is apparent as failure approaches. It is for this purpose that Profile Type III is constructed where only companies which provided data continuously over a long period are included. In constructing this profile, the number of failed companies for which data were available continuously over five years, i.e., years two to six prior to failure, was relatively small. Only 25 failed companies were identified. These failed companies were then matched to non-failed companies on the basis of MLH industrial classification and data availability over a five-year period. Thus, a company which failed in 1979 and had comprehensive data back to 1973 is matched with a non-failed company in the same MLH and with the same years of accounts available. All failures in Profile Type III occurred between 1975 and 1981.

THE COMPUTATION OF FINANCIAL RATIOS

For each company seven ratios were compiled. These are presented in Table 6.2 and are based upon Beaver's analysis. This table contains profitability ratios, solvency ratios and liquidity ratios and a gearing ratio. For the remainder of this chapter each of these will be assessed according to its mean, median and measure of volatility for each of the three profile types.

EMPIRICAL RESULTS: PROFILE TYPE I

In order to determine whether consistent differences exist between the ratio levels of failed and non-failed companies throughout the 1970s the following profile was provided. Failed companies were grouped together according to their date of failure. The means and medians of each ratio of the failed companies for two years prior to failure were plotted against the means and medians of the non-failed companies over the relevant years. A visual inspection is made of the results. *It must be emphasised that in all subsequent graphs, when a company is referred to as failing in year* t, *the last year of financial data shown is for the year prior.* The same rule applies to non-failed

Table 6.2: Ratio definitions

Profitability Ratios	
Ratios	Predicted
1. R1: Pre-tax Profit/Total Assets[a]	Non-failed > Failed
2. R2: Pre-tax Profit before Interest payments and Directors' Fees/Total Assets	Non-failed > Failed
3. R3: Net Profit & Depreciation/Total Assets	Non-failed > Failed
Solvency Ratios	
4. R4: Net Working Capital/Fixed Assets	Non-failed > Failed
Liquidity Ratios	
5. R5: Current Assets/Current Liabilities	Non-failed > Failed
6. R6: Current Assets − Stock/Current Liabilities	Non-failed > Failed
Gearing Ratios	
7. R7: Total Debts[b]/Total Assets	Failed > Non-failed

Notes: a. Total Assets is exclusive of Intangible Assets.
b. Total Debts: government loans + Hire Purchase and Mortgage and Bank Overdrafts + other long-term loans.

companies. Finally it must be recalled that there are relatively few failed firms and so these profiles need to be treated with particular caution.

Profitability Ratios

Pre-tax Profit/Total Assets (R1) (Figure 6.1) showed that differences existed between failed and non-failed companies during the 1970s. The means of this ratio for the failed companies were either negative or slightly positive. They remained consistently below the mean values of the non-failed companies throughout the 1970s. For the non-failed companies, profitability was broadly similar at between 5 and 10 per cent for most years up to 1978 but thereafter a declining trend was observed. The mean values of the failed companies, on the other hand, appeared to exhibit a greater degree of variability over the period in question. Profitability appeared to be highly volatile amongst failed companies — the profiles for ratios R2 and R3 were essentially equivalent to R1 throughout the 1970s and are not shown. Nevertheless, the number of failed companies which experienced losses varied substantially from year to year. For example, none of the nine companies that failed in 1978 made losses according to the R1 profit measure two years prior to failure whereas all of the companies failing in 1976 experienced losses two years prior to failure. It could be argued either that such apparent variations are a chance result stemming from the small number of failed companies in each year or that they reflect macro-economic factors characteristic of certain years. These points will be discussed in further detail later.

An examination of the skewness for ratios R1, R2 and R3 (Table 6.3) showed indications of the presence of extreme values for both failed and non-failed companies throughout the 1970s. The median values (Figure 6.2 for R1 is an example) for all the three profitability ratios of the failed companies generally remained below the median of the non-failed companies during the 1970s. Although the medians, by diminishing the effect of extreme values, were consistently below the means of the non-failed companies, considerable variability was still apparent in all three profitability ratios amongst the failed companies. Some of this apparent variability is clearly due to a small numbers effect. An examination of the lower and upper

193

quartiles (Table 6.3) suggested that, in the majority of cases, non-failed companies experienced higher values than failed companies. This was particularly true with reference to R1 as all the values of the upper and lower quartiles of failed companies fell below the values of those of the non-failed companies throughout the 1970s.

Solvency ratios

The profile of the solvency ratio (R4) (Figure 6.3) shows that apart from the companies which failed in 1977 the differences between the mean values of the two groups did not appear to be as high as would be needed to aid the effective separation of failed and non-failed companies. Although the medians (in Figure 6.4) of the failed and non-failed companies were different in most years, an examination of the quartile data suggests that the solvency ratio did not provide a consistent decision rule which would distinguish between failed and non-failed companies during the 1970s.

Liquidity ratios

The mean values of the two liquidity ratios (R5 is shown in Figure 6.5) for failed companies were generally below the main values of non-failed companies during the 1970s. Whilst the mean value of the current ratio (R5) for the non-failed companies remained around a value of 2:1, the mean values of the failed companies varied substantially. For example, the current ratio of the companies which failed in 1979 was on average 0.8:1, compared with the average value of 2.6:1 for companies failing in 1980.

Although the median data (R5 is shown in Figure 6.6) showed more consistent differences between failed and non-failed companies, the amount of variability amongst failed companies was still marked during the 1970s. The median and lower quartiles of the failure groups generally had lower values than those of the non-failed groups. Curiously, however, in both 1978 and 1980 the liquidity measure R5 for the upper quartile of failed companies actually exceeded that for the upper quartile of the non-failed companies.

Table 6.3: Profile Type I: quartiles

		1975 F	1975 NF	1976 F	1976 NF	1977 F	1977 NF	1978 F	1978 NF	1979 F	1979 NF	1980 F	1980 NF	1981 F	1981 NF
R1	U.Q.	13.6	14.3		15.2	15.7	13.8	8.6	15.2	5.2	14.7	4.6	11.2	− 1.1	9.2
	Med	− 6.2	7.6	− 23.2	7.4	3.8	7.8	4.5	8.0	− 4.6	7.8	0.0	5.8	− 4.3	3.2
	L.Q.	− 15.2	1.0		1.0	− 19.6	1.2	0.0	0.7	− 18.5	2.1	− 15.4	0.4	− 23.7	4.2
R2	U.Q.	25.3	48.9		52.1	57.3	45.0	26.2	49.0	85.5	44.1	75.0	41.4	41.6	42.8
	Med	0.0	31.4	− 13.8	30.6	12.0	30.0	19.4	31.0	21.6	30.9	18.7	26.8	1.6	25.4
	L.Q.	− 6.6	19.1		19.7	0.6	18.4	14.5	19.4	5.1	19.5	10.1	16.0	12.5	13.6
R3	U.Q.	11.5	14.1		13.7	21.0	14.4	12.6	14.8	8.2	15.3	5.0	13.9	3.9	14.5
	Med	− 3.3	8.0	− 17.7	7.8	4.8	8.6	8.4	9.5	5.2	10.3	2.6	8.5	− 1.1	8.1
	L.Q.	− 11.4	3.8		4.0	− 17.2	4.7	5.1	4.3	8.1	5.1	− 4.0	4.0	− 22.3	2.6
R4	U.Q.	70.6	224.9		189.1	199.5	194.1	987.1	166.0	− 0.2	183.6	251.8	187.3	577.7	170.8
	Med	15.4	100.0	− 50.0	93.1	− 12.2	82.9	68.1	71.9	− 90.7	74.4	157.1	77.8	78.3	63.7
	L.Q.	− 17.2	22.6		24.1	− 392.9	518.8	26.1	103.0	− 183.5	17.7	− 12.8	15.9	− 332.0	15.6
R5	U.Q.	144.6	252.2		242.9	162.4	233.0	235.5	229.2	94.4	232.5	283.3	212.6	145.8	232.7
	Med	120.0	160.2	136.7	163.7	93.4	159.4	133.2	149.1	70.5	152.3	126.7	150.8	104.6	154.9
	L.Q.	94.9	119.9		118.8	59.4	112.2	127.6	106.9	33.3	112.7	90.4	111.3	71.2	109.2
R6	U.Q.	105.2	191.7		184.7	109.5	165.9	183.9	154.4	63.2	171.2	216.7	163.1	127.3	168.9
	Med	65.6	116.7	114.0	120.6	67.2	111.9	98.5	107.7	32.3	107.9	118.3	104.0	69.9	107.8
	L.Q.	44.3	72.1		80.1	40.5	76.2	74.3	70.3	16.2	72.2	28.7	70.9	34.3	71.7
R7	U.Q.	37.6	21.8		22.1	131.4	22.3	25.9	23.8	63.2	24.0	30.6	24.3	46.1	24.6
	Med	33.1	5.4	24.0	5.4	36.7	6.9	15.0	10.2	25.3	10.7	22.6	11.3	17.3	10.0
	L.Q.	9.1	0.0		0.0	13.6	0.0	0.0	0.0	2.7	0.0	0.9	0.0	0.0	0.0

Note: U.Q. = Upper Quartile, Med = Median, L.Q. = Lower Quartile.

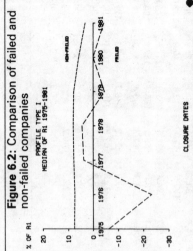

Figure 6.1: Comparison of failed and non-failed companies

PROFILE TYPE I
MEAN OF R1 1975–1981

% OF R1

NON-FAILED

FAILED

CLOSURE DATES

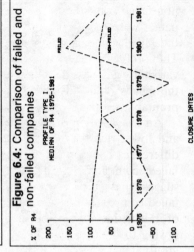

Figure 6.2: Comparison of failed and non-failed companies

PROFILE TYPE I
MEDIAN OF R1 1975–1981

% OF R1

NON-FAILED

FAILED

CLOSURE DATES

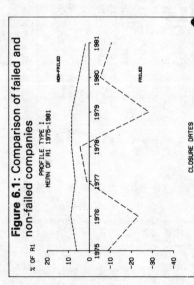

Figure 6.3: Comparison of failed and non-failed companies

PROFILE TYPE I
MEAN OF R4 1975–1981

% OF R4

NON-FAILED

FAILED

CLOSURE DATES

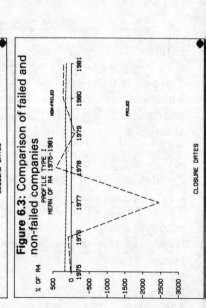

Figure 6.4: Comparison of failed and non-failed companies

PROFILE TYPE I
MEDIAN OF R4 1975–1981

% OF R4

FAILED

NON-FAILED

CLOSURE DATES

Gearing ratios

An inspection of the gearing ratio (R7) (Figure 6.7) showed that differences existed between the mean values of failed and non-failed companies. The mean values of the non-failed companies were very stable and remained below the mean values of the failed companies throughout the period except for 1978. The profile of the ratio indicated considerable year-to-year variability amongst the failed companies which is comparable to the results obtained in the investigation of the profiles of the profitability ratios.

An examination of the medians, (Figure 6.8) and the upper and lower quartiles (Table 6.3) also demonstrated consistent differences between the gearing ratios for the failed and non-failed companies during the 1970s. These results broadly suggest that failed companies incurred more debts than non-failed companies throughout the period even though the extent of indebtedness varied substantially amongst failed companies. Owing to the low number of failed companies in each failure group, it was not feasible to make effective comparison between the standard deviations and histograms of the ratios of the failed and non-failed companies throughout the 1970s.

EMPIRICAL RESULTS: PROFILE TYPE II

This profile type compares the ratios of all the failed companies which provided data at some stage between two and five years prior to failure and non-failed companies which provided data at some stage beween 1977 and 1980.

Profitability ratios

The profiles of all three profitability ratios (R1, Figure 6.9, is an example) exhibit striking differences between the means of the failed and non-failed companies throughout the four-year period. Figure 6.9 shows the profitability of the failed companies to be strongly negative over the four-year period prior to failure although there was considerable year-to-year variability. The means of the non-failed companies were higher than for the failed firms over the four years but showed a slight declining

197

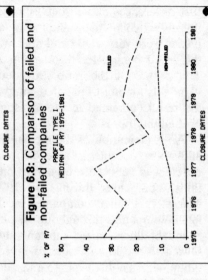

Figure 6.5: Comparison of failed and non-failed companies

PROFILE TYPE I
MEAN OF R5 1975-1981

Figure 6.6: Comparison of failed and non-failed companies

PROFILE TYPE I
MEDIAN OF R5 1975-1981

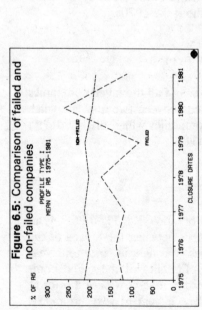

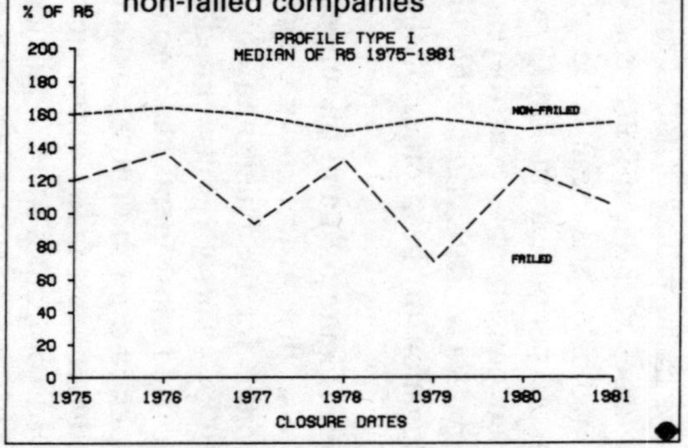

Figure 6.7: Comparison of failed and non-failed companies

PROFILE TYPE I
MEAN OF R7 1975-1981

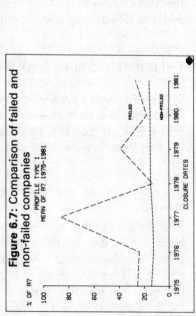

Figure 6.8: Comparison of failed and non-failed companies

PROFILE TYPE I
MEDIAN OF R7 1975-1981

trend particularly in 1980 where the non-failed companies experienced the lowest mean values over the four years. Although the median values in Figure 6.10 showed higher values for the ratios for both failed and non-failed companies the variability was still marked for the failed companies over the four-year period. Again the profiles of ratios R2 and R3 were essentially the same as those of ratio R1.

In general an examination of median profitability measures, of which Figure 6.10 is an example, shows that median profitability for non-failed companies fell between 1977 and 1980. It also shows that median profitability of non-failed companies paralleled that fall and did show a deterioration as failure approached.

Beaver's profile of the Net Profits/Net Assets (Figure 6.11) ratio was the second-best ratio in discriminating between failed and non-failed companies. In the Beaver analysis, failed companies experienced a rapidly declining trend in the mean value of this ratio over a five-year period, whilst during the same period the means of the non-failed companies remained remarkably stable. The numbers of failed and non-failed companies which made losses one year prior to failure amounted to 83.0 per cent and 4.0 per cent respectively.

In the sample used in this text, the numbers of failed and non-failed companies which experienced losses over the four year period are presented in Table 6.4. As the table clearly indicates 68.3 per cent of failed and 35.7 per cent of non-failed companies experienced losses before the deduction of tax (R1) two years prior to failure. These percentages fell to 46.6 per cent and 18.5 per cent respectively after the deduction of tax but before any allowance was given to cover depreciation (i.e. R3). For all three profitability ratios the number of failed companies which made losses rose as failure approached.

These differing results were partly attributable to the characteristics of the two samples. Beaver's sample was selected from a population of relatively large US firms where the rates of failure were very low compared with our population of small manufacturing companies in Northern England. The latter include a relatively large proportion of companies which are likely to fail within the next five years and, therefore, have financial characteristics similar to those of companies which actually failed.

The mean profitability of both the failed and the non-failed

199

Table 6.4: Profile type II: the percentages of failed and non-failed companies which made losses over the four year period

	Years prior to failure			
	5	4	3	2
R1				
Failed	40.0	45.1	42.9	68.3
Non-failed	22.1	16.5	22.7	35.7
R2				
Failed	12.9	22.0	20.0	29.3
Non-failed	4.0	2.8	4.0	5.3
R3				
Failed	25.8	35.3	30.0	46.6
Non-failed	12.0	9.5	13.7	18.5

companies in Beaver's analysis appeared to be lower than the mean value of failed and non-failed companies in the present study. Clearly, there are major differences in time periods and also, to a lesser extent, accounting conventions, but it also supports the view outlined in Chapter 4 that profitability rates in larger companies are generally lower, but less variable, on a year-by-year basis than for smaller companies.

In spite of the conflicting evidence presented above, the profiles analysed so far indicate that differences between the mean profitability ratios of failed and non-failed companies are in the direction predicted by Beaver. The results thus appear encouraging since, according to a Beaver type of comparison, it is possible to distinguish between failed and non-failed companies up to five years prior to failure. In practice, however, no such conclusions can be drawn regarding the predictive ability of the ratios and their significance without having additional information on the standard deviations and the overall distributional overlaps of the ratios.

The values of the standard deviations of all three profitability ratios (R1 as shown in Figure 6.12 is an example) remained relatively stable for the non-failed companies throughout the four-year period. The corresponding values for failed companies demonstrated a far larger degree of instability over the same period and rose as the companies approached failure.

The extent of overlap between failed and non-failed companies is shown in an examination of the histograms (R1, Figure

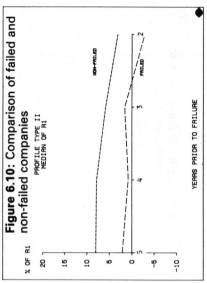

Figure 6.9: Comparison of failed and non-failed companies

PROFILE TYPE II
MEAN OF R1

NON-FAILED

FAILED

YEARS PRIOR TO FAILURE

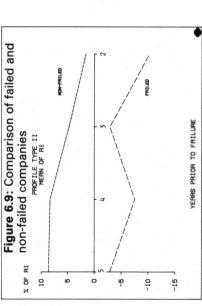

Figure 6.10: Comparison of failed and non-failed companies

PROFILE TYPE II
MEDIAN OF R1

NON-FAILED

FAILED

YEARS PRIOR TO FAILURE

Figure 6.11: Beaver's failed and non-failed companies

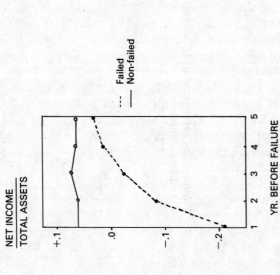

Figure 6.12: Comparison of failed and non-failed companies

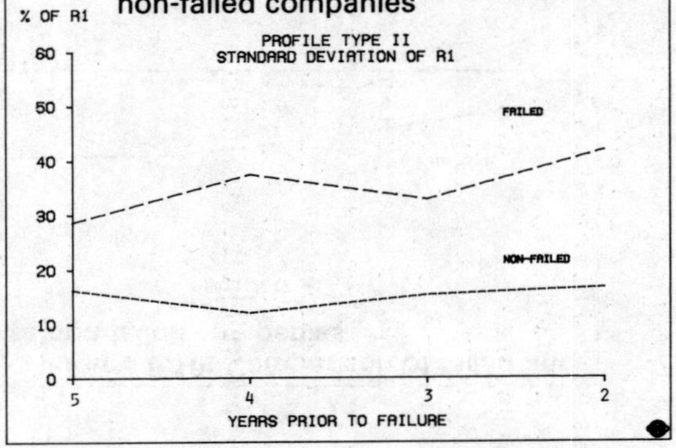

6.13, is an example). These illustrate a substantial distributional overlap for all three profitability ratios (particularly R2 and R3) over the four-year period. Figure 6.13 also shows that both distributions have shifted to the left in the upper histogram — which plots profitability two and five years prior to failure — partly reflecting the overall fall in profitability in the late 1970s. Beaver's histogram for this profitability ratio (Figure 6.14) was stable for non-failed companies over a five-year period (indeed, the values of the ratio actually increased slightly) whereas there was a clear deterioration in the values for failed companies. The amount of distributional overlap was also far less than in the analysis presented here, thus explaining why his profitability ratio performed well in the classification model.

Solvency ratios

The means of the solvency ratio (Figure 6.15) for failed and non-failed companies do not appear either to be significantly different from each other until two years prior to failure. The means of failed companies were above those of non-failed companies five years prior to failure, similar for four years prior, fell below the non-failed companies three years prior and showed a dramatic fall two years prior to failure. Whilst the average value of the solvency ratios for non-failed companies remained around the value of unity the corresponding averages of solvency ratio for failed companies varied substantially within the range of +1.8 to −2.8.

The median profile (Figure 6.16) by diminishing the effects of extreme values, shows both significant differences between failed and non-failed companies and considerably less year-to-year variability, with failed companies experiencing lower median values than non-failed companies throughout the four-year period.

Table 6.5 shows that lower quartile failed companies had a solvency ratio of −7.89 two years prior to failure compared with +1.53 for non-failed lower quartile companies in 1980. On the other hand, upper quartile failed companies had higher values than non-failed companies, except for two years prior to failure when the upper quartile failed companies had a solvency ratio of 1.3 whereas upper quartile non-failed companies had a ratio of 1.7.

Figure 6.13: Distribution of profitability (R1): comparison of failed and non-failed companies

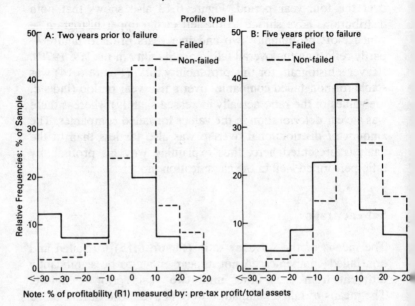

Note: % of profitability (R1) measured by: pre-tax profit/total assets

Figure 6.14: Beaver's distribution of net income/total assets: comparison of failed and non-failed companies

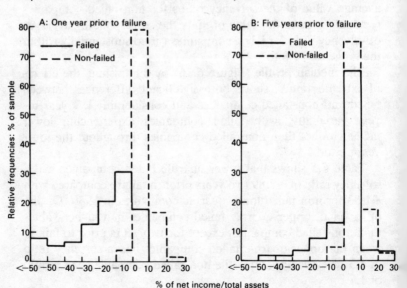

% of net income/total assets

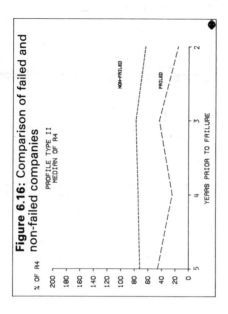

Figure 6.16: Comparison of failed and non-failed companies

PROFILE TYPE II
MEDIAN OF R4

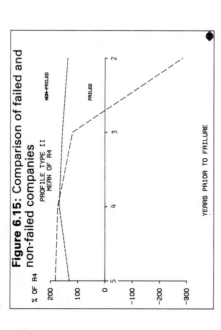

Figure 6.15: Comparison of failed and non-failed companies

PROFILE TYPE II
MEAN OF R4

Table 6.5: Profile type II: quartiles

Years prior to failure	5		4		3		2	
	NF	F	NF	F	NF	F	NF	F
R1								
Upper quartiles	15.3	7.5	14.8	8.8	11.5	11.2	9.2	4.0
Medians	8.0	2.1	7.8	0.8	5.8	1.6	3.1	2.9
Lower quartiles	0.8	— 7.2	2.1	— 10.4	0.4	— 6.9	4.2	— 13.2
Skewness	3.17	— 4.4	— 5.1	— 4.6	— 2.72	— 3.9	3.5	— 5.0
R2								
Upper quartiles	49.2	35.5	44.1	34.4	41.4	40.0	42.7	40.0
Medians	31.0	23.5	30.9	19.8	26.5	17.5	25.2	14.4
Lower quartiles	19.4	12.5	19.5	6.3	15.7	3.8	13.5	0.0
Skewness	2.2	2.6	2.8	1.6	2.3	2.9	0.5	1.4
R3								
Upper quartiles	14.9	10.6	15.3	11.2	13.7	11.8	14.2	7.8
Medians	9.5	5.4	10.3	4.7	8.7	4.7	8.1	1.7
Lower quartiles	4.3	— 1.1	5.1	6.3	4.0	3.4	2.5	5.3
Skewness	5.4	9.3	0.5	— 3.9	— 1.7	— 2.5	— 3.5	— 5.1
R4								
Upper quartiles	166.0	200.5	183.6	218.6	188.6	259.6	171.0	130.3
Medians	71.9	45.6	74.4	24.3	77.8	43.4	63.7	15.7
Lower quartiles	10.3	— 25.9	17.7	— 55.2	16.7	— 29.4	15.3	— 78.9
Skewness	— 0.4	3.8	7.4	1.5	5.3	3.5	6.1	5.9
R5								
Upper quartiles	229.2	200.6	232.6	160.0	213.9	204.4	233.3	145.4
Medians	149.3	115.9	157.4	106.9	151.6	115.5	154.9	112.5
Lower quartiles	107.0	84.7	112.9	74.6	115.5	87.6	109.2	74.7
Skewness	7.8	3.4	6.3	1.7	13.5	3.5	8.7	4.3
R6								
Upper quartiles	153.8	129.8	170.2	112.3	163.6	144.5	168.9	116.8
Medians	107.7	79.7	108.2	78.6	105.3	73.9	107.8	70.1
Lower quartiles	70.5	42.0	72.8	38.5	71.2	36.6	71.9	35.8
Skewness	8.7	3.7	6.9	2.7	13.9	8.3	10.2	5.1
R7								
Upper quartiles	23.7	28.0	24.0	33.9	24.1	35.3	24.6	34.9
Medians	10.0	13.6	10.6	20.4	11.0	20.3	9.9	25.0
Lower quartiles	0.0	0.0	0.0	0.5	0.0	0.0	0.0	2.1
Skewness	1.7	4.4	1.7	2.95	1.4	3.2	2.2	4.8

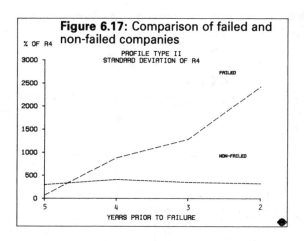

Figure 6.17: Comparison of failed and non-failed companies

The differences between the values of the standard deviations (Figure 6.17) of failed and non-failed companies were marked except for five years prior to failure where failed companies had slightly lower values than non-failed companies. The standard deviations of failed companies rose sharply from 5.0 (five years prior to failure) to above 25.0 (two years prior to failure) whilst, during the same period, the standard deviations of non-failed companies remained between 2.5 and 3.0. The histograms (Figure 6.18) also illustrated considerable overlap between the distributions of the value of the solvency ratio for failed and non-failed companies over the four year period. These values were spread widely between below 0 to over 4.0 for both failed and non-failed over the four-year period.

Hence, despite differences between median values of the solvency ratio for failed and non-failed companies in the majority of cases, the annual variation and the extent of the distributional overlap is so great that it would not be possible to distinguish between failed and non-failed companies without the risk of high Type I and/or Type II errors.

Liquidity ratios

A profile of the liquidity ratios R5 and R6 (R5, Figure 6.19, is an example) illustrates persistent, if insubstantial, differences between the arithmetic means of failed and non-failed companies.

207

Figure 6.18: Distribution of solvency (R4): comparison of failed and non-failed companies

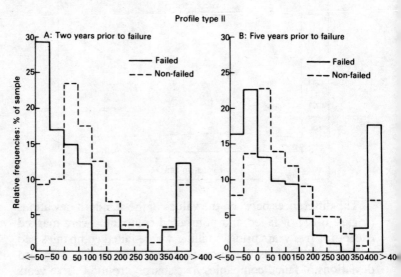

% of solvency (R4) measured by: net working capital/fixed assets

The mean value of the current ratio (R5) for non-failed companies remained relatively stable around the value of 2:1 over the four year period. The mean value of the current ratio of failed companies varied somewhat but never fell below 1.5:1 in any of the four years. It could be argued that such relatively high mean values for failed companies were caused by window-dressing because the ratio included stock (Tamari, 1978). However, the exclusion of stock from the current ratio (R6) only led to a fall in the mean values (R6) of failed companies to 1.2:1. The exclusion of stock resulted in a somewhat greater reduction in the mean values of non-failed companies rather than failed companies but the general profiles over time of R5 and R6 are similar. The evidence does not support the hypothesis that measure R5 is excessively prone to window-dressing. The median values (Figure 6.20) of the current ratios for failed companies were slightly above 1:1. In fact, over half of the failed companies had values above 1:1 for their current ratio two years prior to failure compared with 80 per cent of the non-failed companies in 1980. Non-failed companies had higher median

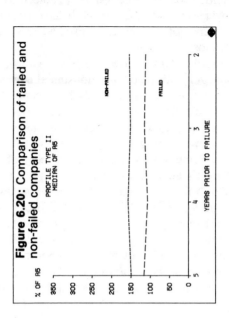

Figure 6.19: Comparison of failed and non-failed companies

PROFILE TYPE II
MEAN OF R5

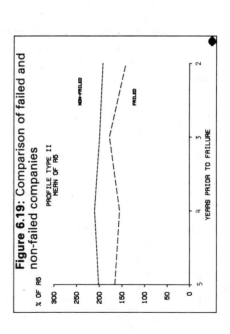

Figure 6.20: Comparison of failed and non-failed companies

PROFILE TYPE II
MEDIAN OF R5

and upper and lower quartile values (Table 6.5) than failed companies over the four-year period. The differences between these values were not, however, as marked as in those of the profitability ratios.

Beaver's profile of the current ratio (Figure 6.21) shows a declining trend for both failed and non-failed companies. In his analysis both groups had substantially higher mean values (2:1 and 3.5:1 respectively) over the five-year period than in our sample. Beaver suggested that these high mean values were caused by window-dressing, but they may also be caused by the presence of extreme values. Only 24 per cent of failed companies in Beaver's analysis had values above 2:1 whilst more than half the non-failed companies had values below 3:1. There was not a single non-failed company in the Beaver study with a value below 1:1 one year prior to failure, compared with 20 per cent of non-failed companies in our study in 1980 which were technically insolvent (i.e., they had values below 1:1).

An examination of the standard deviation value (Figure 6.22 for ratio R5) reveals considerable instability for both failed and

Figure 6.21: Beaver's failed and non-failed companies

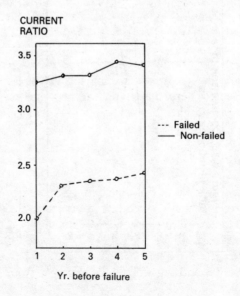

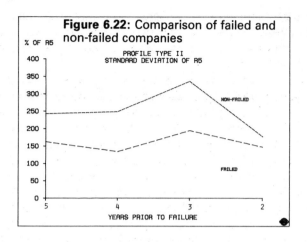

Figure 6.22: Comparison of failed and non-failed companies

non-failed companies over the four-year period. The value of the standard deviations of non-failed companies were within the range of 1.8 to 3.3 compared with 1.2 to 1.7 for failed companies. However, the histograms of both liquidity ratios (Figure 6.23 is an example), illustrate a substantial degree of distributional overlap. Forty three per cent of failed companies and 45 per cent of non-failed companies had values between 1:1 and 2:1 for the current ratio (exhibiting the amount of overlap).

Beaver's histogram (Figure 6.24) of the current ratio, in contrast to the profitability ratio, showed a relatively high degree of distributional overlap. Hence the predictive ability of the current ratio was comparatively weak in his classification model. However, the distributional overlap was even greater in the present study than in Beaver's, implying that the classification results presented here, based on the absolute values of the liquidity ratios, are likely to be inferior to those of Beaver.

Gearing ratios

In the present sample failed companies, on average, undertake higher borrowing than non-failed companies throughout the four-year-periods. As illustrated by Figures 6.25 and 6.26, the mean and medians of the gearing ratio of the failed companies remained consistently above the corresponding values for non-failed companies and demonstrated a rapid upward trend over

Figure 6.23: Distribution of liquidity (R5): comparison of failed and non-failed companies

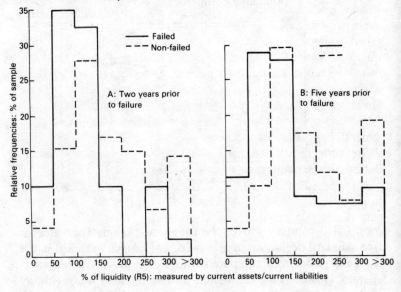

% of liquidity (R5): measured by current assets/current liabilities

Figure 6.24: Beaver's distribution of current ratio: comparison of failed and non-failed companies

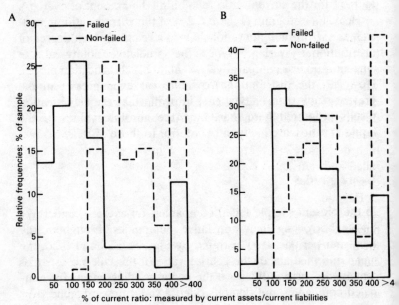

% of current ratio: measured by current assets/current liabilities

the same period. The mean values of the gearing ratio for non-failed companies remained around 0.15 over the four-year period, whilst the values for failed companies rose from 0.2 five years prior to failure to 0.35 two years prior to failure. The non-failed companies also experienced lower values for the upper quartiles. Table 6.5 demonstrates that the upper quartile value of failed companies was 34.9 per cent two years prior to failure compared with 24.6 per cent for non-failed companies in 1980. However, the values of the lower quartiles remained similar for failed and non-failed companies over the four-year period and generally approximated to zero.

Beaver's failed and non-failed companies incurred higher debt than the companies analysed in the present study (Figure 6.27). The mean values of the gearing ratio of failed companies in his sample rose to 0.8 one year prior to failure. Only 6.7 per cent of failed companies in Beaver's analysis had values below 0.35 compared with 37 per cent of failed companies in the present study. For non-failed companies the percentages were 80 per cent in Beaver's analysis and 63 per cent in the present analysis. These percentages indicate that Beaver's failed and non-failed companies experienced far greater relative diversity and hence the use of this measure of gearing will provide a better discriminator for the Beaver companies than for those in the present study.

The values of the standard deviation of the gearing ratio (Figure 6.28) of Northern failed companies rose sharply to over 0.6 two years prior to failure. This particular ratio appears to exhibit considerable variation amongst failed companies whereas standard deviations for non-failed companies remained at around the value of 0.18 which indicates relatively smaller deviations about the mean values. An examination of the histograms (Figure 6.29 (a) & (b)) also demonstrated a relatively high degree of distributional overlap of the gearing ratios for failed and non-failed companies. The amount of overlap, however, decreased slightly as the companies approached failure.

Despite the apparent differences between the mean values of all seven ratios of failed and non-failed companies, the distributional overlaps (as displayed by the standard deviation and the histograms) are considerable, so that it seems unwise to conclude that the absolute values of any of the seven ratios, particularly on a univariate basis, would be capable of adequately discriminating between failed and non-failed companies in any

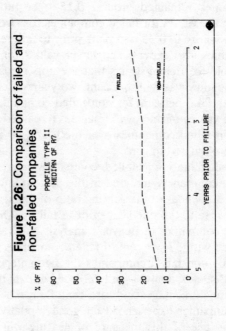

Figure 6.25: Comparison of failed and non-failed companies

PROFILE TYPE II
MEAN OF R7

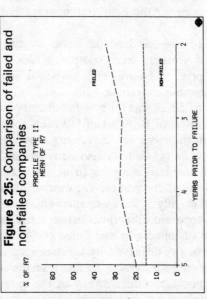

Figure 6.26: Comparison of failed and non-failed companies

PROFILE TYPE II
MEDIAN OF R7

Figure 6.27: Beaver's failed and non-failed companies

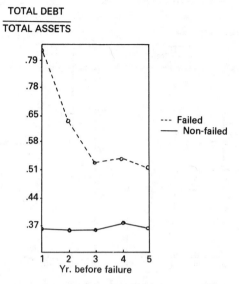

Figure 6.28: Comparison of failed and non-failed companies

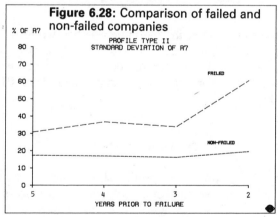

of the four years. The major limitation, however, of Profile Type II is in its method of construction, since there are different companies included in each year. From this it can be difficult to determine, even if the mean value of a ratio declines in the years prior to failure, whether this is attributable to a real decline in companies providing the data, or to the entry into the data set of companies with lower values or to the exit of companies with higher values. There is clearly a need to eliminate

215

Figure 6.29: Distribution of gearing ratio (R7): comparison of failed and non-failed companies

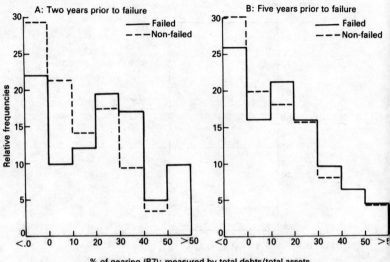

% of gearing (R7): measured by total debts/total assets

entry and exit in order to determine whether, within a group of small companies providing data continuously over a four-year period, any profile deterioration is apparent as failure approaches. It is for this purpose that Profile Type III is constructed.

EMPIRICAL RESULTS: PROFILE TYPE III

Although in Beaver's work profiles showed a declining trend of ratios such as Net Profit/Total Assets over all five years prior to failure, he did not incorporate any trend measures in his classification model. Other studies have shown that the *trends* of ratios, particularly the profitability ratios, over a period of time, are generally more powerful discriminating variables than the *actual* levels of the ratios in any one particular year.

To include trend measures in failure prediction models at least three consecutive years of data are required for every company in the sample, but Beaver was limited by two major disadvantages in his analytical approach. First, his model was constructed so that classification was undertaken annually on a

216

univariate basis. Second, Beaver's sample included shorter-life companies for which data were not available for all years.

This question was addressed by Edmister (1972), who, after testing three hypotheses — viz trends, averages and the level of ratios — concluded that at least three consecutive years of financial data were required in order that the classification of small manufacturing firms between failures and non-failures could be carried out effectively.

Blum (1974), by adopting a measure of volatility, incorporated variability of the ratios on a year-by-year basis to predict financial failure in a multivariate framework. His approach, like Edmister's, also needed at least three years of financial data.

Dambolena and Khoury (1980) analysed a matched sample of 46 failed and non-failed companies taken from Moody's Industrial Manual. They evaluated the effect of inclusion of ratio stability measures such as the standard deviation, the standard error of the mean and the coefficient of variations of ratios over a number of years, within a discriminant function to predict failures. Dambolena and Khoury's profile of stability measures showed striking differences between failed and non-failed companies. They concluded that the inclusion of stability measures (through the inclusion of standard deviation of the ratios over the four years) in their discriminant analysis model improved the classification results significantly.

Keasey and Wynarczyk (1986) examined Dambolena and Khoury's study to assess the extent to which improvements in classification accuracy were real and the extent to which they depended on the inclusion of their particular stability measures and tests. Keasey and Wynarczyk analysed a matched sample of failed and non-failed companies drawn from the sample under investigation here. They concluded that Dambolena and Khoury's approach of analysing stability measures was ambiguous since it was impossible to determine whether the noted improvement of predictive results was due to having more years of financial data (so as to calculate the value of the standard deviations), or simply to the inclusion of the standard deviation measure, *per se.* Furthermore, although the measure of stability (via the inclusion of the standard deviations) did improve the predictive ability of the ratios (though not as significantly as suggested by the work of Dambolena and Khoury) other variables such as averages or simply the inclusion of the

217

ratios of more than one year had similar if not better classificatory success.

Drawing upon earlier studies and the results outlined in this chapter, it appears that the profiles of the major ratios exhibited a greater degree of instability for failed than for non-failed companies. For example, the standard deviations tended to increase as the companies approached failure. This indicated a greater deviation about the mean values where, in contrast to previous studies, the trends of the ratios did not appear to be a major distinguishing characteristic of failed companies.

To examine the roles of stability and variability of the ratios measured by (a) the standard deviations of the ratios over the three-year period and (b) the volatility of the ratios over the same period, the analysis has to be confined to companies for which comprehensive data were available over six to two years prior to failure: *Consequently, Profile Type III was conducted upon a sub-sample of 50 failed and non-failed companies matched by industry and data availability.* Note that, because of these data deficiencies, this does not claim to be a representative profile of *all* small companies.

Several tests were conducted. Firstly, since Type III profiles are constructed *only* for companies providing data continuously over a four-year period, it is possible to compare the mean and median values of such companies with those included in the Type II profiles. Secondly, since it is argued that ratio stability/variability is potentially a significant factor distinguishing failed from non-failed firms, measures of these characteristics are derived. The following methods were used to compute and plot the stability and variability measures. With respect to the standard deviation measure for the second year prior to failure for each failed company, the standard deviations were computed from the mean values of the ratios two, three and four years prior to failure. For the third year prior to failure, they were computed from values of the ratios, three, four and five years prior to failure and so on. The same procedure was followed for non-failed companies. With respect to the volatility measure for the second year prior to failure for every failed and non-failed company, the volatility of the ratios (VIS) was computed as follows:

$$\text{VIS} = |R1_2 - R1_3| + |R1_3 - R1_4|$$

For the third year prior to failure it was computed as:

$$VIS = |R1_3 - R1_4| + |R1_4 - R1_5|$$

Where: $R1_2$ = The value of Ratio one, two years prior to failure.

$R1_3$ = The value of Ratio one, three years prior to failure etc.

Profitability ratios

Figure 6.30 shows the mean values for Profile Type III for the profitability ratio R1, whilst Figure 6.31 shows the median values for the same ratio. It is clear that in all cases (ratios R1, R2, R3) the mean and the median profitability of the failed firms are below those of the non-failed firms in each year. It is also clear that there is considerably greater variability between years for failed than for non-failed companies, the latter group being highly stable. Indeed, all three profiles carried out to date provide support for the hypothesis that highly volatile profitability ratios are characteristic of failed companies across the 1970s (Profile Type I) and over the shorter four years (Profile Type II and III) irrespective of differing sample sizes or specific macro-economic conditions. It can, therefore, tentatively be suggested that highly volatile profitability is a distinctive financial characteristic of failed companies, and that a measure of volatility would yield better classification results than the absolute values of ratios in any given year.

The profile of the volatility measure (Figure 6.32) revealed highly supportive results for the above statement. Failed companies experienced far higher values for the volatility measure. The histogram of the volatility measure of R1 (Figure 6.33) exhibits relatively lower distributional overlap than the absolute values of the ratios over the three-year period. Figure 6.33 shows that, for example, 80 per cent of failed companies had volatility measures of over 0.16 compared with only 16 per cent of non-failed companies two years prior to failure. Furthermore, the same figure displays that not a single non-failed company had volatility values over 0.30 compared with 56 per cent of failed companies. Averages of the ratios over the three-year period (Figure 6.34) demonstrated comparable distributional overlap to the volatility measure.

219

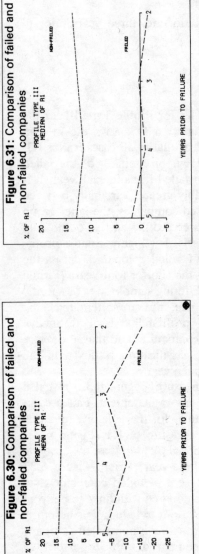

Figure 6.30: Comparison of failed and non-failed companies

PROFILE TYPE III
MEAN OF R1

% OF R1

NON-FAILED

FAILED

YEARS PRIOR TO FAILURE

Figure 6.31: Comparison of failed and non-failed companies

PROFILE TYPE III
MEDIAN OF R1

% OF R1

NON-FAILED

FAILED

YEARS PRIOR TO FAILURE

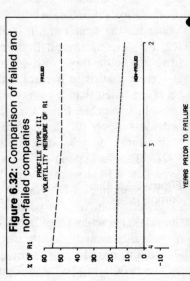

Figure 6.32: Comparison of failed and non-failed companies

PROFILE TYPE III
VOLATILITY MEASURE OF R1

% OF R1

FAILED

NON-FAILED

YEARS PRIOR TO FAILURE

Figure 6.33: Distribution of volatility measure of (R1): comparison of failed and non-failed companies

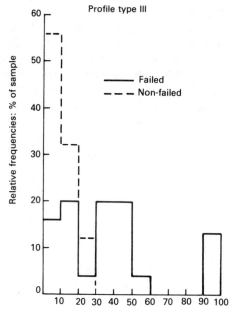

% of volatility measure of R1: over two, three and four years prior to failure

Figure 6.34: Distribution of average measure of (R1): comparison of failed and non-failed companies

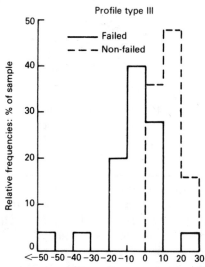

% of average measure of R1: over two, three and four years prior to failure

221

Profile Type III, therefore, demonstrates substantially lower distributional overlap than Profile Type II over the four-year period. In part, however, this may be attributed to the use of a matched sample, in contrast to Profile Type II, where aggregated financial data over a number of years for failed as well as non-failed companies were used. Consequently, shorter life non-failed companies which are more prone to failure were excluded in the Type III Profile. Furthermore, by aggregating the financial data over a longer period, the effect of macro-economic variables is reduced and the performance of the non-failed companies improves. They become more profitable, more liquid, less highly geared, whereas the corresponding values of failed companies remained relatively unchanged. This leads to wider gaps between the levels of the ratios for failed and non-failed companies (as well as reducing the amount of overlap).

Given these limitations, the results obtained from Profiles Type II and Type III, in contrast to Beaver's analysis, do not demonstrate consistent rapidly declining trends in the values of the three profitability ratios in the years prior to failure. The profitability of failed companies is lower than for non-failed companies for all five years prior to failure. Further investigation of failed Northern companies revealed that only 24 per cent of failed companies experienced consistently declining trends in the profitability ratio (R1) over the three-year period (i.e. four, three and two years prior to failure) compared with 4 per cent which experienced a rise. For the remaining failed companies the values of the profitability ratio (R1) varied from year to year (illustrating the superiority of the volatility measure over the trend in distinguishing between failed and non-failed companies in this particular case). Similar results were obtained for R2 and R3.

An examination of the histograms of the standard deviation measure (Figure 6.35) shows that 92 per cent of non-failed companies had standard deviations of R1 below 0.1 compared with 40 per cent of failed companies over the three-year period. Furthermore, none of the non-failed companies had values over 0.17 whereas 56 per cent of the failed companies had values in the range of 0.17 to 1.37 over the same period for the standard deviation measure. However, the above results demonstrated a somewhat greater degree of distributional overlap than the volatility and average measures.

It is, therefore, possible to conclude that as far as the profit-

Figure 6.35: Distribution of standard deviation measure of (R1): comparison of failed and non-failed companies

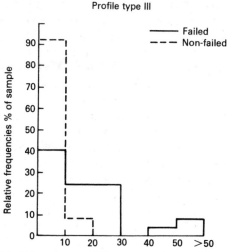

Profile type III

% of standard deviation measure of R1: over two, three and four years prior to failure

ability ratios are concerned, it is most likely that the volatility and average measures would provide superior classificatory results over trends or standard deviation measures and, in particular, the absolute values of the ratios.

Solvency ratio

Despite the clear differences between the mean and median values for the solvency ratio R4 (Figures 6.36, 6.37) of failed and non-failed companies, the histograms demonstrated considerable degrees of distributional overlap. The results suggest that it is not possible to provide a clear decision rule which would efficiently distinguish between failed and non-failed companies using the solvency ratio in a univariate framework.

Liquidity ratios

Companies included in the Profile Type III analysis exhibited comparatively higher mean and median values for liquidity ratios R5 and R6 (Figures 6.38, 6.39) than those included in the

223

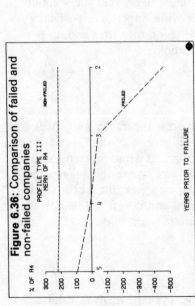

Figure 6.36: Comparison of failed and non-failed companies

PROFILE TYPE III
MEAN OF R4

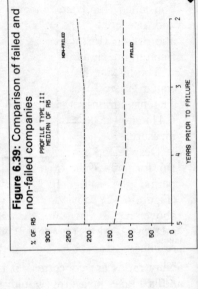

Figure 6.37: Comparison of failed and non-failed companies

PROFILE TYPE III
MEDIAN OF R4

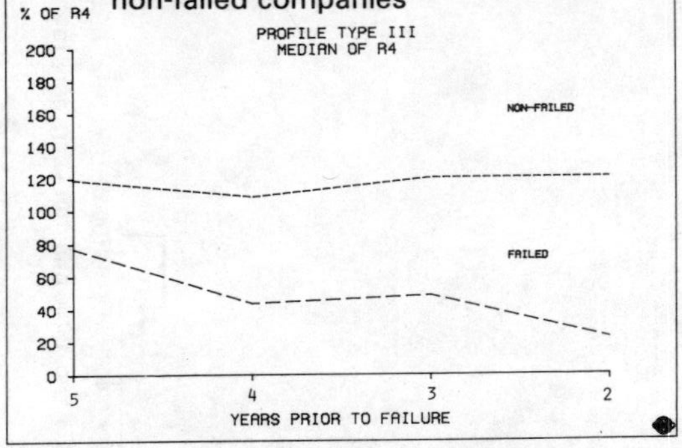

Figure 6.38: Comparison of failed and non-failed companies

PROFILE TYPE III
MEAN OF R5

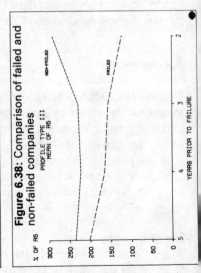

Figure 6.39: Comparison of failed and non-failed companies

PROFILE TYPE III
MEDIAN OF R5

Type II analysis. This was true for both failed and non-failed companies. Amongst Profile Type III companies the mean current ratio of failed companies deteriorated from 2:1 to 1.5:1 over the four-year period whilst the corresponding value for non-failed companies experienced a consistently upward trend and rose from 2.4:1 to 2.9:1 over the same period. An examination of the histograms also demonstrated a slightly declining trend in the values of the liquidity ratios for failed companies.

The histograms of the volatility measure (Figure 6.40) illustrated greater overlap than for the absolute value of the ratio. The histograms of the averages of the current ratio (Figure 6.41) showed less distributional overlap than for the volatility measure.

Despite the instability of the standard deviations of R5 and R6 for failed and non-failed companies over the four-year period, the histograms of the standard deviation measure R5 (Figure 6.42) showed relatively low distributional overlap. The above results suggest the inclusion of standard deviation measures and average measures for R5 could yield satisfactory results.

Figure 6.40: Distribution of volatility measure of R5: comparison of failed and non-failed companies

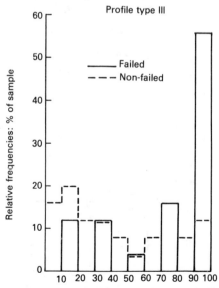

% of volatility measure of R5: over two, three and four years prior to failure

Figure 6.41: Distribution of average measure of (R5): comparison of failed and non-failed companies

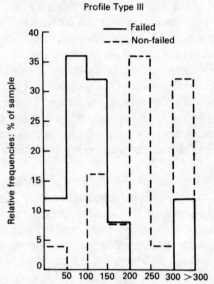

Figure 6.42: Distribution of standard deviation measure of (R5): comparison of failed and non-failed companies

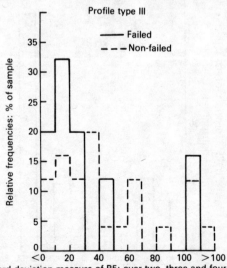

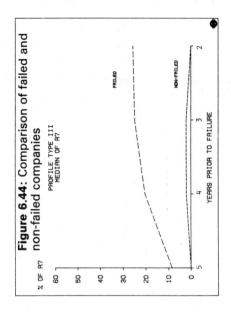

Figure 6.43: Comparison of failed and non-failed companies

PROFILE TYPE III
MEAN OF R7

% OF R7

FAILED

NON-FAILED

YEARS PRIOR TO FAILURE

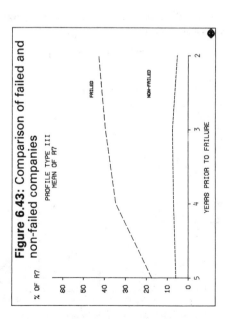

Figure 6.44: Comparison of failed and non-failed companies

PROFILE TYPE III
MEDIAN OF R7

% OF R7

FAILED

NON-FAILED

YEARS PRIOR TO FAILURE

Figure 6.45: Distribution of volatility measure of (R7): comparison of failed and non-failed companies

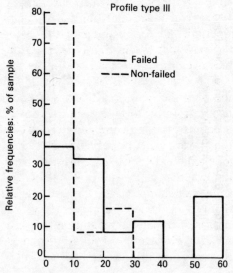

% of volatility measure of R7: over two, three and four years prior to failure

Figure 6.46: Distribution of average measure of (R7): comparison of failed and non-failed companies

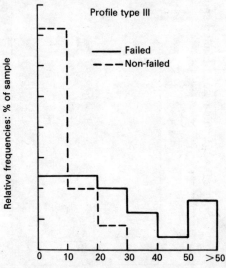

% of average measure of R7: over two, three and four years prior to failure

Gearing ratio

There are marked differences between the gearing ratio R7 (Figures 6.43, 6.44) of failed and non-failed companies over the four-year period. An examination of the histograms also demonstrated a consistent rise in trend of the gearing ratio for failed companies over the four-year period. The values of the gearing ratio of non-failed companies, on the other hand, declined slightly over the period so that distributional overlap was smallest two years prior to failure. Further investigation of the financial accounts of failed companies provided supportive evidence for the above results by revealing that more than half of the failed companies experienced a consistent rise in trend of the gearing ratio, whereas only 7 per cent experienced a decline in trend. In the remaining cases the gearing ratio either remained unchanged or varied from year to year. This conclusion was confirmed by an examination of the histograms of the volatility measure (Figure 6.45) for R7. The histograms of the averages (Figure 6.46) also showed reduced overlap in the

Figure 6.47: Distribution of standard deviation measure of R7: comparison of failed and non-failed companies:

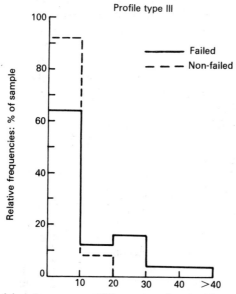

% of standard deviation measure of R7: over two, three and four years prior to failure

distribution of failed and non-failed companies compared with the volatility measure. The histograms of the standard deviation measure (Figure 6.47) demonstrated a comparable amount of distributional overlap to those of the volatility measure.

SYNTHESIS AND CONCLUSIONS

In this chapter a great deal of data has been presented and, in so far as this is possible, a synthesis is presented in Table 6.6. In the first column are the seven ratios broadly grouped between profitability, solvency, liquidity and gearing. The prime purpose of the chapter has been to identify whether according to the three profile types any ratio or group of ratios is able to distinguish consistently between failed and non-failed companies. To answer this question each profile was compared on the basis of mean and median values, the extent to which there was volatility/stability and any evidence amongst failed companies of ratio deterioration as failure approached.

It is perhaps worthwhile discussing both the solvency and chosen liquidity ratios. Whilst both generally indicated that non-failed firms were more solvent and more liquid than failed firms, only for Profile III for the liquidity measures was there any evidence of a reduction in liquidity amongst failed firms as failure approached. To some extent the absence of a clear solvency or liquidity factor surprised us since these are generally thought to be at the heart of corporate failure but, because they may coincide with other factors, this may merely be a reflection of the limitations of a univariate approach.

On the other hand the profitability ratios R1 and R3 and the gearing ratio R7 appear to be relatively good univariate predictors of failure. In general the profitability of failed firms is lower and gearing higher than for non-failed firms and the distributions of the two groups appear reasonably separate. Amongst the profitability ratios R1 appears to perform best.

Interestingly, in view of the Beaver results for the Profile II and III analyses there appears *no* evidence of a rapid decline in profitability amongst failed firms as failure approaches, although failed firms do become more highly geared in their later years. The implication of this result is that the profitability of a failed company, five years prior to failure, is below that of a non-failed company and profitability is therefore a good long-

Table 6.6: Synthesis

Ratios	Mean			Medians			Volatility			Declining trend as failure approaches			Use as discriminator		
	Profile I	Profile II	Profile III	Profile I	Profile II	Profile III	Profile I	Profile II	Profile III	Profile I	Profile II	Profile III	Profile I	Profile II	Profile III
Profitability															
R_1	NF ↗ F	NF >> F	NF >> F	NF >> F	NF >> F	NF >> F	F > NF	F > NF	NF > F	?	No	No	Good	Moderate	Good
R_2	NF ↗ F	NF >> F	NF >> F	NF >> F	NF >> F	NF >> F	F ↗ NF	F ↗ NF	NF >> F	?	?	No	Weak	Weak	Good
R_3	NF >> F	NF >> F	NF >> F	NF >> F	NF >> F	NF >> F	F > NF	F > NF	NF >> F	?	?	?	Moderate	Weak	Good
Solvency															
R_4	NF ↗ F	NF ↗ F	NF >> F	NF >> F	NF >> F	NF >> F	F ↗ NF	F > NF	F > NF	?	?	?	Weak	Weak	Weak
Liquidity															
R_5	NF ↗ F	NF >> F	NF >> F	NF >> F	NF >> F	NF >> F	F > NF	F ↗ NF	NF >> F	?	Perhaps	Yes	Weak	Weak	Moderate
R_6	NF ↗ F	NF >> F	NF >> F	NF >> F	NF >> F	NF >> F	F > NF	F ↗ NF	NF >> F	?	Perhaps	Yes	Weak	Weak	Moderate
Gearing															
R_7	F > NF	F > NF	F > NF	F > NF	F > NF	F > NF	F > NF	F > NF	F > NF	?	Yes	Yes	Good	Moderate	Good

term indicator. Gearing, on the other hand, is a better short-term indicator since it does appear to increase as failure approaches and a high gearing ratio would appear to indicate more immediate problems.

The main conclusion to be drawn from this chapter is that the use of univariate techniques is extremely cumbersome. Only seven ratios have been examined yet the presentation of the results in a comprehensible manner has presented formidable difficulties and, whilst it appears that gearing and profitability measures hold out some promise, it is not possible to measure directly that contribution or to determine the extent to which *combinations* of factors (and ratios which measure those factors) are good predictors of corporate failure.

NOTES

1. A Type I error is predicting a failed company as non-failed whereas a Type II is predicting a non-failed as a failed company.

2. We recognise that there is the possibility of 'phase' problems with this strategy. Take, for example, company A which fails in July 1980 i.e. year t, and provides accounts for the period August 1979 to July 1980. It therefore is deemed to provide accounts for year t (one year prior to failure) whilst its accounts for year $t-1$ (two years prior to failure) cover the period August 1978 to July 1979. On the other hand company B fails two months earlier in May 1980 (year t) and provides accounts for April 1979 to March 1980 but this is referred to as year $t-1$.

Thus although there is only a two-month difference in the date of failure, accounts for year $t-1$ (two years prior to failure) for company A financial data cover August 1978 to July 1979 whereas those for company B cover April 1979 to March 1980. This, of course, is an extreme example, and in the majority of cases similar periods are covered.

3. More sophisticated profile constructions have been suggested to us. For example Norman Strong pointed out that to take account of differences over the trade cycle it might be possible to construct a collection of non-failed companies which has the same proportion of data derived from, say year t, as the sample of failed companies. However, it will be shown that there is little variation in the financial ratios of the non-failed firms and so it was our view that this added sophistication would be unjustified.

7

Multiple Discriminant Analysis

INTRODUCTION

This chapter briefly reviews the major empirical studies using multiple discriminant analysis for predicting company failure. It then uses the technique upon those small manufacturing companies described in Chapter 2. The chapter begins with a very brief non-technical explanation of multiple discriminant analysis which is followed by a discussion of some of the problems of applying this technique to corporate failure. To benefit from this discussion the reader is advised to have studied either the review by Altman *et al.* (1981) or by Steele (1984).

MULTIPLE DISCRIMINANT ANALYSIS: THE TECHNIQUE

Approximately twenty years ago, financial analysts began moving away from the type of univariate approach used in Chapter 6 because of the limitations of relying upon a single ratio. The development of multivariate statistical methods able to deal with combinations of two or more ratios resulted in the application of a technique known as multiple discriminant analysis (MDA) to the prediction of company health. In simple terms, discriminant analysis classifies a company into one of two groups (failed/non-failed) on the basis of a statistic (Z-score) which is a combination of ratios which best separates failed from non-failed companies.

Assume Figure 7.1 represents the best separation possible; the next task is to pick a value or range of values for the Z-score which will be used to classify further companies. Thus, if a value

Figure 7.1: Z-score distribution

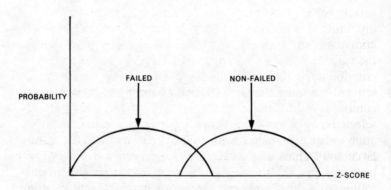

of Z equal to 2 was thought to separate the two categories of companies and a company had to be classified as failed or non-failed, its Z-score would be computed and if it was above 2 it would be classified as non-failed, whereas if it were less than 2 it would be classified as failed.

It must be emphasised that great care must be exercised when utilising the discriminant technique to avoid spurious results. In most applications, the discriminant function is a *linear* function and can be written:

$$Z = \text{constant} + (x_1 . \text{ratio 1}) + (x_2 . \text{ratio 2}) + \ldots + (x_n . \text{ratio n})$$

where x_1, x_2, x_n, etc. are the positive or negative coefficients of the ratios. As shown above, a value or range of values for Z would then be chosen to separate failed from non-failed companies. When a company has to be classified as failed or non-failed the relevant ratios are determined and multiplied by the coefficients in the Z function. This will produce a score which is compared to the critical discriminating Z-score.

Two methods for ratio selection are generally used. The first is to include all possible ratios and select on the basis of a criterion which is usually based on a specified F-value. Secondly, only ratios which on *a priori* grounds are thought to be important are included, but, given the lack of theory over the determinants of failure, the *a priori* approach is little more than guesswork.

The approaches which are usually used depend upon statistical search techniques. For example a 'stepwise forward' discriminant technique begins by selecting the single best discriminating ratio. A second discriminating ratio is selected as the variable best able to improve the value of the discrimination criterion in combination with the first ratio. The third and subsequent ratios are similarly selected according to their ability to contribute to further discrimination. At each step, ratios already selected may be removed if they are found to reduce discrimination when combined with more recently selected ratios. Eventually, either all the ratios will have been selected or it will be found that the remaining ratios are no longer able to contribute to further discrimination. When this point has been reached, the stepwise procedure halts and further analysis is performed using only the selected ratios.

The next step is a test of the predictive accuracy of the discriminant function on a hold-out sample of known failed and non-failed companies. If the predictive accuracy is poor, the original set of ratios, the sample from which the function was derived and/or the form of the Z-function may be changed.

COMPANY FAILURE AND MULTIPLE DISCRIMINANT ANALYSIS

To date there are probably in excess of 100 studies which have attempted to apply discriminant analysis to the prediction of corporate failure. The studies which appeared before 1981 were reviewed by Altman *et al.* (1981), whilst some of the more recent studies are reviewed in Steele (1984). The work by Altman *et al.* provides a thorough review of both the empirical studies and the assumptions underlying the statistical technique of discriminant analysis. We do not propose to replicate this work, but rather to summarise briefly these studies and assumptions and provide further references in the associated notes.

Discriminant analysis assumes that ratios are multivariate normally distributed. Few empirical studies of corporate failure have, however, tested for this in their data.[1] A second

235

assumption is that the dispersion (variance-covariance) matrices are equal.[2] In contrast to regression analysis the coefficients on the selected ratios are *not* uniquely defined. The technique decides which ratios to include, by maximising the ratio of the 'between groups' to 'within groups' variance.

Standard multiple discriminant analysis techniques incorporate *a priori* probabilities to account for two factors; firstly the presence of failures/non-failures in the population and secondly the costs in misclassifying a failure as a non-failure and vice versa[3] so that, for example, the 'priors' can be adjusted to take into account the different costs of Type I and Type II errors.

The purpose of constructing a model of corporate failure is that it should have predictive powers. Unfortunately too few modellers have rigorously tested the validity of their work by the use of future-dated hold-out samples, i.e. by taking the existing derived discriminant function and testing it on a sample of firms in the population and seeing whether it predicts those which will fail over the next, say, two years.[4]

A final general criticism of existing studies is that they exhibit a lack of concern with the process of failure. Indeed we are not aware of any studies that have attempted to determine *when* a business will fail, as opposed to *whether* it will fail. In our view a concern with the former question would lead to a greater emphasis upon the process of failure which we believe to be a most fruitful area for analysis.

Any review of the use of multiple discriminant analysis for predicting corporate failure must begin with the seminal paper by Altman (1968). This paper applied MDA for the first time and showed that the technique was more effective than the results obtained by Beaver's (1967) univariate approach. However, subsequent work by Moyer (1977) indicated that the predictive accuracy of the Altman model on a genuinely post-dated sample of company failures was only 75 per cent, one year prior to failure, compared with the 96 per cent claimed by Altman.

We have noted on several occasions that there is no adequate theory of corporate failure which would assist the selection of ratios on an *a priori* basis. To overcome this, Deakin (1972) took the Beaver univariate ratios and used MDA on 64 companies. He obtained broadly similar results to Beaver, but the use of hold-out samples showed the results were disappointing, particularly for companies that were not to fail for three years or more.

A study by Blum (1974) provided another interesting development in the history of MDA since he used not simply the absolute values of ratios but also their variability. In the context of small companies, we shall see that this is a potentially important and relevant development.

The above studies were all conducted in the United States and the first major attempt to apply MDA to corporate failure in Britain was conducted by Taffler and Tisshaw (1977). This early study appears to have been strongly 'data-driven' since a total of 80 potentially useful ratios were identified and computed and each of these was subject to both a logarithmic and reciprocal transformation. In a later study Taffler (1982) utilised varimax rotated principal component analysis to identify the dimensions of the data set but the exclusively empirical approach used is open to question.[5] Nevertheless Taffler's work on predicting failure amongst large UK companies is of major importance.

The concept of ratio stability, first examined by Blum, was developed by Dambolena and Khoury (1980). They took a total of 19 ratios and for each computed a number of measures of stability such as the standard deviation of the ratio over three- and four-year periods. They claimed that the introduction of ratio stability measures significantly improved the classificatory powers of the model, but as noted in Chapter 6, Keasey and Wynarczyk (1986) question the validity of this statement.

Finally one of the most revealing studies was conducted by Hamer (1983). He compared the performance of the four models outlined by Altman (1968), Blum (1974), Deakin (1972) and Ohlson (1980) when applied to the same data set. The Ohlson study used logit analysis which will be reviewed in Chapter 8. Hamer concluded that all models had broadly the same predictive power and that this was not clearly related to either the choice of ratios or statistical techniques. He suggested that since different ratio sets have little influence, the choice of variables should be determined by data collection constraints.

In conclusion, the literature review indicates extensive work in refining the methodology in discriminant models of failure prediction and also in developing new empirical approaches. The evidence suggests that failure prediction models developed from a 'pure empiricist' approach risk being data-dependent and more attention should now be given to the development of a theoretical framework. As regards statistical methodology, continuous refinements have not produced significantly better results. As Zavgren (1983) writes of Diamond's (1976) pattern recognition model,

> His study is, then, the most advanced of those using discriminant analysis. Such refinements in technique and meticulous adherence to statistical assumptions have failed to produce a significant improvement in predictive accuracy, however, thus seeming to indicate that the benefits to further improvements in the discriminant analysis approach have neared an asymptotic limit. (p.23)

THE PREDICTION OF SMALL COMPANY FAILURE: RESULTS OF DISCRIMINANT ANALYSIS

This section presents new results on the application of multiple discriminant analysis (MDA) to small company failure. Its primary purpose is to determine whether the techniques developed in studies of large companies can be replicated for the small company sector.

The characteristics of the companies to be analysed were described in Chapter 2. It will be recalled that a total of 636 companies were included, of which 177 failed and 459 were trading in 1982 (non-failed). All companies traded at some stage between 1970 and 1982. As noted in Chapter 2, a company was defined as failed if it either had been liquidated or dissolved or had ceased trading, and in the opinion of the researchers and/or the company's accountants was unlikely to trade again. Whilst this data base has been carefully assembled it is important that its limitations are re-emphasised at this point.

As noted in Chapter 6, a major problem of research into small companies is that many of these companies either do not submit accounts or submit incomplete accounts, and that this is particularly, though not exclusively true for failing companies. The scale of the problem will be seen in Table 7.1 by the fact that of the 177 failed companies only seven provided complete financial information in the year prior to failure. A further 154 provided no information whatsoever for the year prior to failure

Table 7.1: Data availability for failed companies compared with non-failed companies

Failed companies

Years prior to failure	Companies with comprehensive annual financial data		Companies which did not submit any annual financial data		Companies which provided partial annual financial data		Total	
	No.	%	No.	%	No.	%	No.	%
1	7	4.0	154	87.0	16	9.0	177	100
2	55	31.0	108	61.0	14	8.0	177	100
3	97	54.8	68	38.4	12	6.8	177	100
4	130	73.4	37	20.9	10	5.6	177	100
5	131	74.0	31	17.5	15	8.5	177	100

Non-failed companies

Financial year	Companies with comprehensive annual financial data		Companies which did not submit any annual financial data		Companies which provided partial annual financial data		Total	
	No.	%	No.	%	No.	%	No.	%
1979	392	85.4	34	7.4	33	7.2	459	100
1978	391	85.2	31	6.8	37	8.1	459	100
1977	386	84.1	32	7.0	41	8.9	459	100
1976	353	77.0	67	14.6	39	8.5	459	100
1975	329	71.7	90	19.6	40	8.7	459	100

whilst the remaining 16 provided incomplete information. Such data deficiencies do not seem to have been a major problem in the large company studies where missing values lead to the company being excluded from the study.

In this study the missing value problem has been handled firstly by *not* generally matching the samples of companies, partly because this would reduce the overall sample size because of asymmetry in account submissions between failed and non-failed companies. Secondly, since the population does not have equal numbers of failed and non-failed companies, we believe the number of companies included to be sufficient to allow for size, sectoral, age and temporal variations. Finally, the asymmetry in the propensity to submit accounts has been included directly in the analysis as an independent predictive variable of failure/non-failure. None the less for the purposes of comparison with other work we do present some results using matched sampling.

As discussed earlier there are a number of statistical assumptions which have to be taken into account if MDA is to be used satisfactorily. One major assumption is that the variables are multivariate normal in their distribution. Whilst the SPSS-X discriminant package which was used does not include a test for multivariate normality the variables were checked for univariate normality — this being a necessary but not sufficient condition for multivariate normality. These tests showed that the majority of variables exhibited negative skewness and so to lessen these effects a log transformation was tested to identify improvements in predictive performance on cross-sectional hold-out samples. It failed to lead to any significant improvement in predictive performance and so our results are based on untransformed variables.

A second choice to be made concerns whether to use a linear or a quadratic discriminant function. In theory the quadratic function should be used when the variance-covariance matrices for the failed and non-failed companies are not equal. Whilst Bartlett's test for homogeneity of variance may be biased in the presence of non-multivariate normality, the test indicated that the dispersion matrices for the sample of small companies were not equal. However a linear rather than a quadratic form was chosen because the latter is more affected by multivariate non-normality than the former, and secondly because use of the quadratic did not improve the predictive results of the cross-sectional hold-out tests.

A third choice is the allocation of the overall sample between the derivation of the function and the conduct of hold-out tests.[6] In this study a total of 485 companies were randomly chosen to calibrate the models and the remaining 151 were used in hold-out tests. Ideally, the last year of available data should not be used when deriving the discriminant function, since it should be used for future-dated hold-out tests. However so few companies which failed presented data in their 'final' year that this type of test could not be satisfactorily conducted and alternative tests were developed.

A fourth choice concerns whether to develop annual discriminant functions or to develop functions according to the year prior to failure. The advantage of annual functions is that they enable the inclusion of sectoral and temporal factors as independent variables. However this requires a much larger data set than is currently available and so we developed functions for each of the various years (up to five) before failure. This means, for example, that if we are constructing a model of firms one year prior to failure this will include data on companies that may have failed at any time between 1972 and 1982, and that the financial data used could be between 1971/72 and 1980/81.

Whilst pooling of data increases the sample size of failed companies it is unclear which non-failed companies should be included. Clearly, matching a set of annual non-failed accounts to every annual set of failed company accounts is the 'best' solution but, as noted above, this would lead to overly reduced final sample sizes. Instead the year 1979 was chosen as the one-year-prior-to-failure sample for all non-failed companies. To recapitulate; failed company data are pooled over the 1972-82 period and each year's accounts are classified according to their number of years from failure. One-year-prior-to-failure data for failed companies are then compared with non-failed company data for 1979, and two-year-prior data for failed companies are compared with 1978, etc. The full comparison is set out in Table 7.2 and is identical to that used for constructing Profile Type II in Chapter 6 except that we now use 1979 as the base year rather than 1980 in order to maximise the sample size. Whilst this strategy precludes the possibility of testing whether companies which failed in 1974 were significantly different from those failing in 1979 it does substantially increase the sample size, particularly for companies supplying data in the one or two years prior to failure. We considered this to be a worthwhile trade-off.

A further choice concerns the size and composition of the variable set. The number of variables to be included is a function of the financial characteristics of the companies and the size of the sample. The empirical literature suggests that the presence of multicollinearity and the variable/sample size ratio can have important consequences for the degree of predictive power obtained. For these reasons the 18 variables listed in Table 7.3 were used as the initial variable set, to reflect both the key characteristics of small companies and the conclusions drawn from other failure studies using MDA. The ratios included differ from those in Chapter 6 where selection took place to ensure comparability with Beaver. The classification of

241

Table 7.2: Comparisons of failed and non-failed firms

Years prior	Data source for failed companies	Data source for non-failed companies
One	Pooled Accounts of all failed companies one year prior to failure	1979
Two	Pooled Acounts of all failed companies two years prior to failure	1978
Three	Pooled Accounts of all failed companies three years prior to failure	1977
Four	Pooled Accounts of all failed companies four years prior to failure	1976
Five	Pooled Accounts of all failed companies five years prior to failure	1975

individual ratios into groupings, such as liquidity, gearing also differs from that in Chapter 6 and a case could be made for individual ratios appearing in different groups or even in more than one group. Nevertheless the grouping which we have chosen is designed to reflect the choices made in other MDA studies.

Once the initial variable set has been chosen there is a further choice between using all variables or a reduced set. The criteria for such a decision are the predictive successes of the two sets, so using Rao's V method[7] of optimally reducing the ratio set, a number of comparisons were undertaken on the predictive success of both the full set and the various reduced sets. The results obtained showed no significant differences in predictive power so reduced ratio sets were used throughout the analysis. These reduced sets were only used because of marginal reductions in computing time and not because of any wish to ease the problem of variable interpretation.

A further choice concerns the specification of the prior probability of failure. Ideally this should equal the probability of failure expected in the period for which the prediction is being made. Without specifying prior probabilities the SPSS-X package automatically sets these equal to the proportion of failed and non-failed firms in the sample. This leads, however, to high Type I errors and so we have chosen instead a prior probability of 0.5 which is rather higher than found in the sample as a whole.

Table 7.3: A categoric list of financial ratios

Liquidity			
Net Working Capital/Total Tangible Assets	X_1	NWC/TTA	
Net Working Capital and Bank Overdraft/ Total Tangible Assets	X_2	NWC+B/TTA	
Cashflow			
Profit Before Tax and Depreciation/Total Tangible Assets	X_3	PBTD/TTA	
Profit Before Tax and Depreciation/Total Debt	X_4	PBTD/TD	
Gearing			
Long-term Liabilities/Total Tangible Assets	X_5	LTL/TTA	
Long-term Liabilities and Bank Overdraft/ Total Tangible Assets	X_6	LTL+B/TTA	
Total Debt/Total Tangible Assets	X_7	TD/TTA	
Interest/Profit Before Tax and Interest	X_8	I/PBTI	
Profitability			
Profit Before Tax and Directors' Remuneration/ Total Tangible Assets	X_9	PBTR/TTA	
Profit Before Tax and Directors' Remuneration/ Total Debt	X_{10}	PBTR/TD	
Profit Before Tax, Interest and Directors' Reumuneration/ Total Tangible Assets	X_{11}	PBTIR/TTA	
Profit Before Tax, Interest and Directors' Remuneration/ Total Debt	X_{12}	PBTIR/TD	
Profit Before Tax/Total Tangible Assets	X_{18}	PBT/TTA	
Asset Structure			
Current Assets/Total Tangible Assets	X_{13}	CA/TTA	
Current Liabilities/Total Tangible Assets	X_{14}	CL/TTA	
Current Assets/Current Liabilities	X_{15}	CA/CL	
Quick Assets/Current Liabilities	X_{16}	QA/CL	
Quick Assets/Total Tangible Assets	X_{17}	QA/TTA	

The results are presented in the following form. First discriminant functions for each of the five years prior to failure are derived from the ratios listed in Table 7.3. These models are developed from data for 485 companies (the primary sample) and the classification results presented. Of the 485 companies 139 failed and 346 were non-failed. The predictive ability of this model can then be tested against the 151 companies in the hold-out sample, of which 38 failed and 113 were non-failed. However, whilst such cross-sectional hold-out tests are better than reclassifying the primary sample, they give an accurate picture of the predictive power of the functions only if the process of failure is stationary over time.

A more powerful test is the use of a future-dated hold-out test of the following form. This takes the full sample of 636 companies and the objective is to determine the proportion of the companies which actually failed in 1979 which could have been predicted as failures using financial data for a year prior to 1979.

A full description of the technique is shown in Table 7.4, but the two year prior can be taken as illustrative. It uses MDA upon those companies which failed in 1979 and which provided data in 1978 ($t-1$) together with companies which never failed (at least until after 1982) and which also provided data for 1978. This is called the *two* year prior model even though it utilises data for year $t-1$ because, as noted in Chapter 6, some companies which fail in calendar year t also provide data for the financial year up to failure. Since financial data for year t are for the year immediately prior to failure, year t is referred to as one year prior, year $t-1$ as two years prior, etc. It is very important that this, initially confusing, distinction is recalled in reading the subsequent text.

To test the extent of time dependence, the coefficients and variables derived from the two-year-prior model are then applied to 1979 (one-year-prior data) and a prediction obtained. A similar procedure can be conducted for the three-year model which is used on 1978 data to predict failure or non-failure.

A second sub-section of tests examines whether the inclusion of more years of prior information in any given year function improves its predictive performance. The sub-section also analyses whether inclusion of ratio averages, ratio trends and ratio volatility improves predictive performance. The tests of predictive success will include reclassification of the derivation sample and cross-sectional hold-out tests. The third sub-section analyses whether simple rules, such as that all companies not submitting accounts could be classified as failures, improve the predictive power of the models. The final sub-section analyses whether sectoral and age variations are important.

Finally whilst the ratios used in any specific discriminant function will be given, the coefficients used to form the functions will not, since this may underpin a future commercial

Table 7.4: Methodology for future-dated hold-out tests

Year of Failure	Two years prior Calendar year $t-$ 1979	Three years prior Calendar year $t-$ 1979	Four years prior Calendar year $t-$ 1979	Five years prior Calendar year $t-$ 1979
Stage 1	Take financial data for financial year 1978 ($t-1$) both for companies failing in 1979 and for non-failed companies. This is the two-year-prior model.	Take financial data for financial year 1977 ($t-2$) both for companies failing in 1979 and for non-failed companies. This is the three-year-prior model.	Take financial data for financial year 1976 ($t-3$) both for companies failing in 1979 and for non-failed companies. This is the four-year-prior model.	Take financial data for financial year 1975 ($t-4$) both for companies failing in 1979 and for non-failed companies. This is the five-year-prior model.
Stage 2	Select ratios and coefficients from the two-year-prior model.	Select ratios and coefficients from the three-year-prior model.	Select ratios and coefficients from the four-year-prior model.	Select ratios and coefficients from the five-year-prior model.
Stage 3	Apply two-year-prior model to 1979 (one-year-prior) data.	Apply three-year-prior model to 1978 (two-year-prior) data.	Apply four-year-prior model to 1977 (three-year-prior) data.	Apply five-year-prior model to 1976 (four-year-prior) data.
Stage 4	Obtain prediction	Obtain prediction	Obtain prediction	Obtain prediction

enterprise. The results are presented to demonstrate fruitful avenues of research rather than to provide a 'self-service' small company failure prediction model.

MDA ON ONE YEAR'S FINANCIAL DATA

MDA was used to determine the predictive power of the 18 ratios listed in Table 7.3. The results shown in Table 7.5, obtained by a reclassification of the derivation sample, appear promising. Type I and Type II error rates diminish as failure approaches and the overall error rate is comparable to the large company studies. The poor performance of the functions in predicting failures is to be expected since the cut-off point between failure and non-failure is designed to minimise the overall error rate when numbers of failed and non-failed firms differ. An inspection of the variables included in each of the prior models shows that three of those included in the one-year-prior model are cash flow and liquidity variables. In later years only one such variable is included, except in the two-year-prior model where two appear. The asset structure, gearing and profitability ratios appear in most years but with a correspondingly lower frequency in earlier years. *A priori* these variables would be expected to be better long-term predictors of failure whereas liquidity/cash flow variables should be better short-term predictors and in this sense the functions displayed in Table 7.5 support *a priori* reasoning. Nevertheless the grouping of variables with cash flow, liquidity, etc. in Table 7.3 is a matter of judgement and so it would be unwise to place too much weight upon the results of this table alone.

The cross-sectional hold-out results are shown in the third section of Table 7.5. One and two-year-prior tests were not conducted because of a shortage of failed companies supplying data for those years. However the satisfactory feature of the hold-out tests is that the bias towards non-failure predictive success displayed in the reclassification results is somewhat reduced, whereas the disappointing feature is that predictive power increases with distance from failure. This may be partly attributable to the quality of small company information declining as failure approaches, but it cannot be a complete explanation.

The earlier section argued that results based on reclassi-

Table 7.5: Classification results using MDA

	One year prior		Two years prior		Three years prior		Four years prior		Five years prior	
	Total cases used	% of cases correctly classified	Total cases used	% of cases correctly classified	Total cases used	% of cases correctly classified	Total cases used	% of cases correctly classified	Total cases used	% of cases correctly classified
Reclassification of original sample										
Non-failed	286	96.2	298	90.6	290	81.7	263	87.1	241	82.2
Failed	11	63.6	39	56.4	73	54.8	91	40.7	95	47.4
Total	297	95.0	337	86.4	363	76.3	354	75.4	336	72.3
Ratios selected by stepwise reduction method	$X_1, X_2, X_3, X_5, X_8, X_{14}, X_{18}$		X_3, X_8, X_{14}, X_{17}		$X_1, X_3, X_8, X_{10}, X_{14}, X_{16}$		$X_2, X_5, X_8, X_{12}, X_{14}, X_{16}$		$X_4, X_6, X_8, X_9, X_{11}, X_{14}, X_{15}$	
Classification of cross-sectional hold-out sample										
Non-failed					93	58.5	78	80.8	72	87.5
Failed					20	60.0	24	41.7	24	54.2
Total					113	58.8	102	71.6	96	79.2

fication or cross-sectional hold-out tests can give spurious indications of the predictive power of discriminant functions and so a future-dated hold-out sample of the type described in Table 7.4 is conducted. The hold-out test results are shown in Table 7.6, the top half of which shows the results of the unmatched sampling and the lower half shows the matched sampling results.

To be included in the two-year-prior analysis the company which failed in 1979 had to have provided data in both 1979 and 1978. Similarly the non-failed company also had to provide data for 1979 and 1978. MDA was conducted on the 1978 data, from which variables and coefficients were derived. These were then applied to the 1979 data which were classified into either the failed or the non-failed group. The results show that the three failed companies were correctly classified compared with only 10.4 per cent of the non-failed companies. This is likely to reflect the fact that the prior probability continued to be set at 0.5. The three-year-prior model, where MDA is conducted on 1977 data and the variables and coefficients derived are applied to 1978 data, shows that all eleven failed companies were correctly classified compared with 47 per cent of non-failed companies.

Broadly similar results are obtained by the use of matched sampling. This is shown in the lower half of Table 7.6. Matching could not adequately take place for the two-year-prior model because of the shortage of failed firms providing data in that year. However taking, for example, the five ratios derived from the 1976 data for all companies a Z-score is computed for each of the 20 companies, half of which failed and half of which did not fail in 1979. The results show that using the four-year-prior model 80 per cent of the failures and 60 per cent of the non-failures would have been correctly identified using the 1976 model and 1977 data.

The unmatched sample results confirm the earlier cross-section results that overall predictive success increases the further away from failure the prediction is made. Nevertheless the overall success rate hides different predictive success rate trends for the failed and non-failed companies. Failure prediction seems to improve whereas non-failure prediction declines as the event approaches.

An analysis of the variables included in the models shows that profitability, gearing and asset structure ratios are of prime

Table 7.6: Future-dated hold-out tests

	Two years prior		Three years prior		Four years prior		Five years prior	
	Total cases used	% of cases correctly classified	Total cases used	% of cases correctly classified	Total cases used	% of cases correctly classified	Total cases used	% of cases correctly classified
Unmatched sample								
Non-failed	356	10.4	350	46.6	321	62.0	283	69.3
Failed	3	100.0	11	100.0	12	83.3	11	63.6
Total	359	11.1	361	49.6	333	62.8	294	69.1
Ratios selected by stepwise reduction method	$X_6, X_9, X_{11}, X_{15}, X_{17}$		$X_3, X_6, X_7, X_8, X_9, X_{11}, X_{14}, X_{15}, X_{17}$		$X_8, X_{11}, X_{15}, X_{16}, X_{18}$		$X_3, X_5, X_6, X_8, X_9, X_{10}, X_{11}, X_{12}, X_{13}, X_{16}, X_{18}$	
Matched sample								
Non-failed	10	10.0	10	40.0	10	60.0	10	70.0
Failed	3	100.0	10	100.0	10	80.0	10	70.0
Total	13	25.5	20	70.0	20	70.0	20	70.0
Ratios selected by stepwise reduction method	$X_6, X_9, X_{11}, X_{15}, X_{17}$		$X_3, X_6, X_7, X_8, X_9, X_{11}, X_{15}, X_{17}$		$X_8, X_{14}, X_{15}, X_{16}, X_{18}$		$X_3, X_5, X_6, X_8, X_9, X_{10}, X_{11}, X_{12}, X_{13}, X_{16}, X_{18}$	

importance, whilst cashflow is of minor importance and liquidity measures are absent. This confirms our earlier univariate conclusions.

It will be recalled that the use of matched samples was suspected of giving both better overall results and a better mix of Type I and Type II errors. This is tested in the lower half of Table 7.6 which indeed indicates an improvement both in overall predictive success and in the error mix. It must question the results of matched studies since, in practice, the numbers of failed and non-failed companies are unlikely to be identical. Furthermore even the proportion of failures and non-failures is not known and so the sample composition which might be most appropriate for deriving the discriminant functions also may not be known. It may be possible to examine historical trends in failure rates but these may be an inadequate guide to current conditions.

The development of a series of year-prior models is, of course, not helpful to the decision maker unless either one specific year model dominates all others or unless each model is equally successful. To test for this each of the year-prior models shown in Table 7.5 was applied to 1978 data in order to attempt to predict failures/non-failures in 1979. In overall terms the one-year-prior model would be expected to out-perform others if only because it contains the most recent information. A progressive deterioration is to be expected in predictive power for the 'older' models.

The results of this are shown in Table 7.7 which demonstrates that, in fact, the opposite is true and the three-and four-year-prior models give the best predictions on 1978 data. We interpret this as being because the calibration of one-and two-year-prior models is based on relatively few cases which themselves may be unrepresentative of failed firms. On the other hand, the three-and four-year-prior models are calibrated on larger numbers of failures and are perhaps composed of rather more companies whose performance contains the seeds of their ultimate decline.

Overall the three-and four-year-prior models, which emphasise profitability, gearing and asset structure appear the most promising but it is disappointing that none of the models addresses the question of when, as opposed to whether, a firm will fail. We attempted to investigate whether dating was possible by testing whether firms which failed became pro-

Table 7.7: Robustness/Stability tests

	One years prior		Two years prior		Three years prior		Four years prior		Five years prior	
	Total cases used	% of cases correctly classified	Total cases used	% of cases correctly classified	Total cases used	% of cases correctly classified	Total cases used	% of cases correctly classified	Total cases used	% of cases correctly classified
Non-failed	388	10.6	384	50.0	390	61.5	384	67.4	390	41.5
Failed	10	90.0	10	90.0	10	90.0	10	70.0	10	70.0
Overall	398	12.5	394	51.0	400	62.3	394	67.5	400	42.3

Note: The above figures are based on using the discriminant models described in Table 7.5 to predict failures/non-failures in 1979 using 1978 data.

gressively more likely to be classified as failures as the event approached. Given our results in Table 7.7 that the three-and four-year-prior models were the best predictors it should not be a surprise that no trend was apparent and dating proved difficult.

DISCRIMINANT MODELS USING MORE THAN ONE YEAR OF FINANCIAL INFORMATION

Averages, trends and summary measures

The work of Edmister (1972) and the analysis in Chapter 6 on univariate ratios suggest the instability of small companies may make MDA inefficient if based on a single year's financial data. Hence we now construct discriminant functions which include more than a single year of financial ratios. The predictive success of the discriminant functions will be judged on the simpler reclassification and hold-out tests since these showed broadly similar results to the more complex future-dated hold-out samples. For unmatched samples the inclusion of more years' data and of summary statistics varied little across the different model years so only the results for the third-year-prior-to-failure model will be presented.

The additions to a single year's financial information consisted of additional years of data, averages derived from those years, trends for financial ratios and a measure of ratio stability. For a single financial ratio these summary statistics were defined as follows:

$$\text{Averages} = \frac{(R_1 + R_2 + R_3)}{3} \qquad \text{Where } R_i = \text{ratio value for year } i$$

$$\text{Trend} = \frac{R_3 - R_1}{R_1}$$

$$\text{Stability} = |R_3 - R_2| + |R_2 - R_1|$$

The effect of inserting these variables into a three-year-prior model can be determined from Tables 7.8, 7.9 and 7.10. The summary statistics are defined for the years three to five and the additional years of pure ratio information are drawn from years four and five. In each case this is because data for the first and second years prior to failure may be unreliable.

Row 1 of Table 7.8 shows five different models using both year-prior data and the summary statistics outlined above on unmatched sample data. The first box shows the reclassification rates obtained using only three-years-prior data. The second shows the results using three-, four-and five-years-prior data. The third box uses only averages, the fourth uses only trend data and the fifth uses only volatility measures. The table shows that whilst more years of ratio information or individual summary measures offer improved overall accuracy only more years of ratio information or averages offer improved accuracy with no substantial imbalance between Type I and Type II errors. For the models presented in this row, the asset structure variables clearly dominate the average and volatility model, but no other patterns are apparent.

The lower half of Table 7.8 builds upon the three-year-prior model in Box 1 of Row 1, and the three-, four-and five-year-prior model in Box 2. In the second row the first box shows the classification results of adding an average to the three-year-prior model, the second shows the effect of adding a trend measure and the third shows the effect of adding a volatility measure. Boxes four and five take the three-, four-and five-year model and add averages and trends respectively. The second row of Table 7.8 shows that, using the reclassification measure, the combination of ratios from a single year, together with an individual summary measure provides improved overall accuracy and generally a better mix of Type I and Type II errors. The third-year-prior-plus-averages model in Box 1 and the third-year-prior-plus-trends model in Box 2 both highlight the importance of asset structure variables.

Discriminant functions based on several years of financial ratios plus summary measures have greater classificatory accuracy than those based on financial data alone. However the effect of adding summary measures to the three-years-prior model is greater than adding them to the three-, four-and five-years-prior model. In fact, the three-years-prior-plus-averages model slightly out-performs the three-, four- and five-years-prior-

253

Table 7.8: Classification results for three-year-prior discriminant models which may include more than one year of financial information — Part I

	Ratios for 3rd year prior		Ratios for 3rd, 4th and 5th years prior		Averages only		Trends only		Volatility only	
	Total cases used	% correctly classified	Total cases used	% correctly classified	Total cases used	% correctly classified	Total cases used	% correctly classified	Total cases used	% correctly classified
Non-failed	290	81.7	219	85.4	219	83.6	219	88.6	219	90.8
Failed	73	54.8	49	58.5	49	63.3	49	30.6	49	32.7
Overall	363	76.3	268	80.3	268	79.8	268	78.0	268	79.5
Ratios stepwise selected	$X_{31}, X_{33}, X_{38}, X_{310}, X_{314}, X_{316}$		$X_{32}, X_{34}, X_{39}, X_{314}, X_{316}, X_{46}, X_{414}, X_{56}, X_{511}$		$A_3, A_7, A_{10}, A_{13}, A_{14}, A_{16}$		$T_1, T_3, T_4, T_7, T_8, T_9, T_{13}, T_{18}$		V_3, V_8, V_{13}, V_{17}	

	Ratios for 3rd year prior + Averages		Ratios for 3rd year prior + Trends		Ratios for 3rd year prior + Volatility		Ratios for 3rd, 4th and 5th years prior + Averages		Ratios for 3rd, 4th and 5th years prior + Trends		Ratios for 3rd, 4th and 5th years prior + Volatility	
	Total cases used	% correctly classified	Total cases used	% correctly classified	Total cases used	% correctly classified	Total cases used	% correctly classified	Total cases used	% correctly classified	Total cases used	% correctly classified
Non-failed	219	85.8	219	88.1	219	90.0	219	84.9	219	92.2	219	87.2
Failed	49	63.3	49	65.3	49	67.3	49	63.3	49	65.3	49	71.4
Overall	268	81.2	268	83.9	268	85.2	268	81.0	268	87.3	268	84.3
Ratios stepwise selected	$X_{33}, X_{34}, X_{313}, X_{314}, X_{316}, X_{317}, A_3, A_9, A_{13}, A_{17}$		$X_{31}, X_{34}, X_{310}, X_{314}, X_{316}, X_{317}, T_2, T_3, T_4, T_8, T_9, T_{13}, T_{18}$		$X_{31}, X_{33}, X_{34}, X_{38}, X_{39}, X_{314}, X_{316}, X_{317}, V_2, V_3, V_7, V_8, V_{13}, V_{14}$		$X_{314}, X_{316}, X_{317}, X_{38}, X_{34}, X_{41}, X_{46}, X_{48}, X_{414}, X_{417}, X_{53}, X_{56}, X_{511}, X_{518}, A_4, A_8$		$X_{31}, X_{33}, X_{314}, X_{316}, X_{317}, X_{318}, X_{41}, X_{46}, X_{53}, X_{57}, X_{511}, X_{518}, T_2, T_3, T_4, T_8, T_9, T_{10}, T_{18}$		$X_{31}, X_{34}, X_{38}, X_{314}, X_{316}, X_{46}, X_{115}, X_{52}, X_{57}, X_{511}, V_4, V_7, V_8, V_9, V_{11}, V_{14}, V_{17}$	

Note: With individual years of ratio information — the first subscript refers to year from which they are drawn, thus X_{31} is ratio X_1, for the three years prior.

Table 7.9: Classification results for three-year-prior discriminant models which may include more than one year of financial information — Part II

	Ratios for 3rd year prior + Averages + Trends		Ratios for 3rd year prior + Averages + Volatility		Ratios for 3rd year prior + Trends + Volatility		Ratios for 3rd, 4th and 5th years prior + Averages + Trends	
	Total cases used	% correctly classified	Total cases used	% correctly classified	Total cases used	% correctly classified	Total cases used	% correctly classified
Non-failed	219	91.8	219	87.7	219	90.9	219	92.2
Failed	49	63.3	49	67.3	49	67.3	49	67.3
Overall	268	86.6	268	84.0	268	86.6	268	87.7
Ratios stepwise selected	$X_{33}, X_{34}, X_{38}, X_{313}, X_{314}, X_{316}, X_{317}, A_3, A_9, A_{13}, T_2, T_3, T_4, T_8, T_9, T_{18}$		$X_{33}, X_{34}, X_{38}, X_{313}, X_{314}, X_{316}, X_{317}, A_6, A_9, A_{11}, A_{13}, V_2, V_3, V_7, V_8, V_9, V_{11}, V_{14}, V_{17}$		$X_{31}, X_{33}, X_{34}, X_{39}, X_{314}, X_{315}, T_2, T_3, T_4, T_8, T_9, T_{11}, T_{13}, T_{18}$		$X_{33}, X_{34}, X_{313}, X_{314}, X_{316}, X_{317}, X_{318}, X_{41}, X_{48}, X_{52}, X_{53}, X_{57}, X_{59}, X_{518}, T_2, T_3, T_4, T_8, T_9, T_{10}, T_{18}$	

	Ratios for 3rd, 4th and 5th years prior + Averages + Volatility		Ratios for 3rd, 4th and 5th years prior + Trends + Volatility		Ratios for 3rd year prior + Averages + Trends + Volatility		Ratios for 3rd, 4th and 5th years prior + Averages + Trends + Volatility	
	Total cases used	% correctly classified	Total cases used	% correctly classified	Total cases used	% correctly classified	Total cases used	% correctly classified
Non-failed	219	89.0	219	92.2	219	92.7	219	92.7
Failed	49	73.5	49	67.3	49	67.3	49	69.4
Overall	268	86.2	268	87.7	268	88.1	268	88.4
Ratios stepwise selected	$X_{34}, X_{38}, X_{310}, X_{313}, X_{314}, X_{316}, X_{46}, X_{415}, X_{52}, X_{54}, X_{57}, X_{59}, X_{514}, X_{15}, V_4, V_7, V_8, V_9, V_{11}, V_{14}, V_{17}$		$X_{31}, X_{33}, X_{34}, X_{314}, X_{316}, X_{317}, X_{318}, X_{415}, X_{53}, X_{55}, X_{511}, X_{513}, X_{518}, T_2, T_3, T_9, V_8, T_{12}, T_{15}, T_{18}, V_3, V_4, V_6, V_7$		$X_{33}, X_{34}, X_{311}, X_{313}, X_{314}, X_{315}, X_{318}, A_5, A_9, A_{13}, V_3, V_7, V_8, V_{17}, T_2, T_3, T_4, T_5, T_8, T_9, T_{12}, T_{18}$		$X_{313}, X_{314}, X_{316}, X_{317}, X_{318}, X_{43}, X_{44}, X_{53}, X_{55}, X_{59}, X_{518}, V_3, V_9, V_8, V_{17}, A_{13}, T_2, T_3, T_8, T_9, T_4$	

Note: With individual years of ratio information — the first subscript refers to year from which they are drawn

Table 7.10: Cross-sectional hold-out results for three-year-prior models which may include more than one year of financial information

	Ratios for 3rd year prior		Averages		Ratios for 3rd year prior + Averages	
	Number of cases used	% correctly classified	Number of cases used	% correctly classified	Number of cases used	% correctly classified
Non-failed	93	58.5	59	81.4	59	76.3
Failed	20	60.0	15	73.3	15	73.3
Overall	113	58.8	74	79.9	74	75.7

	Ratios for 3rd year prior + Averages + Volatility		Ratios for 3rd year prior + Trends + Volatility		Ratios for 3rd year prior + Averages + Trends + Volatility	
	Number of cases used	% correctly classified	Number of cases used	% correctly classified	Number of cases used	% correctly classified
Non-failed	59	62.7	59	55.9	59	66.1
Failed	15	73.3	15	53.3	15	40.0
Overall	74	65.2	74	55.4	74	62.6

plus-averages model. Similar results are obtained for the volatility measure, whereas the trend variables do give marginal increases in accuracy.

Table 7.9, Row 1, takes the three-year-prior model and adds combinations of averages, trends and volatility, while Row 2 takes the three-, four-and five-year-prior model and also adds similar combinations. It shows that it is possible to increase reclassification success by including additional variables. However the cost of such success may be increased multicollinearity and the possibility of unstable 'predictive' functions. To examine this question several functions from Tables 7.8 and 7.9 were tested on a cross-sectional hold-out sample. The results are shown in Table 7.10 and indicate that the improvement in reclassification success obtained by increasing the number of types of variables need not be maintained in this form of test.

In conclusion a single year of financial information plus a summary measure tends to give good overall results and a satisfactory mix of Type I and Type II errors. However the predictive results achieved are generally somewhat lower than those obtained in the large firm studies.

NON-SUBMISSION OF DATA AND THE PREDICTION OF FAILURE

By now it should be clear that the major problem with predicting the failure of small companies is that not all submit annual accounts. Whilst it may be legitimate for large company studies to ignore this problem, the scale of non-submission amongst small firms means that ignoring it could lead to bias. This section will analyse whether it is possible to employ a simple rule of thumb for classifying companies for which no information is available. The rule proposed is that every company which does not submit full accounts for a given year will be classed as a failure for that year. This rule has been chosen purely for its simplicity in order to determine how previous results would be affected.

The first row of Table 7.11 shows how the basic ratio reclassification results of Table 7.5 are affected by the rule, highlighting the increase in the number of failed companies now considered in the three years prior to failure. There are also slight increases in the sample sizes of the non-failed companies but there is no pattern to the increases. Given the nature of the rule adopted, and the propensities not to submit accounts, the mix of Type I and Type II errors show the expected improvements for all years. Whilst the mix of errors shows a general improvement, the overall classificatory success only shows improvement of non-failed companies not submitting accounts one, four and five years prior to 1979. However, the slight loss in classificatory success for a number of the years should be compared with the improved mix of errors, the number of cases included and the possible non-optimal nature of the decision rule utilised. At this stage the simple rule of thumb suggested seems a reasonably successful way of dealing with small company non-submission.

Cross-sectional hold-out tests for the simple rule are conducted in Row 1 of Table 7.12. First it should be clear that the introduction of a non-submission variable now makes it feasible to provide predictions for one and two years prior to failure. The mix of Type I and Type II errors for these years is satis-

257

Table 7.11: A non-submission variable and the prediction of failure: reclassification results

Model type	Sample	One year prior		Two years prior		Three years prior		Four years prior		Five years prior	
		Total cases used	% correctly classified	Total cases used	% correctly classified	Total cases used	% correctly classified	Total cases used	% correctly classified	Total cases used	% correctly classified
Ratios	Non-failed	305	90.2	300	89.9	295	80.3	280	81.8	261	75.9
	Failed	126	96.8	102	83.3	92	64.1	91	40.7	95	47.4
	Total	431	92.1	402	88.3	387	76.5	371	71.7	356	68.3
Ratios and	Non-failed	227	94.6	222	94.1	219	90.0				
Volatility	Failed	72	87.8	65	73.9	84	80.9				
Measures	Total	299	93.0	287	89.5	303	87.5				
Ratios, Volatility	Non-failed	227	95.4	222	95.0	219	90.9				
Measures and	Failed	72	87.8	65	73.9	84	80.9				
Trends	Total	299	93.6	287	90.2	303	88.2				

Table 7.12: A non-submission variable and the prediction of failure: cross-sectional hold-out results

Model type	Sample	One year prior		Two years prior		Three years prior		Four years prior		Five years prior	
		Total cases used	% correctly classified	Total cases used	% correctly classified	Total cases used	% correctly classified	Total cases used	% correctly classified	Total cases used	% correctly classified
Ratios	Non-failed	106	85.2	97	71.4	95	57.3	81	77.8	75	84.0
	Failed	30	90.9	27	73.3	26	69.2	24	41.7	25	52.0
	Total	136	86.5	124	71.8	121	59.9	105	69.6	100	76.0
Ratios and	Non-failed	72	57.2	63	57.0	61	53.1				
Volatility	Failed	25	71.0	22	60.9	21	66.6				
Measures	Total	97	60.8	85	58.0	82	56.6				
Ratios, Volatility	Non-failed	72	58.4	63	58.1	61	54.1				
Measures and	Failed	25	71.0	22	60.9	21	66.6				
Trends	Total	97	61.6	85	58.8	82	57.3				

factory and the overall rate of predictive success, although not as high as the basic ratio and non-submission reclassification results of Tables 7.5 and 7.11, is well above that which could be achieved by a random model. For three years prior, the results are not as good as the two sets of reclassification results, but are slightly better than the cross-sectional hold-out results without the inclusion of a non-submission variable. For four and five years prior the 'non-submission' cross-sectional hold-out results in Table 7.12 are worse than the 'basic' ratio reclassification results. Hence, the addition of a non-submission variable to the basic ratio discriminant model would seem useful primarily for the three years immediately prior to failure.

The addition of a non-submission variable is likely to have a similar effect on the other discriminant models discussed in this chapter as on the basic ratio model, since all models suffer from the non-submission problem. To test this hypothesis, a non-submission variable has been added to two models from Tables 7.8 and 7.9. Rows 2 and 3 of Table 7.11 show that for the third year prior to failure the reclassification results for the models are slightly better when a non-submission variable is included. Furthermore, results are presented for one-and two-year-prior models because the addition of the non-submission variable makes the sample of failed companies large enough to be considered. The results show that one to three years prior to failure it is possible to obtain fairly high levels of reclassification success for small companies, once it is recognised that there is an asymmetry in the propensity for failed and non-failed companies to submit accounts.

Whilst improvement in reclassification success is one indicator of the 'power' of a variable, the cross-sectional hold-out tests are a better indicator of the usefulness of a non-submission variable. Rows 2 and 3 of Table 7.12 indicate that the cross-sectional hold-out results for the two extended models are substantially less than the reclassification results. Nonetheless, they are still an improvement on the cross-sectional hold-out results for the ratios, volatility and trends model without a non-submission variable shown in Table 7.10. Overall, the conclusion is that a non-submission variable is a useful addition to discriminant functions for small company failure predictions for the three years immediately prior to failure.

PREDICTING SMALL COMPANY FAILURE WITH REFERENCE TO INDUSTRY, AGE AND INFLATION EFFECTS

The sample used to develop the discriminant functions discussed so far in this chapter has grouped together companies from all industrial sectors. This might be thought unsatisfactory since, for example, companies in mechanical engineering may fail for reasons different from those in the paper and printing industry. To analyse the importance of a sectoral classification for the development of predictive discriminant models, results for basic ratio models for the third year prior to failure for five broad industrial sectors are shown in Row 1 of Table 7.13. The results show that the aggregated total reclassification success rate, 84 per cent, is higher than that achieved for a model built on the total sample (76 per cent in Table 7.5) and the overall success rates for individual sectors in Table 7.13 are broadly similar. Furthermore, whilst individual sectors differ on the mix of Type I and Type II errors, in total they are markedly superior to the mix obtained with the single non-sectoral model (Table 7.5). The models for the different sectors vary in terms of the variables included; for example, all financial categories appear in the timber model, but liquidity measures are significantly absent in the mechanical engineering model.

The cross-sectional hold-out sample results shown in Row 2 of Table 7.13 for the industry-specific basic ratio discriminant models reveal that when aggregated they are better than those achieved by developing a three-year-prior model on the overall sample of industries, i.e., 58.8 per cent in Table 7.5 compared with 67 per cent in Table 7.13. However, the overall success rates and the mix of Type I and Type II errors vary markedly between sectors, so that although the general level of predictive success could be raised by developing sectoral discriminant models, such a policy runs the risk of a wide variance of results for the differing sectors.

In Chapters 4 and 5 the age of companies was identified as an important variable in explaining performance (Johnson, 1986). Given the generally high rate of failure amongst young companies, it could be argued that failure prediction rates would be improved by developing separate models for different age groups of companies. Since failure rates for companies less than five years old have been shown to be significantly higher

261

Table 7.13: Classification results at industry level: three years prior

Classification of original sample	Mechanical Engineering		Metal Manufacture		Timber		Paper & Printing		Other		Total	
	No. cases	% correctly classified	No. cases	% correctly classified	No. cases	% correctly classified	No. cases	% correctly classified	No. cases	% correctly classified	No. cases	% correctly classified
Non-failed	57	96.4	38	86.5	33	84.4	36	85.7	126	84.8	290	87.4
Failed	10	80.0	13	76.9	9	88.9	7	57.1	34	62.9	73	70.4
Overall accuracy		94.0		84.1		85.4		81.0		80.1		84.0
Ratios selected by the stepwise method	$X_4, X_5, X_6, X_8, X_{10}, X_{11}, X_{12}, X_{15}, X_{16}$		$X_2, X_3, X_4, X_9, X_{13}, X_{16}, X_{18}$		$X_1, X_3, X_7, X_{10}, X_{12}, X_{13}$		$X_3, X_{12}, X_{13}, X_{17}$		X_1, X_3, X_{12}, X_{14}			

Classification of cross-sectional hold-out sample	Mechanical Engineering		Metal Goods not Elsewhere Specified		Timber		Paper and Print		Others		Total	
	No. cases	% correctly classified	No. cases	% correctly classified	No. cases	% correctly classified	No. cases	% correctly classified	No. cases	% correctly classified	No. cases	% correctly classified
Non-failed	21	72.2	22	82.4	13	75.2	11	42.9	26	52.5	93	66.1
Failed	5	50.0	3	100.0	0	0	0	0	12	72.7	20	71.1
Overall accuracy		67.9		84.5		75.2		42.9		58.9		67.0

than those for more mature companies (Ganguly, 1985), separate discriminant models were developed for each of these two groups. As in previous models the variables included were those in Table 7.3 and the final discriminant function was selected by stepwise reduction. Cross-sectional hold-out tests were conducted in addition to a reclassification of the original sample. To aid comparability with the previous results, discriminant models were only developed on basic ratios alone and for three-years-prior data.

An analysis of the first row of Table 7.14 shows that overall classificatory success for the short life companies is less (74%) than for the longer life companies (82%). An examination of the ratios included in the short life model shows a conspicuous absence of any liquidity variables. Instead the asset structure variables appear frequently in both this and the long life model. It is encouraging that the Type I and Type II errors are similar for both models and that the overall classification rates are high and of similar magnitude. Furthermore, the overall success rate of 81 per cent is somewhat better than the 76.3 per cent achieved by developing a discriminant function without an age dimension (in Table 7.5).

Although the classification results for the original sample were somewhat better for the long life model than the short life, matters are reversed substantially for the cross-section hold-out tests — although the inclusion of only 19 short life companies in

Table 7.14: Reclassification and cross-sectional hold-out results: short-life model

Reclassification	Short-life		Long-life		All cases	
	No. of cases	% correctly classified	No. of cases	% correctly classified	No. of cases	% correctly classified
Non-failed	32	75.0	258	87.3	290	85.9
Failed	18	72.2	55	61.0	73	63.0
Total	50	74.0	313	82.3	363	81.3
Ratios selected by stepwise reduction	$X_5, X_{11}, X_{13}, X_{17}$		$X_2, X_4, X_8, X_{12}, X_{13}$ X_{14}, X_{16}, X_{17}			
Cross-sectional hold-out tests						
Non-failed	14	75.0	79	52.3	93	55.9
Failed	5	80.0	15	80.0	20	80.0
Total	19	76.3	94	56.7	113	60.2

the hold-out test must cast doubt on the validity of these results. When the results of the hold-out sample for the two models are aggregated, they are similar to the results obtained by developing a single discriminant function for all ages of companies both in terms of the mix of Type I and Type II errors and in terms of the total predictive success rate (60.2 per cent as compared to 58.8 per cent).

In summary, there seems less to be gained by developing separate discriminant functions for differing ages of companies than taking into account more years of data and formulating summary statistics.

Finally, given that the data used throughout this text come from a period of high inflation, models based on ratios adjusted for inflationary effects might be expected to achieve higher predictive success rates than models based purely on historic cost data. However, Keasey and Watson (1986) found that making current cost adjustments to the historic cost ratios and including specific current cost ratios did not generally improve the predictive success rates for small company failure. They attribute this to the fact that the current cost adjustments do little to alter the variance within and between the distributions of failed and non-failed companies.

CONCLUSIONS

This chapter briefly reviewed existing large firm studies which have used multiple discriminant analysis (MDA) for predicting corporate failure. It then presented the results of applying MDA to data on small companies.

In our review in this chapter and elsewhere we have emphasised the absence of either a satisfactory static or dynamic theory of the *process* of failure. The empirical models that exist have therefore tended to rely on 'brute empiricism' in ratio selection, with the risk that the results could become sample dependent. Furthermore the use of MDA does not assist the development of a theoretical model because the technique does not allow the coefficients or variables selected to be examined for an economic rationale.

The problems in developing a predictive model of small firm failure include all the above together with several additional problems. First, small companies generally have an undiversified, narrow product range and frequently only a few major customers for their products, making them more akin to sub-contractors than independent manufacturers. This reliance upon a few products renders them vulnerable to even quite mild economic fluctuations. Second, their financial structure and access to capital differs radically from large companies. Whereas large companies should have relatively easy access to long-term capital (either equity or loans), often the only source of capital for the small company — other than the owner's own resources — is bank overdrafts and extended credit from suppliers, the latter being particularly unpredictable. Third, as we noted in Chapter 3, the managerial structure of many small companies often consists of the owner and his wife, so that any unpredictable occurence such as illness or other personal problems can lead to the company's collapse, almost irre-spective of its financial health. This suggests that qualitative data, such as managerial structure, may be important for the prediction of small company failure, a matter which we investi-gate in Chapter 9.

Actual failure depends upon the reactions of creditors, bankers (and increasingly) government agencies, etc. to the company's difficulties but it is not clear that the financing agencies react to small company distress in the same way or as consistently as they do to large company distress. Furthermore, a large proportion of small company failures are young, and the absence of any data on their performance means that failure prediction models cannot be calibrated.

Whilst recognising the presence of such problems this chapter reports the results of our attempts to use MDA in building a predictive model of small company failure. We have constructed a number of models, based on a large number of different years of data. To some extent this complexity has been imposed upon us by the availability of data, notably the absence of published accounts for failed companies one and two years prior to failure. In fact only seven out of 177 failed companies submitted full accounts in the year prior to failure and only 55 two years prior to failure. Since it is likely that those submitting would be atypical, then models based on this data could be biased. Hence, although data on the year prior to failure should provide the most recent information, the 'best' models used three-year-prior data in order to increase sample size. It also has to be re-emphasised that it is *not* possible to identify whether the small firm failures in, for example, 1975 differ from those in 1980. Because of data shortages the financial data for all failed firms, irrespective of when they failed, were classified as being either one, two, three, four or five years prior to failure. The one-year-prior data were then compared with 1979 data for non-failed firms, the two-year-prior data compared with 1978 data for non-failed firms and the three-year-prior data compared with 1977 data for non-failed firms.

A summary selection of the results of the various reclassification and cross-section hold-out tests is shown in Table 7.15. All the results shown are based on the three-year-prior model, i.e. comparing financial data for 1977 for companies which never failed (up until 1982) with financial data for the third year prior to failure of companies which failed at any stage between 1971 and 1982. The top row of the table shows the results based on a reclassification of the original sample and the second row shows the results based on a cross-section hold-out test. The first box in both rows shows the results of the standard model indicating success rates of 76.3 per cent and 58.8 per cent in the reclassificatory and hold-out samples respectively. It is against these standards that more sophisticated models have to be examined.

From Table 7.15 it appears that, in the context of a hold-out test, the ratios-plus-averages model is the most successful, achieving a correct classification rate of 75.7 per cent, whereas none of the other models achieved a success rate significantly higher than that of the standard model, although the industry model did achieve a rate of 67 per cent, three years prior to failure. It will be apparent that only the standard model, the industry model and the age model use the same number of cases. In order for readers to reacquaint themselves with the reasons for this, each box shows the table in the text from which it has been drawn.

The problem of small companies not submitting financial data in the years immediately prior to failure was 'overcome' by the rule that all companies not submitting accounts were presumed to fail in that year. In the test we showed that, for the *one*-year-prior model, a significant improvement in predictive power was obtained with this rule. However as we show in Row 2 when this rule is applied to the three-year-prior model, it actually leads to a reduction in predictive power compared with the standard model.

Table 7.15: Summary table of best ratios: reclassification and cross-sectional hold-out results: three-year-prior model

Reclassification of original sample	Standard model (Ratios only) (Table 7.5)		Ratios + Averages (Table 7.8)		Ratios + Non-submission + Volatility + Trends (Table 7.11)		Industry model (Table 7.13)		Age model (Table 7.14)	
	Number of cases	% correctly classified	Number of cases	% correctly classified	Number of cases	% correctly classified	Number of cases	% correctly classified	Number of cases	% correctly classified
Non-failed	290	81.7	219	85.8	219	90.9	290	87.4	290	85.9
Failed	73	54.8	49	63.3	84	80.9	73	70.4	73	63.0
Total	363	76.3	268	81.2	303	88.2	363	84.0	363	81.3
Ratios included	1 Profitability 1 Gearing 2 Asset Structure 1 Liquidity 1 Cash Flow						No pattern in each of the industrial sectors		Primarily Asset Structure ratios in both long-life and short-life model	

Cross-sectional hold-out tests	1 (Table 7.5)		2 (Table 7.10)		4 (Table 7.12)		5 (Table 7.13)		6 (Table 7.14)	
	Number of cases	% correctly classified	Number of cases	% correctly classified	Number of cases	% correctly classified	Number of cases	% correctly classified	Number of cases	% correctly classified
Non-failed	93	58.5	59	76.3	61	54.1	93	66.1	93	55.9
Failed	20	60.0	15	73.3	21	66.6	20	71.1	20	80.0
Total	113	58.8	74	75.7	82	57.3	113	67.0	113	60.2

In the final two boxes the results for the three-year-prior model with sectoral and age components are shown. As noted above, there is some improvement with the use of a sectoral model but the age model brings few improvements compared with the standard.

Overall the results obtained when MDA is applied to small company failure prediction are weaker than those obtained in the large company studies, particularly in the years immediately prior to failure. In part, this is due to problems over data and partly because fewer small firms exhibit clear trends as failure approaches. Furthermore, the limitations with the use of MDA and the absence of any underlying theoretical model suggest that either alternative techniques or different data are required if significant improvements in predictive power are to be obtained.

Despite these problems, however, it needs to be emphasised that our 'best' model bears favourable comparison with most of the large company results, since in a cross-sectional hold-out test we were able to predict with 75 per cent accuracy failed from non-failed companies three years ahead. We regard this as a very worthwhile achievement.

NOTES

1. See Lachenbruch, Sneeringer and Revo (1973), Gilbert (1968) and Moore (1973).

2. Again, testing this assumption has rarely been undertaken, even though Gilbert (1969) and Wahl and Kronmal (1977) show that if dispersion matrices are unequal the quadratic may be superior to the linear form of discriminant analysis.

3. Eisenbeis (1977), however, shows that inappropriate prior probabilities can lead to some very misleading classification results.

4. The lack of use of future-dated hold-out samples may either be because standard discriminant analysis does not explicitly incorporate a time dimension or because of the unwillingness of researchers to place themselves in the position of practitioners having to use such models!

5. Other questions have been raised over the statistical approaches in these models. For example, the use of 'winsorising' the extreme values and the excluding of non-failed companies which were deemed problematical are both dubious procedures used.

6. A cross-sectional hold-out test is one where a discriminant function's predictive power is ascertained on a different but time-coincident sample of firms.

7. With Rao's V, a generalised distance measure, the variable selected is the one which contributes the largest increase in V when added to the variables already in the discriminant function.

8

Factor, Probit and Logit Analysis

INTRODUCTION

An alternative to using multiple discriminant analysis is the use of conditional probability models to estimate the probability of occurrence of a choice or outcome, conditional on the attribute vector of the choice or outcome set that is available. The second half of this chapter will show that although conditional probability models have a number of advantages over multiple discriminant analysis they are generally unable to reduce the multi-dimensionality of the problem of corporate failure. This implies that either a theory or some form of dimensionality reduction technique will have to be employed to ensure that the variable choice set is of the right form before using the conditional probability models. The earlier chapters argued that the development of theory leaves much to be desired and so the first half of this chapter will outline a dimension reduction technique, factor analysis. It presents a factor-analytic classification of small company financial ratios which can then be used as a starting point for the prediction of small company failure via conditional probability models.

FACTOR ANALYSIS: THE TECHNIQUE AND EXAMPLES

Factor analysis (or its close cousin, principal component analysis) is used when the research is concerned with discovering which variables in a data set form coherent sub-groups that are relatively independent of one another. Inspection of sets of variables that are correlated with one another can reveal a great deal about hypothetical structures that may have generated the combination of outcomes that were measured by the observed variables.

Given an array of correlation coefficients for a set of variables, factor-analytic techniques determine whether some pattern of relationships exists such that the data may be reduced to a smaller set of factors that may be taken as the source variables. All of the variants of factor analysis follow three steps to reach the above goal: first, a correlation matrix is derived; second, initial factors are extracted; third, the initial factors are rotated to a terminal solution which achieves simple factors.

After relevant variables have been defined and selected most forms of factor analysis produce a product moment correlation matrix. From the correlation matrix, new variables may be defined as exact mathematical transformations (principal component analysis) of the original data, or inferential assumptions may be made about the structuring of variables and their source variation (classical factor analysis). With either technique the initial factors are derived so that the factors are orthogonal and the data are reduced as far as possible.

Principal component analysis simply makes what would be the 'best' linear combination of variables, where 'best' means that a particular combination of variables accounts for more of the variance in the data as a whole than any other linear combination of variables. The first principal component, therefore, is the best summary of linear relationships exhibited in the data. The second component is defined as the second best linear combination of variables, under the condition that the second component is orthogonal to the first.

Subsequent components are defined similarly until all the variance in the data is exhausted. Unless at least one variable is perfectly determined by the rest of the variables in the data, the principal component solution requires as many components as there are variables for factor-analytic purposes. Hence, the analyst normally retains only the first few components, which account for the vast majority of the variance, for further rotation/interpretation.

Classical factor analysis differs because it is based on the premiss that the observed correlations are mainly the result of some underlying regularity in the data-common deteminants. It is hoped that the common determinants will not only account for all the observed relations in the data but will also be smaller in number than the variables. The basic postulate of factor analysis is, therefore, the existence of a residual variance, which is not accounted for by common factors and does not contribute to the intercorrelations of the variables. However, the extent of the unique variance or its complement, community, is not known. It has to be estimated from the data and it is this step that usually differentiates the variants of factor analysis.

Regardless of whether or not the factors are defined or inferred, the exact structure of the factors is not unique. One factor solution can be transformed into another — there are several statistically equivalent ways to define the underlying dimensions of the same set of data. Therefore, the choice of rotation is the one which gives the terminal factors which suit the needs of the problems. The major options available to the analyst are an orthogonal rotation method or an oblique rotation method. Orthogonal factors are simpler to handle but the oblique factors are thought to be more realistic.

In the context of corporate failure prediction the best known work utilising factor analysis is by Pinches, Mingo and Caruthers (1973). They (PMC) utilised factor analysis (employing financial ratios as variables and industrial firms as cases) first to develop classifications of financial ratios and second to measure the long-term stability/change in these classifications over the 1951-1969 period. To look at both of these questions, they used data from the US Compustat data tapes for 221 industrial firms for which 48 financial ratios were available for the years of 1951, 1957, 1963 and 1969. They applied a common log transformation to all financial ratios to improve normality and reduce outliers.

To develop classifications, data matrices for the years 1951, 1957, 1963 and 1969 were factor analysed to produce patterns of financial ratios for each of the years. Utilising factor analysis, oblique rotation to the final factor matrix and the decision rule that only variables which factor loaded at more than 0.7[1] were to be included, PMC derived financial structures for each of the years. A reduced form of their results is shown in Figure 8.1 below. Rather than showing every variable which loaded at 0.7 or more, Figure 8.1 illustrates the two variables most highly correlated (highest factor loading) with each factor.

The reduced space represented by the seven factors consistently accounted for a high amount of information contained in the original data matrix — 91% in 1951, 92% in 1957, 87%

Figure 8.1: Financial ratios and factor loadings defining seven financial ratio patterns for industrial firms

	Factor Loadings			
Ratio Number: Ratio Name	1951	1957	1963	1969
Factor 7 — Return on Investment				
32 Net income/Net worth	.96	.97	.85	.97
44 Total income/Total capital	.96	.97	.85	.97
Factor 2 — Capital Intensiveness				
34 — Net worth/Sales	−.85	−.85	−.82	−.88
36 — Sales/Total assets	.97	.85	.79	.89
Factor 3 — Inventory Intensiveness				
23 — Inventory/Sales	.64	.96	.90	.97
37 — Cost of goods sold/Inventory	−.57	−.95	−.96	−.97
Factor 4 — Financial Leverage				
7 — Debt/Total capital	.99	.99	.93	.97
47 — Debt/Total assets	.99	.96	.91	.97
Factor 5 — Receivables Intensiveness				
11 — Receivables/Inventory	−.99	−.99	−.99	−.99
20 — Receivables/Sales	−.90	−.89	−.80	−.82
Factor 6 — Short-term Liquidity				
15 — Current assets/Current liabilities	.77	.82	.80	.91
46 — Current assets/Total assets	−.91	−.79	−.73	−.78
Factor 7 — Cash Position				
12 — Cash/Total assets	.89	.87	.80	.91
26 — Cash/Fund expenditures	.99	.99	.85	.91

in 1963 and 92% in 1969. Furthermore, the derived factors are easy to interpret in terms of accepted accounting practice/ thought. However whilst factor analysis may capture the key characteristics of long-life companies, it is less clear whether the derived factors will represent the population of companies existing at any one point in time since, by requiring companies to have data over an 18-year period, companies which are born and which die within such a period are excluded. For large US companies exclusion of the birth and death process over such a period may hardly alter the results, but the process is likely to be much more important for small UK companies.

To examine the stability of the derived factors over the sample period, PMC analysed the means of the financial ratios for stability, instability, or trending in a given direction. They then used differential factor analysis to determine how many of the companies shared in the process. If a ratio had an upward trend over the period and most companies have shared in the process, then the difference measure representing the change between the two endpoints of the process showed a small variance — and a subsequent high differential loading. If the companies did not share in the trend, the difference measure showed a high variance and a low differential factor loading.

PMC's analysis of the means revealed that downward shifts in the level of Return on Investment, Capital Intensiveness, and Cash Position were shared by most firms as was the upward trend in Financial Leverage and Receivable Intensiveness. Inventory Intensiveness and total Short-term Liquidity showed no significant trends.

THE FINANCIAL STRUCTURE OF SMALL UK MANUFACTURING COMPANIES

This section undertakes similar tests to PMC on the financial structure of the collection of small manufacturing companies, the characteristics of which were described in Chapter 2. It will determine if the financial structure is stable/unstable throughout the 1970s but, given the above comments concerning the potential importance of the birth and death process, the analysis will be conducted both for companies providing data for at least a seven-year period and for those providing only three years of data. For both samples of companies the factor analysis and differential factor analysis will use the ratios listed in Table 8.1 as the primary data set.

The ratios were chosen from the information commonly available in small company accounts and on the basis that they should capture most facets of a company's financial structure. Only sales-based ratios are excluded on the grounds that turnover figures are not consistently provided by small companies.

Factor analysis and differential factor analysis with orthogonal and oblique final rotations were conducted on these ratios. Throughout the analysis the oblique and orthogonal rotations gave essentially the same results and so only the orthogonal results will be presented here.

Table 8.2 shows the results of a factor analysis for 116 companies which provided data for the years 1974, 1976, 1978 and 1980. The raw data for any two consecutive years were averaged and factor analysis then conducted. The eight derived factors account for approximately 90 per cent of the information contained in the raw data of the ratio set. Therefore, the results presented here compare well with those of Pinches, Mingo and Caruthers. As is to be expected, given the different

Table 8.1: Variables used in factor analysis

V1 — Current Assets/Current Liabilities
V2 — Current Assets — Stock/Current Liabilities
V3 — Net Profit/Total Assets
V4 — Total Debt (includes bank overdraft)/Net Worth (i.e. Share Capital & Reserves)
V5 — Total Debt (includes bank overdraft)/Total Assets
V6 — Net Profit/Current Liabilities
V7 — Fixed Assets/Total Assets
V8 — Current Assets — Current Liabilities/Total Assets
V9 — Pre-tax Profit + Depreciation/Total Debt
V10 — Pre-tax Profit + Depreciation/Total Assets
V11 — Pre-tax Profit before Directors' Fees + Interest/Total Debt
V12 — Pre-tax Profit before Directors' Fees + Interest/Total Assets
V13 — Pre-tax Profit/Total Assets
V14 — Net Profit + Depreciation/Total Assets
V15 — Net Profit + Interest/Total Assets
V16 — Total Debt (excludes bank overdraft)/Total Assets
V17 — Current Assets/Total Assets
V18 — Current Liabilities/Total Assets
V19 — Current Assets — Stock/Total Assets
V20 — Current Assets — Current Liabilities/Fixed Assets
V21 — Net Profit/Net Worth
V22 — Net Profit/Fixed Assets
V23 — Fixed Assets/Net Worth
V24 — Net Profit/Current Assets — Current Liabilities
V25 — Pre-tax Profit/Net Worth
V26 — Current Assets — Current Liabilities/Current Liabilities
V27 — Net Profit + Interest/Net Worth
V28 — Net Profit + Depreciation/Net Worth
V29 — Net Profit + Interest/Total Debt

---

nature of the underlying ratio set, the derived factors are somewhat different from those of the PMC study. Nonetheless, six of the derived factors are readily interpretable in terms of standard accounting theory/thought.

The decision rule used to determine which variables to include under each factor heading was, firstly, to include ratios if they had a factor loading of more than 0.70 for at least two of the three years; second, if a factor had ratios which loaded at 0.70 or more for only one of the years then all ratios which loaded at this level or more were included; third, if a factor had no ratios which loaded at 0.70 or more for any of the years then the factor was not included. By utilising such a decision rule it is clear that the ratios for each factor will tend to exhibit exaggerated similarity and stability. However, some decision rule has to be adopted if all ratios are not to be listed under each factor

Table 8.2: Financial ratios and factor loadings for single-plant independent manufacturing firms which had complete data for the years 1974, 1976, 1978, 1980

Ratio number	Ratio name	Factor loading		
		1975	1977	1979
Factor 1 — Return on Investment				
V3 *	Net Profit/Total Assets	.96	.94	.94
V6	Net Profit/Current Liabilities	.77	.74	.86
V10	Pre-tax Profit + Depreciation/Total Assets	.88	.87	.86
V13	Pre-tax Profit/Total Assets	.89	.88	.88
V14	Net Profit + Depreciation/Total Assets	.91	.89	.92
V15	Net Profit + Interest/Total Assets	.94	.91	.93
V22	Net Profit/Fixed Assets	.73	.58	.66
Factor 2 — Liquidity				
V1 *	Current Assets/Current Liabilities	.95	.94	.06
V2	Current Assets − Stock/Current Liabilities	.93	.93	.04
V18	Current Liabilities/Total Assets	−.84	−.79	−.27
V26 *	Current Assets − Current Liabilities/ Current Liabilities	.95	.94	.06
Factor 3 — Solvency				
V4	Total Debt/Net Worth	−.94	−.07	−.27
V21	Net Profit/Net Worth	.97	.08	.06
V23 *	Fixed Assets/Net Worth	−.95	−.35	−.28
V25	Pre-tax Profit/Net Worth	.95	.10	.05
V27	Net Profit + Interest/Net Worth	.95	.08	−.01
Factor 4 — Asset Structure				
V7 *	Fixed Assets/Total Assets	−.94	−.08	−.94
V17	Current Assets/Total Assets	.94	.06	.95
Factor 5 — Debt Coverage				
V9 *	Pre-tax Profit + Depreciation/Total Debt	.93	−.09	.98
V11	Pre-tax Profit before Directors' Fees + Interest/Total Debt	.94	−.14	.96
V29	Net Profit + Interest/Total Debt	.83	−.04	.97
Factor 6 — Gearing				
V5	Total Debt/Total Assets	.49	−.14	.71
V16 *	Total Debt − Bank Overdraft/Total Assets	.46	−.11	.83
Factor 7				
V12	Pre-tax Profit before Directors' Fees + Interest/Total Assets	.48	.01	.73
V19 *	Current Assets − Stock/Total Assets	.72	.19	.68
Factor 8				
V24 *	Net Profit/(Current Assets − Current Liabilities)	.09	.89	.98
	Percent of variance explained by the 8 factors	88.5	88.7	90.9

Note: a. 116 cases for each year.
* indicates ratio which has highest overall factor loading with a given factor.
Ratio List, therefore, equals V3, V1 or V26, V23, V7, V9, V16, V19, V24

and each factor is to take on its own identity. If the above decision-rule is accepted then it is clear from Table 8.2 that only the Return on Investment factor exhibits stability over the whole period, whilst liquidity and solvency show marked instability. Further discussion of factor stability will be left until the differential factor analysis section. The variable which loaded highest with each factor is starred and overall the set of starred ratios offers few surprises.

It was argued above that factor-analysing data for companies with accounting information available over a long period of time may give a false impression of the overall average financial structure of small companies since births and deaths are ignored. Table 8.3 presents the results of an identical factor analysis to that in Table 8.2, except that companies included in Table 8.3 needed only to have data available for two years. Thus a company providing data in both 1974 and 1976 is shown in the table as 1975, whilst one providing data for both 1976 and 1978 is shown as 1977. Comparing the two tables it is clear that allowing for births and deaths leaves the overall derived financial structure essentially unaltered, except that only five factors are now directly interpretable and a slightly lower percentage of the information contained in the raw data is explained by the derived factors. Whilst both of these differences are to be expected, given the structures of the two data sets, the high stability shown by the factors in Table 8.3 is more surprising and difficult to explain.

Although the derived financial structures are similar for the two data sets, the two starred ratio sets only include four common ratios (V3, V1 or V27, V9, V25) and it is an empirical question whether differences in the final ratio set are material. This will shortly be resolved when the two data sets are used separately to predict failure/non-failure via a logit model.

Whilst it is possible to compare the financial structures of the two data sets it is not possible to compare their financial trends and company participation in the financial trends. To derive a trend, time-series data are needed for each company and this prevents the derived financial trends and differential factor analysis for the 'birth and death' data set differing from those of the 'continuous' data set. Thus, the analysis of trends and participation in trends is restricted to the 'continuous' data set.

Differential factor analysis, as discussed by Pinches, Mingo and Caruthers, was conducted by taking the difference in value

277

Table 8.3: Financial ratios and factor loadings for single-plant independent manufacturing firms which had data for at least two consecutive years for 1974, 1976, 1978 and 1980

Ratio number	Ratio name	Factor loading		
		1975	1977	1979
Factor 1 — Return on Investments				
V3 *	Net Profit/Total Assets	.95	.95	.94
V6	Net Profit/Current Liabilities	.80	.83	.48
V10	Pre-tax Profit + Depreciation/Total Assets	.89	.90	.88
V13	Pre-tax Profit/Total Assets	.85	.89	.90
V14	Net Profit + Depreciation/Total Assets	.94	.94	.92
V15	Net Profit + Interest/Total Assets	.94	.93	.93
Factor 2 — Liquidity				
V1 *	Current Assets/Current Liabilities	.96	.94	.05
V2	Current Assets — Stock/Current Liabilities	.90	.87	.06
V8	Current Assets — Current Liabilities/Total Assets	.79	.80	.17
V18	Current Liabilities/Total Assets	−.82	−.79	−.26
V26 *	Current Assets — Current Liabilities/ Current Liabilities	.96	.94	.05
Factor 3 — Solvency				
V4	Total Debt/Net Worth	−.72	−.80	−.16
V21	Net Profit/Net Worth	.93	.96	.06
V25	Pre-tax Profit/Net Worth	.96	.95	.05
Factor 4 — Asset Structure				
V7	Fixed Assets/Total Assets	−.90	−.87	−.94
V17 *	Current Assets/Total Assets	.92	.88	.94
V19	Current Assets — Stock/Total Assets	.72	.74	.49
Factor 5 — Debt Coverage				
V9 *	Pre-tax Profit + Depreciation/Total Debt	.93	.95	.99
V11	Pre-tax Profit before Directors' Fees + Interest/Total Debt	.89	.35	.98
V29	Net Profit + Interest/Total Debt	.81	.93	.98
Factor 6				
V20	Current Assets — Current Liabilities/Fixed Assets	.87	.82	−.12
V22 *	Net Profit/Fixed Assets	.86	.81	−.01
Factor 7				
V11	Pre-tax Profit before Directors' Fees + Interest/Total Debt	.02	.70	.07
V12 *	Pre-tax Profit before Directors' Fees + Interest/Total Assets	.04	.74	.68
V19	Current Assets — Stock/Total Assets	.14	.10	.74
V24	Net Profit/(Current Assets — Current Liabilities)	.76	−.10	−.02
Factor 8				
V16	Total Debt — Bank Overdraft/Total Assets	−.21	.75	.18
V24 *	Net Profit/(Current Assets — Current Liabilities)	.12	.46	.91
	Percent of variance explained by the 8 factors	85.4	83.7	88.3
	Cases for each year	206	236	212

Note: * indicates ratio which has highest overall loading with a given factor.
Ratio List, therefore, equals V3, V1 or V26, V25, V17, V9, V22, V12, V24

278

between 1974 and 1980 for each ratio for each company and then factor analysing the resulting difference ratio set. The number and type of factors were equivalent to those presented in Table 8.2. Every ratio listed under each factor in the table and those that had a higher differential factor loading were included to form a new financial structure matrix. For the ratios listed the raw mean values for 1974 + 1976 = 1975, 1976 + 1978 = 1977, 1978 + 1980 = 1979 were derived and t-tests conducted to see if there were any significant differences between the values for 1975 and 1979.

An analysis of Table 8.4 shows that the Return on Investment factor was essentially stable over the mid to late seventies and the majority of firms shared in the stability. The one exception to this conclusion is the decline shown by Pre-Tax Profit/Total Assets. This points to the overall conclusion that small companies seem to have suffered slightly declining profitability ratios over the late seventies. A similar overall conclusion may be drawn for the liquidity factor (although factor loadings over the period showed some instability) with the proviso that fewer companies in total seem to have shared the same experience. The other factors apart from asset structure, also showed stability. With factor 8 most of the companies seem to have been part of the stability, as shown by the high differential factor loading coefficients. Whereas, with factor 7 fewer companies experienced stability, as the differing trends of the various firms have counterbalanced each other to give an overall picture of stability. One of the most striking results shown in Table 8.4 is the relative increase in fixed assets and the relative decrease in current assets over the mid-seventies. From the differential factor loadings it is clear that many companies had varying movements around the trend and it is difficult to think of an explanation for this trend and the 'noise' surrounding it.

Overall these results demonstrate that classification of ratios can be empirically determined and that such classifications are 'reasonably' stable over the period. It also shows that whilst analysis of continuing, as opposed to 'birth and death', company data does not lead to very different factors, the derived ratio sets can differ. We now turn to the question of whether the different derived ratio sets give different results for the prediction of failure/non-failure.

Table 8.4: Differential factor analysis and means

	Differential factor loading	1975	1977	1979
Factor 1 — Return on Investment				
V3 Net Profit/Total Assets	.96	.046	.048	.040
V6 Net Profit/Current Liabilities	.87	.138	.135	.127
V10 Pre-tax Profit + Depreciation/				
Total Assets	.90	.110	.112	.093
V13 * Pre-tax Profit/Total Assets	.89	.065	.067	.045
V14 Net Profit + Depreciation/				
Total Assets	.95	.091	.093	.088
V15 Net Profit + Interest/Total Assets	.96	.062	.064	.061
V22 Net Profit/Fixed Assets	.81	.211	.209	.185
Factor 2 — Liquidity				
V1 Current Assets/Current Liabilities	.63	1.675	1.642	1.614
V2 * Current Assets — Stock/				
Current Liabilities	.62	1.136	1.063	1.023
V8 Current Assets — Current Liabilities/				
Total Assets	.61	.183	.182	.175
V18 Current Liabilities/Total Assets	−.33	.472	.459	.458
V26 Current Assets — Current Liabilities/				
Current Liabilities	.63	.675	.642	.614
Factor 3 — Solvency				
V4 Total Debt/Net Worth	−.67	1.597	0.959	1.038
V21 Net Profit/Net Worth	.67	−.050	.138	−.047
V23 Fixed Assets/Net Worth	−.66	2.520	1.448	1.445
V25 Pre-tax Profit/Net Worth	.64	−.058	.277	−.017
V27 Net Profit + Interest/Net Worth	.62	.092	.227	.075
Factor 4 — Asset Structure				
V7 * Fixed Assets/Total Assets	−.38	0.336	.350	.357
V17 * Current Assets/Total Assets	.40	0.654	.640	.632
V19 ** Current Assets — Stock/Total Assets	.41	.430	.408	.394
Factor 5 — Debt Coverage				
V9 Pre-tax Profit + Depreciation/				
Total Debt	.62	1.840	1.995	2.181
V11 Pre-tax Profit before Directors' Fees				
+ Interest/Total Debt	.65	4.037	3.561	3.522
V29 Net Profit + Interest/Total Debt	.51	0.874	1.084	1.289
Factor 6 — Gearing				
V5 Total Debt/Total Assets	.43	.197	.198	.205
V16 Total Debt — Bank Overdraft/				
Total Assets	.58	.074	.072	.071
Factor 7				
V12 ** Pre-tax Profit before Directors' Fees				
+ Interest/Total Assets	.06	.238	.224	.203
V19 ** Current Assets — Stock/Total Assets	.10	.430	.408	.394
V20 Current Assets — Current Liabilities/				
Fixed Assets	.34	1.155	1.181	1.127
Factor 8				
V24 Net Profit/(Current Assets —				
Current Liabilities)	.96	−.366	.351	.149

Notes: * — significant difference at 95% two-tailed t-test for 115 degrees of freedom for 1975 and 1979 means.
** — significant difference at 99% two-tailed t-test for 115 degrees of freedom for 1975 and 1979 means.

PROBIT AND LOGIT MODELS

Chapter 7 noted that the major problem with using multiple discriminant analysis (MDA) for predicting company failure was that it does not explicitly identify the predictive power of individual variables. MDA is primarily designed to provide a failure/non-failure prediction, rather than estimating the probability of failure/non-failure. These problems are overcome by using conditional probability models. The above section derived financial structures via factor analysis and so this section will provide a brief, mainly non-technical exposition of conditional probability models, followed by a review of two US studies and one UK study which have used conditional probability models to analyse/predict large company failure. Finally the results of applying a logit model of failure to our small manufacturing company data base will be presented.

Conditional probability models are used to estimate a relationship between a set of attributes describing an entity and the probability that the entity will be in a given final state. The simplest form of probability model to describe initially is the linear probability model with a single explanatory variable:

$$Y_i = \alpha + BX_i + E_i \ldots \tag{8.1}$$

(Where X_i = value of attribute-ratio for company i)

$Y_i = 1$ — if company fails

    0 — if company does not fail

E_i = independently distributed random variable with 0 mean — assume X_i is fixed or, if random, is independent of E_i

The interpretation of equation 8.1 as a linear probability model comes about when the expected value of each dependent variable observation Y_i is taken.

$$E(Y_i) = \alpha + BX_i \ldots \tag{8.2}$$

Since Y_i can take on only two values, 1 and 0, the probability distribution of Y_i can be described by letting $P_i = \text{Prob}(Y_i = 1)$ and $1 - P_i = \text{Prob}(Y_i = 0)$. Then $E(Y_i) = 1(P_i) + 0(1 - P_i) = P_i$.

281

Thus, the regression equation can be interpreted as describing the probability that an entity will end up in a given state, given information about the entity's attributes.

Whilst the linear probability model has a simplistic appeal it also has a number of problems. First, the error term is heteroscedastic and although this does not lead to biased or inconsistent parameter estimates, the estimates will be inefficient. Utilising a weighted least squares technique to correct for the heteroscedasticity is not ideal because the predicted probabilities could lie outside the 0 to 1 range and the technique is sensitive to specification error.

The difficulties associated with the linear probability model indicate the need for alternative model specifications. Since the most disturbing problem with the technique is the possibility of predicted values outside the 0 to 1 range, it is natural to use alternative techniques for which all predictions must lie within this range. Since the major concern of the analysis is to interpret the 'dependent' variable as the prior probability of an entity ending up in a given final state, it seems natural to use some notion of probability as the basis of the transformation. The process of transformation should, therefore, translate the values of the attribute X, which may range in value over the entire real line, to a probability which lies in the interval (0,1).

The transformation should also have the property of monotonicity — these properties suggest the use of cumulative probability functions. The resulting probability distribution can be represented as equation 8.3.

$$P_i = F(\alpha + BX_i) = F(Z_i) \dots \tag{8.3}$$

Where F is the cumulative probability function and X is stochastic. Whilst there are a number of possible cumulative probability distributions which could be used, attention will be restricted to the normal and logistic.

The probit probability model is associated with the cumulative normal probability function. Let Y represent a dummy variable equal to unity when a company fails and 0 when it does not fail. Further assume that for each company Z_i^* represents the critical cutoff value which translates the underlying attribute into a final end state. Specifically,

Company fails if $Z_i > Z_i^*$
Company does not fail if $Z_i \leqslant Z_i^*$

The probit model assumes that Z_i is a normally distributed random variable, so that the probability that Z_i is less than (or equal to) Z_i^* can be computed from the cumulative normal probability function

$$P_i = F(Z_i) = \frac{1}{\sqrt{2\pi}} \int_{-\infty}^{Z_i} e^{\frac{-s^2}{2}} ds \tag{8.4}$$

where s is a random variable which is normally distributed with mean zero and unit variance.

To obtain an estimate of the index Z_i apply the inverse of the cumulative normal function to equation 8.4.

$$Z_i = F^{-1}(P_i) = \alpha + BX_i \ldots \tag{8.5}$$

It is possible to interpret the probability P_i resulting from the probit model as equivalent to the probability that a standard normal variance will be less than or equal to $\alpha + BX_i$.

An alternative to the probit model, and one often used because of computational savings, is the logit model. The logit model is based on the cumulative logistic probability function and is as follows:

$$P_i = F(Z_i) = F(\alpha + BX) = \frac{1}{1 + e^{-Z_i}} = \frac{1}{1 + e^{-(\alpha \; | \; DX_i)}}$$

where: e = the base of natural logarithms
P_i = probability of a firm failing
X_i = firm's attributes

As with the probit model the above is estimated using maximum likelihood techniques.

It should now be clear that if the decision maker requires

283

only the dichotomous classification of failing or non-failing, then MDA may be adequate. An estimate of financial risk may be helpful, however, because the user is able to alter his decision variable to suit the degree of risk. Martin (1977) suggests that cumulative probability models provide significantly better probability estimates, in terms of classification accuracy, than either linear or quadratic discriminant functions.

PROBIT AND LOGIT MODELS OF COMPANY FAILURE PREDICTION

The only major British model where a linear probability regression model was used was constructed by the Bank of England. Its purpose was to develop a working predictive model, to evaluate empirically earlier company failure prediction models and to incorporate funds' flow variables into the analysis. The model is described in Earl and Marais (1979) and the Bank's experience with the model is described in the Bank of England Quarterly Bulletin (1982).

The sample used was 38 quoted companies drawn from the manufacturing and distribution sectors which failed between 1974-77, which were compared with 53 non-failed companies randomly selected from the Datastream sample of the top 1,000 UK industrial companies for the period 1973-77. Forty-seven conventional ratios, and 12 constructed from the sources and uses of funds statement, were used in a linear probability regressive model (multiple regression analysis with a 0-1 dependent variable).

On reclassifying the original sample the model achieved a 92 per cent overall success rate one year prior to failure. Realising the potentially spurious nature of the results Earl and Marais tested the model on a hold-out sample of 10 industrial failures in 1978 and 19 non-failed companies including a number known to be having problems; the overall success rate for correct classification was reduced to approximately 62 per cent.

This model highlights both the importance of using hold-out samples and that linear probability models are imperfect for two reasons. First, because the probability estimates are not constrained to the 0-1 interval, it is possible to achieve the ludicrous result of a company having a negative or greater than one probability of failure; second, although the coefficient estimates are not biased they are not efficient and this is why it is preferable to use either a probit or logit model.

The major US studies using logistic models are by Ohlson (1980) and Zavgren (1983, 1985). Ohlson's sample included US companies, selected from the Wall Street Journal Index, failing between 1970 and 1976. Companies which did not report statements for the entire sample period were eliminated, leaving a sample of 105 failed companies. In the non-failed sample, each of 2,058 non-failed companies contributed one year of data used to derive the logistic function.

Ohlson did not use theory or a dimension reduction technique to limit his variable list. His list of nine variables was chosen on the basis of 'simplicity' (Ohlson p.118), but this may have caused problems for his analysis. For example, a number of. his ratios used total assets in either the denominator or numerator, thus possibly causing a problem of spurious multi-collinearity with its concomitant problems of interpreting the significance of individual variables.

Three models were estimated by Ohlson: the first to predict failure within one year, the second to predict failure within two years if the firm did not fail in the first year, and the third to predict failure in one or two years. Classification errors were assessed using the same set of data from which the models were estimated rather than undertaking any hold-out tests. Ohlson justified this testing on the grounds that the sample size was large and this would reduce bias.

The misclassification rates for the first model were 17.4 per cent for the non-failed companies and 12.4 per cent for the failed companies in the year prior to the failure date, which are somewhat higher than those achieved by discriminant analysis studies.

Ohlson also discussed the importance of accounts submission lags and found that they could be quite considerable for companies showing high probabilities of failure (up to 13 months) and that the lags can increase as failure approaches, a point which we develop in the next chapter.

A recent study by Zavgren (1985) attempts to derive a model of corporate failure which utilises a dimension reduced data set, logistic analysis and an evaluation of the information content of the different functions prior to failure. The companies included in the sample were selected from those on the

Compustat New York Stock Exchange Over-the-Counter and Research tapes. Forty-five failed companies were matched with 45 healthy companies on the basis of four digit industry code and asset size. The variables used in the analysis were those derived by Pinches *et al.* (1973, 1975) factor analysis.

Utilising a logit model, the minimum total classification error rates for the original derivative sample were: 18% —one year prior, 17% — two years prior, 28% — three years prior, 27% — four years prior and 20% — five years prior. For a hold-out sample of 16 companies which failed in 1979-1980 matched with non-failed companies, the various models for the one to five years prior achieved an average error rate of 31 per cent.

One interesting aspect of the Zavgren study is that she looks at the information content of the different year prior models by using information theoretic measures. She found the amount of information increases over the five-year period to failure by an average 18 per cent for failed companies and 16 per cent for non-failed. However, it needs to be noted that the sample selection procedure included only companies which had complete and up-to-date information.

One of the benefits of conditional probability models is that they allow an interpretation of the significance of individual variable coefficients and Zavgren found the acid test ratio to be important for short-term prediction of failure, and efficiency ratios such as the asset turnover, receivables turnover and inventory turnover to be important for longer-term predictions.

PREDICTING UK SMALL COMPANY FAILURE: LOGISTIC RESULTS

Earlier in this chapter we derived the major financial factors of two sets of companies, one of which provided data over a seven-year period (termed complete) and one which provided data only over a three-year period (termed incomplete). For each of the factors the ratio which loaded highest (the most correlated) will be a variable in the following logistic functions. On the basis of the variable sets used, each of the logistic functions (complete and incomplete) should capture most of the financial characteristics of small companies with each of the variables having the maximum chance of independence. The overall variable set, inclusive of both 'complete' and 'incomplete', is listed in Table 8.5.

For each variable set (complete and incomplete) a logistic function was estimated on a sample of 500 companies for each of the five years prior to failure. The 'complete' function results will be discussed first.

The results presented in Table 8.6 show that each of the year-prior functions is at least significant at the 95 per cent level[2]. However, whilst the overall functions are significant, only one or two variables, apart from the constant, from each function are significantly[3] different from zero. In the three-to five-year prior functions the significant variables capture notions of liquidity and asset structure, whereas the two-year prior function replaces the liquidity variable with a profitability variable and the one-year prior function has only a capital gearing ratio as significant. Given the familiar data problems in constructing a one-and two-year prior model it would be unwise to draw any strong inferences from these models. The three-to five-year prior functions suggest that companies are more likely to fail if they have a low level of liquidity and low levels of fixed assets.

Table 8.7 presents the 'prediction' results of the reclassification of the original sample using the functions depicted in Table 8.6. Since no end-user was specified, the 'cut-off' probability for deciding whether or not a company had failed was that which minimised the overall error. Since non-failed companies outnumber failed companies, this means the errors for non-failed companies are biased downwards and those for

Table 8.5: Variables used in the logistic analysis

V1	= Current Assets/Current Liabilities
V3	= Net Profit/Total Assets
V7	= Fixed Assets/Total Assets
V9	= Pre-tax Profit + Depreciation/Total Debt
V12	= Pre-tax Profit before Directors' Fees + Interest/Total Assets
V16	= Total Debt (excludes bank overdraft)/Total Assets
V17	= Current Assets/Total Assets
V19	= Current Assets − Stock/Total Assets
V23	= Net Profit/Fixed Assets
V24	= Fixed Assets/Net Worth
V25	= Net Profit/Current Assets — Current Liabilities
V26	= Pre-tax Profit/Net Worth

Table 8.6: Probability of non-failure: logit function for complete data/basic ratios

	V3	V1	V24	V7	V9	V16	V19	V25	Constant
Coefficient 1 year prior	2.243	−.254	−.038*	−.041	.291	−1.70	−.873	−.012	−3.046*
Standard error	1.285	.153	.017	1.611	.246	1.649	1.482	.045	1.285
Coefficient 2 years prior	2.364*	.170	−.001	1.691*	.208	−.217	−.552	.104	−.353
Standard error	1.00	.183	.010	.823	.114	1.165	.700	.070	.582
Coefficient 3 years prior	.890	.442*	.002	2.366*	.106	−.353	.679	−.011	.933*
Standard error	.516	.185	.012	.605	.063	1.183	.542	.024	.446
Coefficient 4 years prior	.873	.538*	−.020	2.104*	.031	−1.269	.170	.013	.848
Standard error	.495	.185	.011	.592	.025	.905	.536	−.012	.443
Coefficient 5 years prior	.270	.357*	.011	1.212*	.026	.403	.684	.042	.866*
Standard error	.494	.140	.015	.560	.021	.966	.511	.040	.423

Note:
a. Significance level of overall function via log (likelihood): Year 1 — 19.334
Year 2 — 41.889
Year 3 — 43.199
Year 4 — 48.901
Year 5 — 22.093

With 8 degrees of freedom the Chi-squared values are: χ^2 95%   99%   99.5%
15.51   20.09   21.96

failed companies are biased upwards. The reclassification results presented in columns one to three of Table 8.7 show that somewhat better classification rates have been achieved than those obtained in the large firm studies. However, the results are no better than those achieved by using MDA upon the same sample of small companies. In fact, MDA achieved similar overall classificatory success but with a far more equal mix of Type I and Type II errors.

Columns four to six of Table 8.7 present the preferred cross-sectional hold-out results for a total sample of 150 companies, using the cut-of probability chosen in the reclassification analysis. The results compare favourably with the reclassification results and are even slightly better, overall, than those achieved by MDA.

Table 8.7: Validation results for complete data/basic ratios

	Percentages of companies correctly classified/predicted											
	Reclassification of original sample			Prediction on cross-sectional hold-out sample			Prediction on future-dated hold-out sample			Robustness tests		
	F	NF	Overall	F	NF	Overall	F	NF	Overall	F	NF	Overall
One year prior	100	93	94	100	100	100	0	93	91	0	100	50
Two years prior	28	97	88	71	84	83	43	83	82	33	83	58
Three years prior	41	92	81	19	83	72	29	88	87	33	100	67
Four years prior	13	97	73	7	97	81	0	100	97	0	100	58
Five years prior	7	100	69	0	95	75						

However the criterion for the choice of 'cut-off' probability leads to high Type II errors (failures classified as non-failures).

The results in columns seven to nine are a surrogate for future-dated hold-out tests. The 1-5 year functions derived and presented in Table 8.5 were applied to 1978, 1977, 1976 and 1975 data, respectively, and used to predict whether companies would be failures/non-failures in 1979. Thus, although the functions were derived by pooling, data used to form the predictions were for years prior to the predicted event. The results are encouraging since, overall, they are no worse than those achieved in the cross-sectional and reclassification tests, and somewhat better than those achieved by MDA. The robustness of the functions was further checked by selecting ten companies which failed in 1979 and ten companies which were non-failed in 1979. The one-year-prior function was applied to 1976 data, the three-year-prior function to 1978 data, the four-year-prior function to 1977 and the two-year-prior function to 1975 data. Although the initial sample was matched, the final sample for each year may not have been because of missing data. The results presented in the final three columns of Table 8.7 show that knowing the date of failure, and which function to apply to a given year of data, are critical to achieving good 'prediction' results. However, the logit results show above average success and are better than those achieved by MDA. The use of a logistic function thus seems to offer a promising method of predicting small company failure.

The variable set used to form the above logistic functions was factor analysed from companies which had complete data for seven years, but this excludes short-life companies and those which, for some reason other than failure, did not provide data for all years. Table 8.8 provides logit coefficients on the factor-analysed ratio set for all companies including those providing incomplete records. The functions have similar levels of overall significance as those for the 'complete' functions. Furthermore, for the two, three and four-year-prior functions the same 'types' of variables are significant; namely, liquidity and asset structure variables. For the one-year-prior to failure function there are no significant variables and for the five-year-prior model a liquidity and return on capital variable are significant. This supports the results in Chapter 6 where univariate analysis showed that low levels of profitability were a good long-term indicator of failure. In other words, the significant variables for

Table 8.8: Probability of non-failure: logit function for incomplete data/basic ratios

	V3	V1	V26	V17	V9	V23	V12	V25	Constant
Coefficient 1 year prior	.952	−.137	−.207	2.219	.269	.295	−.958	−.011	−1.300
Standard error	2.260	.207	.188	1.488	.338	.232	.534	.056	.838
Coefficient 2 years prior	2.984*	.141	−.007	−1.923*	.227	−.086	−.459	.095	−2.076*
Standard error	1.254	.181	.036	.724	.116	.133	.302	.071	.553
Coefficient 3 years prior	.974	.427*	−.004	−1.860*	.113	.003	−.078	−.012	−1.397*
Standard error	.674	.191	.033	.517	.065	.057	.371	.023	.380
Coefficient 4 years prior	1.047	.595*	.043	−1.727*	.034	−.041	.022	.012	−.839*
Standard error	.565	.193	.046	.498	.026	.038	.299	.012	.326
Coefficient 5 years prior	−.123	.320*	.140*	−.799*	.031	.015	.526	.057	.314
Standard error	.633	.140	.061	.448	.022	.118	.392	.041	.290

Note:
a. Significance level of overall function via log (likelihood): Year 1 = 19.968
Year 2 = 42.617
Year 3 = 39.565
Year 4 = 46.294
Year 5 = 26.469
With 8 degrees of freedom the Chi-squared values are: χ^2 95%   99%   99.5%
15.51 20.09 21.96

Table 8.9: Validation results for incomplete data/basic ratios

	Percentages of companies correctly classified/predicted										
	Reclassification of original sample			Prediction on cross-sectional hold-out sample			Prediction on future-dated hold-out sample			Robustness tests		
	F	NF	Overall	F	NF	Overall	F	NF	Overall	F	NF	Overall
One year prior	33	100	98	100	82	83	29	99	98	29	100	64
Two years prior	0	100	86	0	100	93	0	100	98	0	100	50
Three years prior	0	100	80	0	100	83	0	100	98	0	100	50
Four years prior	54	83	74	0	100	83	29	84	82	20	100	67
Five years prior	16	93	69	7	95	76						

the two sets of functions are not dissimilar. Table 8.9 shows the overall prediction results of the 'incomplete' functions are marginally better and more consistent than those of the 'complete' functions but the mixes of Type I and Type II are more unequal. Surprisingly, these adjustments have not led to an unambiguous improvement in the prediction of small company performance.

The previous chapter on MDA concluded that 'summary' measures capturing several years of financial information could improve the predictive power of discriminant functions. A number of alternatives were tried for both the 'complete' and 'incomplete' variable sets one, two and three years prior. Tables 8.10 and 8.11 present the 'best' functions in terms of overall predictive accuracy. For the complete data set, Table 8.10 shows that asset structure remains significant whilst the standard deviation of the liquidity variable (as defined in Chapter 7), replaces liquidity as the other significant variable in the three-year-prior function.

One danger of including summary measures is the increased possibility of multicollinearity leading to unstable parameter estimates. This is illustrated in the one-year-prior model where, once summary measures are included, no single variable is significant despite the overall significance of the function.

Similar findings were obtained from including companies with 'incomplete' data, as shown in Table 8.11, except that here a summary measure is significant only for the three-year-prior function. Reclassification and cross-sectional hold-out results only are presented for the functions shown in Tables 8.10 and

Table 8.10: Probability of non-failure: logit function for complete data/basic ratios, stability, trends

	V3	V1	V24	V7	V9	V16	V19	V25	Standard deviation of V3	Standard deviation of V1	Trend for V16	Constant
Coefficient 1 year prior	−3.704	5.014	.175	6.096	−.019	−7.528	−.018	.016	−2.101	−4.798	−.218	2.322
Standard error	2.355	3.096	.169	4.121	.092	4.242	2.912	.160	1.966	4.292	.194	3.115
Coefficient 2 years prior	2.634	.690	−.001	4.196*	.454	.887	.299	.041	.643	−3.258*	−.018	1.228
Standard error	1.950	.470	.090	1.217	.353	1.831	.950	.097	.891	1.446	.046	.882
Coefficient 3 years prior	.792	.446	.005	2.640*	.028	.864	.784	−.082	.047	−2.177*	−.067	.778
Standard error	.843	.250	.013	.860	.067	1.708	.682	−.060	.189	.936	.040	.614

Note:
a. Significance level of overall function via log (likelihood): Year 1 = 26.934
Year 2 = 71.595
Year 3 = 43.047

With 11 degrees of freedom the Chi-squared values are:

	95%	99%	99.5%
χ^2	19.68	24.73	26.76

Table 8.11: Probability of non-failure: logit function for incomplete data/basic ratios, stability, trends

	V3	V1	V26	V17	V9	V23	V12	V25	Standard deviation of V3	Standard deviation of V2	Trend for V9	Constant
Coefficient 1 year prior	−3.479	2.093	.017	−.971	.008	.425	−.710	−.002	−.902	−6.722	−.109	−2.432
Standard error	2.744	1.966	.227	2.484	.086	.323	.838	.081	1.667	4.570	.140	2.154
Coefficient 2 years prior	4.578	.809	−.033	−4.644*	.573	−.194	−.686	.021	.759	−1.372	−.012	−3.179*
Standard error	2.656	.509	.042	1.307	.410	.196	.754	.078	.929	1.989	.045	.967
Coefficient 3 years prior	.519	.374	.046	−1.927*	.208	.097	−.035	−.077	.056	−1.996	−.076*	−1.831*
Standar error	1.340	.257	.070	.745	.067	.144	.473	.057	.256	1.160	.038	.531

Note:
a. Significance level of overall function via log (likelihood): Year 1 — 20.408
Year 2 — 73.807
Year 3 — 39.724

With 11 degrees of freedom the Chi-squared values are:

χ^2 95% 99% 99.5%
19.68 24.73 26.76

Table 8.12: Validation results for basic ratios, trends and stability measures

	Percentages of companies correctly classified/predicted											
	Reclassification of original sample			Prediction on cross-sectional hold-out sample			Reclassification of original sample			Prediction on cross-sectional hold-out sample		
	F	NF	Overall	F	NF	Overall	F	NF	Overall	F	NF	Overall
One year prior	21	98	82	0	94	92	0	100	80	0	100	97
Two years prior	35	98	89	25	95	91	0	100	85	0	100	94
Three years prior	0	100	98	0	100	82	0	100	98	0	100	82

8.11 because the other forms of test gave essentially the same general picture. Table 8.12 shows the overall results for the 'complete' and 'incomplete' functions are similar, although the 'incomplete' functions gave a more unequal mix of Type I and Type II errors. The criteria for the choice of a cut-off probability were the same as in Tables 8.7 and 8.9. For the 'complete' data functions the addition of summary measures generally improves both overall reclassification and cross-sectional hold-out results. For the 'incomplete' functions the use of summary measures means the reclassification results are essentially unchanged whereas the cross-sectional hold-out results are slightly improved. It therefore appears that the inclusion of summary measures marginally improves the success rate of logit functions in predicting small company performance.

Finally, an age variable was added to the above sets of functions but it was neither individually significant nor did it improve the overall significance of the functions or the classificatory/predictive success of the functions, and so the results are not shown.

CONCLUSIONS

This chapter has reviewed those studies which have used factor, probit and logit for predicting corporate failure amongst large companies. It has also applied these techniques to a study of corporate failure amongst small businesses in order to determine whether this provides any additional dimension of understanding to that provided either by univariate analysis or by MDA.

In these matters it confirms the results of the large firm studies which indicate that the use of logit methods does not bring significantly greater overall predictive power than the use of MDA. Their advantage lies with a greater ability to isolate groups of variables which are associated with failure and non-failure.

Using our logit models both for complete information companies and incomplete information companies, liquidity measures consistently appear in the models. This contrasts with the results obtained from the univariate analysis which suggested that liquidity was a relatively poor discriminator. The incomplete information models, however, also suggested that profitability was a good long-term indicator of failure, and this result was also obtained in the univariate analysis.

NOTES

1. 'A loading of .70 was chosen since the square of this times 100 equals approximately 50%. Variables with less than 50% common variation with the rotated factor pattern were considered too weak to report.' (Pinches, Mingo and Caruthers, 1973, p.390.)

2. Under maximum likelihood estimation the significance of individual variables can be determined via asymptotic t-values. A good approximation, and the one used in this study, to a 95% level of significance is if a variable coefficient is twice that of its standard error.

3. The overall significance of a function under maximum likelihood estimation is usually determined by a variant of the likelihood ratio tests. These are calculated as follows: suppose we impose g restrictions on the k-elements of the parameter vector $= 0$ (set some elements to zero). Let $\ln L\ (\hat{\theta})$ be the sample log-likelihood computed from the unrestricted maximum likelihood parameter vector. Let $\ln L\ (\theta^*)$ be the sample log-likelihood computed when the g restrictions are imposed in estimating maximum likelihood estimators. Then the statistics

$$-2 \ln [L\ (\theta^*)/L(\hat{\theta})] = -2 [\ln L(\hat{\theta}) - \ln (\theta^*)] \sim \chi^2\ (g)$$

is asymptotically distributed as a Chi-square with g degrees of freedom.

9

Qualitative Information and the Prediction of Small Company Failure

INTRODUCTION

Previous chapters, with the exception of Chapter 3, have relied solely upon financial ratios in order to construct a failure prediction model. Some success at predicting the failure of small companies has been achieved utilising this method. However, sole reliance upon accounting information has theoretical and practical limitations (especially in relation to the financial statements of small companies) which in turn raises questions concerning its reliability as a practical decision aid.

As we have noted, the lack of a clearly defined theory linking corporate failure to accounting variables creates the problem that the potential number of accounting ratios which could be included in a prediction model is immense. Without a theory to determine which explanatory variables to include, the researcher has to employ statistical search procedures. Whilst being able to determine which variables in the specific sample most adequately discriminate between failed and non-failed companies, such a routine does not ensure that these explanatory variables will be equally valid for other samples.

Further conceptual problems arise because corporate failure may be the culmination of an extended period of declining economic performance. The symptoms of this decline, as reflected in the financial variables, may differ depending upon the point in the failure process that the company has reached. Thus, the resulting discriminant functions for the various years prior to failure often contain different variables and/or coefficients. In consequence, they may produce conflicting results with hold-out samples and there is no guarantee that, say, a three-year-prior function will adequately model companies only one year away from failure. To be of maximum practical use these models presuppose that the decision-maker knows how many years prior to failure the companies actually are. Yet if the decision maker already knows this, he would have no need of a failure prediction model!

The financial accounts of small companies present a number of additional practical problems which limit their use as explanatory variables. Two major problems relate firstly to the lack of independent confirmation of the figures presented in the accounts owing to the lack of a system of internal control inherent in small companies and secondly to the time lag between the accounting year end and the actual drawing-up and submission of the accounts to Companies House. These issues and the associated empirical evidence were examined in some detail in Chapter 3 of the present work. The role of information on reporting lags and its incorporation into a failure prediction model are discussed in the following section.

A third and very serious problem is that since the introduction of the UK 1981 Companies Act, this information source is generally no longer publicly available. One of the provisions of the Act is a reporting concession which allows small companies to submit only an 'abridged' set of accounts to Companies House. These abridged accounts consist of only a highly aggregated balance sheet and accompanying notes which are of limited analytic value. Thus, a failure prediction model which incorporates financial variables whose components are not included in the new aggregated balance sheet will be of little practical use, unless the user is able to obtain access to the full set of accounts which still have to be produced for the company's shareholders.

In the absence of financial information from which to construct ratios, other sources of information will need to be utilised in order to assess risk and the likelihood of company failure. An empirical investigation into the usefulness of these alternative or 'qualitative' sources of information as a means by which to predict company failure was begun in Chapter 3. In this chapter that work is extended and linked to the type of financial ratio analysis described in previous chapters. This 'qualitative' analysis broadly encompasses the following areas:

(a) the characteristics of and changes in the ownership and management structure;
(b) the financial reporting submission lags;
(c) the incidence of audit qualifications and changes in auditors;
(d) the existence of loans secured on the company's assets.

The chapter is subdivided as follows. The next section reviews the previous research, which includes the univariate analyses already presented in Chapter 3. This provides the framework within which to discuss a range of possible qualitative explanatory variables and the reasons why they may be useful in the prediction of small company failure. Following that is a summary of the research method to be used. The empirical results are given in the third section and some concluding remarks are presented in the last.

PREVIOUS RESEARCH ON QUALITATIVE INFORMATION AND COMPANY PERFORMANCE

Most studies concerned with aspects of company performance have generally relied solely upon financial ratios, not merely to provide measures or indicators of performance, but also as predictors of the future performance of the companies studied. This is understandable in terms of data availability, costs, objectivity and previous empirical success. However, Argenti (1976) argues that, in terms of understanding and underlying causes of failure, financial ratios are generally of limited use. In order to direct the search for possible qualitative explanatory variables we undertake a brief review of Argenti's model.

Argenti argues that financial ratios, whilst often being a suitable tool for highlighting some of the associated symptoms, are unable to yield insights into the causes of business failure. This is because financial ratios are merely symptoms of the underlying failure process. Furthermore, financial ratios are likely to become less reliable as failure approaches because of 'creative accounting' practices used by the failing company's management who attempt to hide the poor financial condition of the company from outside investors and creditors. This form of manipulation of the accounts is likely to be a particularly acute

298

problem in respect of the small company sector because of the close day-to-day involvement in the running of the business by its shareholders/directors.

These considerations led Argenti to produce a dynamic model of business failure which did not rely upon financial ratios. He viewed failure in terms of the interaction of a number of inherent defects in the actual organisation and financial structure of the company with changes in the macro-economic environment and the occurrence of 'normal business hazards' such as strikes and the loss of a large customer. The major inherent managerial defect identified by Argenti was the 'autocrat' or 'one-man-band', where a single individual dominated the controlling board of directors and rarely heeded the advice of others. Such an autocrat would inevitably make mistakes which, because of certain financial defects such as a poor or non-existent financial information system and high gearing, would eventually weaken the company to such an extent that it could not survive normal business hazards or an economic downturn.

This framework allowed Argenti to identify three 'trajectories' or typical paths which companies experienced in the period leading up to failure. The appearance of the various symptoms, such as creative accounting, increased gearing and declining performance, and the trajectory followed by any particular company depended primarily upon its age and size. However, apart from a few case studies of large companies, such as Rolls-Royce, Argenti provided little in the way of empirical evidence to support his thesis.

This lack of empirical evidence concerning the inherent deficiencies characteristic of failing companies must place a question mark over his thesis of business failure. However, Argenti's model does provide a framework which directs the search for possible qualitative explanatory variables. In addition, his model contains a number of propositions which are in principle testable such as the presence of an autocrat controlling the company, the lack of an adequate financial information system, the manipulation of the financial accounts and high gearing levels. To test the above hypotheses empirically, adequate proxies which measure these factors in failing and healthy companies are obviously required.

To our knowledge, there has been no research concerning the hypothesised presence of an autocrat in control of failing companies. However, it seems reasonable to assume that, *ceteris paribus*, an autocratic regime will be more likely to be present in companies which have few active directors or outside shareholders. In this situation where there are few internal constraints upon managerial behaviour and limited alternative sources of power, it is easier for a charismatic individual to dominate a company. Furthermore, a company with an autocrat in control is more likely to experience a net outflow of managerial personnel as failure approaches. As the pressures and uncertainties associated with failure build up and so sour working relationships, it is to be expected that some directors will leave and it is highly unlikely that new directors will be either sought or found to replace them.

Recent research by Carsberg *et al.* (1985) has indicated that few small companies have any form of internal management accounting information beyond the most rudimentary. Furthermore, the major source of financial information on which managerial decisions are based consists of the information contained in the annual financial accounts. In this respect then, most small companies may be said to have inadequate accounting information systems as it is generally recognised that the historical cost information on which these statements are based is of limited relevance for many managerial decisions.

It is to be expected that the greater the delay between the actual drawing up of these annual accounts and the period to which they refer, the less useful they become for almost any purpose. Companies with long delays between the accounting year end and the final certification of the accounts by the auditors may be assumed to have a poor accounting information system. Indeed, the Carsberg *et al.* study found that 80 per cent of the small companies examined had their accounts prepared by their auditor and, until the final accounts were produced, the company's management had little up-to-date financial information. A long delay in the drawing up of the accounts is also likely to be indicative of a company with a poor internal system of accounting information. Whittred and Zimmer (1984) argue that the major reasons for such delays in the drawing-up of the accounts are that the company's book-keeping records are incomplete, inaccurate or inconsistent which necessitates considerable additional time spent on preparation and auditor/ client negotiation.

A study by Lawrence (1983) into the timeliness of financial

reporting and financial distress in large companies also supports the proposition that failing companies tend to take longer to produce their annual financial statements than healthy companies. However, when Whittred and Zimmer examined the ability of the audit lag to predict company failure, they found that neither alone, nor in conjunction with conventional bankruptcy prediction models, did it do so.

Argenti also suggested that failing companies would attempt to manipulate their financial statements in order to hide the state of the company from outsiders such as creditors and customers. One obvious delaying tactic to prevent outsiders discovering the truth about the company's condition which Argenti did not mention was the fact that companies may simply delay submitting their accounts to Companies House.

Empirically it has been found to be the case that failing companies take significantly longer than healthy companies to publish their accounts. For large quoted companies this is unlikely to be an important predictor of failure because of the existence and enforcement of legal and stock market regulations concerning the publication of the annual accounts. A study by Whittred (1980) into the relationship between reporting lags and share price movements indicated that excessive reporting delays are interpreted by investors as 'bad news' and the company's share price suffers a fall without the bad news actually being published. The study also found that the submission lag did not improve the ability to predict financial distress in large companies. With small unquoted companies, however, the above sanction does not exist. Consequently the practice of delaying the submission of the accounts is more widespread.

It seems likely that if, as Argenti believes, failing companies engage in 'creative accounting' in order to appear financially 'sound', the auditors of these companies, if they are truly independent, would be more likely to qualify their audit reports. Hence, failing companies would be significantly more likely to receive qualified audit reports than healthy companies.

A number of share price reaction and experimental studies have looked into the effect that qualified audit reports have upon investor's and lender's decisions, with Crasswell (1985) providing a useful recent review. However, none of these studies has addressed the issue of whether a qualified audit report may aid the prediction of failure.

Impending failure may also lead to a switching of auditors.

301

For example, reporting disputes or anticipated qualified audit reports, management changes, the size of the audit fee and 'insurance' motives may all lead to pressure to change auditors. These issues were, however, investigated by Schwartz and Menon (1985) who did not find that changes in auditors were associated with past audit qualifications or management changes. They concluded that the greater propensity of failing companies to change auditors was due to a reordering of client preferences and increasing audit fees to reflect the additional insurance costs. Their results, however, do not rule out the possibility that failing companies change auditors because of reporting disputes and anticipated audit qualifications. Furthermore, because this study was conducted on large companies which are audited by large firms of auditors it has limited relevance to the small company sector. Small companies are generally audited by small firms of auditors with, as we noted in Chapters 3 and 5, differing perceptions of what constitutes 'true and fair' reporting. Thus, if small companies are in dispute with their present auditors they may be more willing to 'shop around' to find an auditor willing to accept 'less stringent' reporting practices.

From the above review of the previous research into qualitative information, it is apparent that this is an area which has received very little attention from academic researchers. The work that has been undertaken has, once again, been exclusively concerned with large companies. Furthermore, only a small proportion of this work has concerned itself with the issue of examining the possible role of these factors for predicting and understanding company failure.

In Chapter 3, which was concerned with an examination of the ownership and management structure of small companies, tabulations were presented concerning the preparation of their accounts and their major sources of finance. The chapter also contained univariate analyses of the relative importance for failing/non-failing companies of most of the factors discussed above. To avoid the reader having to return continually to Chapter 3 we now briefly summarise its main findings.

Failing and non-failing companies differ in several important respects. Firstly, failing companies tend both to have fewer directors and to experience a net outflow of directors in the period leading up to eventual failure. Secondly, failing companies take longer than non-failing companies to submit their accounts to Companies House. Thirdly, failing companies tend to receive more audit qualifications to their last set of available accounts than non-failing companies. Finally, failing companies are more likely to have a secured loan (particularly one held by a bank) than non-failing companies.

RESEARCH METHOD AND QUALITATIVE VARIABLES

The univariate results of the publicly available qualitative information summarised above indicate that failing and non-failing companies exhibit marked differences in many respects. This supports the work of Argenti and other research in this area, even though most of it has been directed towards large companies. The remainder of this chapter tests whether these observed differences between failing and non-failing companies are substantial enough to enable an interested decision maker to discriminate adequately and reliably between financially healthy and failing companies, either alone or in conjunction with convential ratio analysis. The research design to be used is described below.

The research method utilised is logit analysis, a general description of which is found in the previous chapter. Whilst the majority of research into company failure has used discriminant analysis, its use would be inappropriate here since it assumes the variables used are multivariate normal in their distribution. This condition will not be fulfilled by the qualitative data used in this analysis because nine of these variables are dichotomous variables (taking on a value of 0 or 1 depending upon the applicability of the item for each individual company). The form of the qualitative variables suggests that logit analysis is a more appropriate estimating procedure (Lachenbruch, Sneeringer and Revo, 1983).

As in previous chapters the dependent variable to be explained is failure/non-failure. The classification of the independent variables used to produce the logit function and the models in which they appear are:

Model 1: Financial Ratios only,
Model 2: Qualitative Information only,
Model 3: Financial Ratios and Qualitative Information

The financial ratios used in models 1 and 3 consist of 28 ratios covering various aspects of company performance such as profitability, liquidity and gearing. These are listed in Table 9.1. The qualitative information used in models 2 and 3 is shown in Table 9.2 and consists of 18 items of information available from the accounts and accompanying documents filed at Companies House. Each item attempts to capture the non-financial aspects of company performance discussed earlier. In order to reduce the problems associated with multicollinearity, a stepwise exclusion technique based upon the maximum likelihood ratio was used to determine which variables should be included in the final logit function. The decision rule specified for variable exclusion was a probability of Chi-square of 0.5. This was chosen to maximise the explanatory power of the functions whilst, hopefully, minimising the problems of multicollinearity.

The matched sample of 146 companies (73 failures and 73

Table 9.1: Financial ratios used in logit analysis

R1 — Current Assets/Current Liabilities
R2 — Current Assets − Stock/Current Liabilities
R3 — Net Profit/Total Assets
R4 — Total Debt (inclusive of overdrafts)/Total Assets
R5 — Total Debt (inclusive of overdrafts)/Net Worth (Equity)
R6 — Net Profit/Current Liabilities
R7 — Fixed Assets/Total Assets
R8 — Current Assets − Current Liabilities/Total Assets
R9 — Pre-tax Profit + Depreciation/Total Debt
R10 — Pre-tax Profit + Depreciation/Total Assets
R11 — Pre-tax Profit before Directors' Fees + Interest/Total Debt
R12 — Pre-tax Profit before Directors' Fees + Interest/Total Assets
R13 — Pre-tax Profit/Total Assets
R14 — Net Profit + Depreciation/Total Assets
R15 — Net Profit + Interest/Total Assets
R16 — Total Debt (exclusive of overdrafts)/Total Assets
R17 — Current Assets/Total Assets
R18 — Current Liabilities/Total Assets
R19 — Current Assets − Stock/Total Assets
R20 — Current Assets − Current Liabilities/Fixed Assets
R21 — Net Profit/Net Worth
R22 — Net Profit/Current Assets − Current Liabilities
R23 — Fixed Assets/Net Worth
R24 — Pre-tax Profit/Net Worth
R25 — Current Assets − Current Liabilities/Current Liabilities
R26 — Net Profit + Interest/Net Worth
R27 — Net Profit + Depreciation/Net Worth
R28 — Net Profit + Interest/Total Debt

Table 9.2: Non-financial variables used in logit analysis

Q1.   Age of company (in years)
Q2.   Number of current directors
Q3.   Have there been any new directors over the 3-year period? (No — 0 Yes — 1)
Q4.   Has a director left the company over the 3-year period? (No — 0 Yes — 1)
Q5.   Number of non-director shareholders
Q6.   Has there been any new share capital introduced? (No — 0 Yes — 1)
Q7.   Has there been any change of auditors in the 3-year period?
      (No — 0 Yes — 1)
Q8.   Has the company had a qualified audit report in prior 2 years?
      (No — 0 Yes — 1)
Q9.   Has the company received a qualified audit report in current year?
      (No — 0 Yes — 1)
Q10. Has the company received a 'Going Concern' qualification?
      (No — 0 Yes — 1)
Q11. Is there a secured loan on the company's assets? (No — 0 Yes — 1)
Q12. Is there a secured loan on the company's assets held by a bank?
      (No — 0 Yes — 1)
Q13. Average audit lag (in months) over the 3-year period
Q14. Average submission lag (in months) over the 3-year period
Q15. Average lag (in months) between auditor's signature and submission
Q16. Final-year audit lag (in months)
Q17. Final-year submission lag (in months)
Q18. Final-year lag (in months) between auditor's signature and submission

non-failures) used to obtain the univariate results reported in Chapter 3 was used to obtain the initial logit functions. Information on a further 20 companies (ten failures and ten non-failures) was obtained for use in the hold-out tests but no attempt was made to incorporate the relative costs of misclassification of failed and non-failed companies.

Model 1, utilising only financial ratios, acts as a control or benchmark by which to compare Model 2 which utilises only qualitative information. This was necessary because the results presented in Chapters 6 to 8 cannot be used to make valid comparisons with the qualitative information considered here since they are based upon data taken 1,2, ... n years prior to failure. Thus, companies which did not produce accounts for the individual years prior to failure were excluded from the analysis for that particular year.

This is inappropriate for the present analysis which incorporates the effects of differing behaviour such as reporting lags. Financial and qualitative information for failed companies has been taken from the last three years of published accounts available before failure, with the last year of available accounts often being two or three years prior to eventual failure. The financial and qualitative information on these failed companies is therefore not restricted to a common period prior to failure.

Basing the predictive function upon the most recent information available for each company has a number of practical advantages. First, the decision maker is not forced to exclude companies merely because they have not submitted their latest set of accounts to Companies House. Secondly, this method produces only a single predictive function rather than a series which can contain different variables and coefficients, which may produce conflicting results and, furthermore, presupposes that the decision maker knows which function to use.

Model 3 incorporates both financial ratios and qualitative information. It is designed to test whether the two information sets working together are able to produce superior results to those obtained from either of the individual information sets. That is, irrespective of the relative predictive content of models 1 and 2, either data set may contain incremental information not present in the other. Thus, the two data sets may be complements rather than substitutes.

THE EMPIRICAL RESULTS

Table 9.3 presents the numbers and percentages of correctly classified companies for the three models from the original sample of 146 companies. The numbers and percentages of correctly classified failed and non-failed companies are shown under the columns headed F and NF respectively. The overall percentage of correctly classified companies is shown in parentheses. The classifications are based upon a cut-off probability which minimises the overall classification error rate. These cut-off probabilities are shown at the foot of Table 9.3(a). Table 9.3(b) shows the variables selected, their coefficients and standard errors and the overall significance of each of the logit functions.

Comparing the results of models 1 and 2 it is apparent that the qualitative information contained in model 2 does not succeed in correctly classifying a greater number of cases than the benchmark, model 1. However, its poorer performance in terms of the number of correct classifications is marginal.

The financial variables selected for inclusion in model 1 are similar to those selected in previous chapters. Little discussion

Table 9.3: Logit models and classification results for the original sample

(a) Original sample classifications results based on 146 cases

	Financial ratios only				Non-financial information only				Ratios & non-financial information			
	F		NF		F		NF		F		NF	
	No.	%	No.	%	No.	%	No.	%	No.	%	No.	%
	56	76.7	56	76.7	55	75.3	55	75.3	60	82.2	60	82.2
Optimum cut-off probability		(76.7) .576				(75.3) .746				(82.2) .777		

(b) Variables selected, coefficients and significance tests

Variables	Ratios		Non-financial data		Ratios & Non-financial data	
	Coefficient	SE	Coefficient	SE	Coefficient	SE
R4 Total Debt/Total Assets	.7048	(.5550)			.8760	(.6891)
R7 Fixed Assets/Total Assets	−.9493	(.6103)			−1.4197	(.7636)
R10 Pre-tax Profit/Total Assets	−.2003	(.1787)			−.2579	(.1803)
R26 Profit before Interest/Equity	−.1240	(.1293)				
R28 Profit before Interest/Total Debt	−.4104	(.3201)			−.4433	(.3217)
R2 Quick Ratio					.1187	(.0560)*
Q14 3-year average submission lag			.0639	(.0181)*	.1483	(.0384)*
Q2 No. of directors			−.2166	(.1012)*	−.2273	(.1257)
Q10 Going concern qualification					.4569	(.6918)
Q12 Bank floating charge			.7845	(.2283)*	.8923	(.3018)*
Q18 Audit to submission lag					−.0841	(.0347)*
Q8 Prior year's qualification			−1.2804	(.6268)*		
Q9 Current year's qualification			1.3177	(.5937)*		
Constant	.6014		.5828		.6785	
Log likelihood ratio significant at	99%		99%		99%	

Note: An asterisk indicates significance at the 95% confidence level.

of this function is therefore required other than to note that whilst none of these variables is individually significant at the 95 per cent confidence level, in total the function is significant at the 99 per cent level. This suggests that, despite the use of the stepwise analysis, multicollinearity may still be present. However, whilst this may cause problems for the determination of the significance of individual variables, it does not affect the predictive accuracy of the model and it is this which should form the basis of comparison between models.

The variables included in the qualitative information function, model 2, are individually significant at 95 per cent levels of confidence. In addition, the overall function is significant at 99 per cent. Furthermore, the variables included and their signs are in the predicted direction.

There is an increased probability of failure for companies with fewer directors, with longer average submission lags and for those which have secured loans held by a bank. Furthermore, this probability of failure increases if the company has received an audit qualification to its last set of accounts but had not received any audit qualifications in either of the prior two years.

If the company has received qualifications in all three years, the increased probability of failure is marginal as the coefficients of the two variables are similar but of opposite signs. Again, this makes intuitive sense as a minority of auditors (primarily large firms) as a matter of policy habitually issue a 'small company' audit qualification to all their small clients. Thus, in these cases where companies receive audit qualifications every year irrespective of their accounting practices, one would not expect the audit qualification to make any difference to the ability to predict financial distress. However, for companies whose auditors do not normally issue qualifications, the issuing of a qualification in the final set of accounts indicates that the auditor is no longer satisfied about some aspect of the company's reporting practices. This is consistent with Argenti's contention that as failure approaches some companies engage in 'creative accounting' practices and are therefore more likely to receive some form of audit qualification.

The classification results for model 3, which is based upon both data sets, are superior to those obtained from either of the individual models. The model is able to predict correctly some 82 per cent of the companies in the sample. This superiority is evident both in terms of overall correct classifications and in correctly classifying failed and non-failed companies. Furthermore, a number of the variables, mainly the non-financial information items, are significant at 95 per cent levels and the overall function is significant at 99 per cent confidence levels. These results tend to indicate that the two information sets are complementary as each contains additional information not present in the other.

The variables included in model 3 differ slightly from those contained in models 1 and 2. Four of the five financial ratios from model 1 are also included in model 3 with the signs and the order of magnitude of the coefficients being similar. The only ratio in model 3 not included in model 1 is a liquidity ratio which is significant at the 95 per cent level. Three of the five qualitative variables included in model 2 are also present in model 3 and again the signs and sizes of the coefficients, apart from the three-year-average submission lag, are unaltered materially. The two audit qualification variables are not included in the model 3 function. However, the 'going concern' qualification is included and this has the predicted sign. The other qualitative variable not present in model 2 but which is included in model 3 is the 'audit-to-submission lag'. The sign on this coefficient implies that the longer the period that companies delay the submission of their accounts once they have been signed by the auditor, the less likely they are to fail. This is counter-intuitive, but sensitivity tests indicate that excluding this variable has very little effect upon the logit function.

To test whether the above results were sample-dependent, data were obtained for an additional 20 companies (ten failed and ten non-failed). The relevant variables for each company were then multiplied by the logit function coefficients obtained from the original sample. The same optimum cut-off points as for the original sample were used for each function. The numbers and percentages of correctly classified companies for each model are shown in Table 9.4.

As may be seen from the table, in terms of the overall correct classification rates, the qualitative information set, model 2, provides a better overall prediction rate and a more equal mix of Type I and Type II errors than model 1. Furthermore, the more extensive model 3 does not provide a better overall prediction rate than model 2. However, as is generally the case in hold-out tests, the overall correct classification rates for all three

Table 9.4: Hold-out sample classification results (20 cases)

Financial ratios only				Non-financial information only				Ratios and non-financial information			
F		NF		F		NF		F		NF	
No.	%	No.	%	No.	%	No.	%	No.	%	No.	%
3	30.0	8	80.0	7	70.0	6	60.0	8	80.0	5	50.0
	(55.0)				(65.0)				(65.0)		

models are considerably reduced. These results, in conjunction with the original sample results, suggest that the qualitative information examined in this chapter is able to predict failure at least as well as the traditional financial ratio model. Furthermore, these results tend to support several of Argenti's and others' hypotheses concerning the nature of the failure process.

CONCLUSION

This chapter has examined the extent to which predictions of small company failure from publicly available qualitative information can be made, either alone or in conjunction with financial ratios. Qualitative factors are potentially of importance partly because of the uncertainties over financial data but primarily because the available financial information may be of reduced value because of the recent changes in the UK reporting requirements for small companies. The qualitative variables examined were chosen because our own and previous research had indicated that these variables may be capable of capturing a number of underlying causes and symptoms associated with business failure. The results, whilst being of a tentative nature, indicate that at least as good predictions may be obtained from this qualitative data as can be achieved from using traditional financial ratios. Furthermore, when this qualitative information is used in conjunction with financial ratios, the results suggest that this information can have incremental explanatory power.

10

Conclusion

THE CONTEXT

The wide range of topics covered in the previous chapters does not fall clearly into neat academic categorisations such as 'industrial economics', 'accounting' or even 'policy studies'. Clearly the material covered is closest to industrial economics but, judging from recent textbooks in this subject, such as Waterson (1984), or Clarke (1985), small firms are irrelevant to the discipline since in neither book is the topic explicitly referenced.

In many respects this reflects the lament by Carlsson (1985) that industrial economics has been hijacked by those in the tradition of industrial organisation, to the exclusion of those interested in industrial dynamics. Carlsson attributes this to a concern amongst economists with markets and to a view of the firm primarily in terms of its impact upon market aggregates such as prices and quantities. The seminal work by Chamberlin (1933) in articulating the relationship between market structure on the one hand and prices, profitability and efficiency on the other has been followed by more than half a century of rigorous analysis. Judging by current research and student reading the prime area of interest is the structure-conduct-performance relationship.

This text, however, has taken as its focus the firm rather than the industry, and has been concerned with the processes of change both within the firms and within a population of firms. In this sense it is a study of what Carlsson calls 'industrial dynamics'.

The approach has several advantages. It enables a direct

assessment to be made of the magnitude of economic change initiated by new and small firms, but most importantly it enables us to ask similar questions of the performance of small firms to those which have been asked of large firms. In principle it is possible to ask whether, for example, large firms grow faster than smaller firms or whether they are more profitable. In the past these questions have been asked of very large firms so that even the 'small' firms in these studies would normally be classified, within the whole spectrum of firms in an economy, as large. For example in the UK the sampling frame has tended to be quoted public companies (Singh and Whittington, (1968); Singh, (1971)) so that new businesses are taken to be those which are newly quoted on the Stock Exchange — even though they were often trading for many years prior to quotation.

The recent major upsurge of interest in small firms amongst governments caught researchers unawares. Unfortunately it has meant that public policies to promote small firms have moved well in advance of research. Instead of public policy being grounded on thorough empirical research it has, in many countries, taken the form of ill-formed acts of faith. In the absence of information on the performance of small firms there has been a tendency, even amongst academic economists, to assume that small firms with perhaps ten or 100 employees perform similarly to small quoted companies. For example in a recent set of readings on *Small Business: Theory and Policy* by Levicki (1984) several leading economists contribute articles on small firms yet a majority contain only references to analyses of quoted companies.

Throughout this book we have emphasised that a small firm is not simply a scaled-down version of a large firm. Small firms differ from large because they are more likely to be owned and managed by the same individuals or group of individuals. They are more likely to be restricted by financial and managerial resources and they lack market power. Furthermore they lack the diversity of range of products and market. All these factors are reflected in the almost tenfold difference in probability of failure between large and small firms. This, in turn, means that a small firm is much more likely to be new than is a large firm, because there is a 'turnover' of small firms.

These differences which produce a high probability of failure present major problems in analysing the performance of small firms, particularly in making comparisons between their performance as a group and the performance of large firms as a group. Problems arise in deriving a fully representative sample of small firms, and particularly in examining the changes in that sample over time because of the large numbers which cease to trade. The problem has several dimensions. If the performance of small firms is examined over a period of time two strategies can be adopted. The first is to examine only 'survivors' but this leads to an upward bias on performance measures. The second is to include both firms which fail and firms that are born, but here substantial problems arise in ensuring that these 'births' and 'deaths' are representative of 'births' and 'deaths' in the small firm sector. In this sector of the economy, the recording of such events is imperfect, especially the coverage of short-life firms.

In this book an examination has been made of single-plant independent manufacturing companies which traded at some stage in Northern England between 1965 and 1978. This means that it is an examination of only a subset of small *firms*. It does not include the numerous firms which have the status of sole proprietorships or partnerships, but since publicly available data are not available on such firms their exclusion is forced upon us. Companies were only included in the data base if they provided more than a single year of financial data between 1971 and 1981 and a single year of employment data between 1965 and 1981. However, since only public data were used it can be unclear when such companies began and when they ceased to trade. Hence it is not always possible to be fully satisfied that even the present sample is fully 'representative' of small companies.

These matters were fully discussed in Chapter 2 which concluded that the current collection of small companies used in the subsequent analysis was slightly biased towards the 'plodding men of business'. There were fewer 'high flyers' and also a lower proportion of short-life failures than a fully random selection. Nevertheless every effort has been made to ensure that the sample was a set of accurate snapshots over time of the small company population.

OWNERSHIP AND CONTROL

If high failure rates are characteristic of small companies, so equally is the closeness of ownership and control. The Bolton Committee (1971) identified three characteristics of a small business — legal independence, a small share of the market, and ownership and control in the hands of a single individual or group of individuals. All three characteristics are found in the present collection of companies and were explored in Chapter 3.

The closeness of the relationship between ownership and control in small companies presents problems for auditors whose prime function is to act on behalf of the shareholders in producing a set of annual accounts. Where however the shareholders and the directors of the company are the same individuals (two-thirds of all companies in the sample have no non-director shareholders) the auditors' responsibility is unclear. This may lead some auditors to avoid the type of thorough audit that should be undertaken, for fear of losing the account which, in turn, risks the small company receiving less than adequate information about its true financial position. The evidence in Chapter 3 suggests this may be particularly true of small companies audited by local firms of accountants.

A second characteristic noted by Bolton was that small businesses were legally independent in the sense of their shares not being owned by another enterprise. The role played by the local bank manager, however, is as important as that of major shareholders in quoted companies. The fortunes of the small company depend as much on the goodwill of its bank manager and its suppliers of trade credit as on the actions of the two or three directors who are nominally the owners of the business. The evidence presented in Chapter 3 suggests that the banks are frequently the prime movers in bringing about small company failure — particularly where they have a floating charge on the assets of the business.

THE PERFORMANCE OF SMALL COMPANIES

Even amongst those small companies which survive over a number of years there are several respects in which their performance differs from that of the large. First, there is clearly

314

much greater variability, from year to year, in the rates of profitability and growth of small companies than there is amongst larger companies. Second, amongst small companies profitability appears to be more persistent over time than does asset growth. Third, amongst small companies profitability appears to increase with size, whereas in the large firm studies the reverse was the case. Fourth, amongst small firms it appears that growth is slightly higher amongst the smallest firms whereas the large firm studies have, overall, shown no constant relationship between growth and size. Finally, superimposed upon all such relationships amongst smaller firms is the role of age, where it is broadly true that younger firms are more likely to be profitable and to grow faster than older firms. For all these reasons even the surviving small firm cannot be viewed as a scaled-down version of a larger firm.

THE MOTIVATIONS FOR SMALL BUSINESS GROWTH

In any study of industrial dynamics the relationship between profitability and growth is of central importance. Several views of this relationship are found in the literature, with the most familiar being the traditional theory of the firm operating in perfectly competitive markets and having to maximise profits. An alternative view is of large companies which are not compelled by competitive conditions to maximise profits, and where management is divorced from ownership. Here management may attempt to maximise other objectives from which they personally benefit more directly such as sales, departmental status etc. Finally Hay and Morris (1984) suggest that unquoted companies may attempt to maximise growth in assets, but subject to a security constraint. This means that the owners of the company will want to maximise their own income from the company without risking the company becoming attractive to any potential outside purchaser.

Different factors operate in genuinely small companies where there is a highly imperfect mechanism for acquisition. Here the objective of an individual who is the director of a single company may be to maximise his time-discounted stream of income. The central objective would therefore be to maximise the income which can be removed from the company at any one point in time without endangering future streams and particularly without risking the viability of the business. In practice this income will be paid using the most tax-efficient combination of dividends, directors' fees and repayments of directors' loans. Not surprisingly, given these objectives, Chapter 5 shows that the most likely outcome for any windfall gain in trading profit will be that it will be removed from the company and put into the pockets of the directors.

Matters may be more complicated because, as Chapter 5 shows, individuals may be the directors of several companies. Many have a portfolio of companies, some of which may be prospering at any point in time, others may be ceasing to trade, whilst others may be newly started. In this sense therefore it is important to make a distinction between *business* or *corporate failure* on the one hand and entrepreneurial or director failure, on the other. The former reflect the closure of a business for whatever reason, but in no sense could this be viewed as a failure by directors who may continue to own other highly successful companies. For this reason business failure, for which statistical data are presented in Chapters 1 and 2, is likely to be an overestimate of the extent of entrepreneurial failure.

This is illustrated by the apparently conflicting results of the analyses reported in Chapters 3 and 5. In Chapter 3 it was shown that 26.5 per cent of all companies had professional directors i.e. individuals who gave their occupation as that of 'Company Director'. When a distinction was made between failed and non-failed companies it was shown that only 20 per cent of directors of non-failed companies were professionals compared with 34 per cent of those in failed companies. We commented that this could reflect the lack of commitment by professional directors to individual companies, with the failure of one company merely resulting in a shuffling of the personal portfolio of assets of company directors.

In Chapter 5, however, it was shown that fast growth companies were much more likely to have professional directors than slow growth companies. Directors of fast growth companies had an average of 4.5 other directorships, whereas directors of non-fast growth companies only had an average of 0.9 other directorships.

These results indicate that the more successful small company directors have a portfolio of businesses from which wealth is derived, with the balance of that portfolio changing according to different trading conditions. It also emphasises the extent to which business failure is likely to exceed entrepreneurial failure. Finally it also demonstrates that public policies designed to create windfall profits for small companies are likely to result in increased economic activity within that firm in only a few cases.

SMALL BUSINESS FAILURE: SOME GENERAL COMMENTS

It is clear that small business failure is both frequent and potentially damaging, yet central to the efficient operations of the market economy. We have also argued above that the failure of businesses has to be distinguished from, and is almost certainly more frequent than, entrepreneurial failure.

When we began our studies into small firm failure two questions concerned us. First, we were unhappy about the absence of any clear theoretical model of the process by which business failure occurred, either in a small or a large firm. Argenti's early models were helpful descriptions, rather than models, and we were disappointed at the use of statistical techniques which did little to probe those factors that actually brought about failure. However we have to admit that our progress in producing a satisfactory model of small firm failure has been extremely limited and we, like our predecessors, have had to have recourse to statistical search procedures.

A second question, which in many respects caused us even greater concern, was whether it was desirable, even if it were technically possible, to predict small firm failure. A number of scenarios could be drawn, depending on the probability of correct predictions and the stage in the business life at which the prediction was made. An examination of these scenarios can be tentatively made within the conventional welfare economics framework.

Assume the most simple case. Here the prediction is made prior to the business starting. It predicts with perfect accuracy that the business will fail within three years, but that over that time it will generate a positive stream of profits. Even here, however, it is unclear whether the establishment of the business leads to net *social* benefits. The gains are that the individual may have been unemployed and, assuming he was producing no output, the community benefits from this extra output. A second consideration is the injection of competition into the market place which a new business provides, which could lead to lower prices and profits. Finally there may be psychological benefits to the person starting the business in the sense that he or she may feel they are contributing towards economic welfare. This, in turn, may lead to reductions in social unrest, crime, health disorders etc.

On the other hand if the business is certain to fail shortly after start-up this will impose social and possibly private costs. The private costs may occur if the new entrepreneur sinks personal savings into the establishment of this business and incurs personal losses. There may also be losses to creditors if, when the business fails, it is unable to pay off its creditors fully. Social costs may be incurred if the entry of the business results in reducing the profits of existing firms, so that some are forced out of business perhaps with no advantage to consumers. Therefore, because it is difficult to establish the net benefits of an additional business being in existence, it is equally difficult to place an unambiguous value on a perfectly correct prediction.

In the case where a small firm failure prediction model exists, *and we assume it is used by the financial institutions,* then they will be unlikely to lend to a business which is certain to fail with losses to the creditors. It is however still possible for that business to begin yet it remains unclear, on *a priori* grounds, whether there is a net social gain from new businesses being formed, even if only the private resources of the entrepreneur are used.

Once these simplifying assumptions are relaxed the water becomes even muddier. For example, the effect of assuming the predictions of the model are imperfect leads to errors of classifying failures as non-failures (Type I error) and non-failures as failures (Type II errors). The relative costs of these two types of errors have to be assessed, although if the model is used it is reasonable to assume it leads to better predictions than would be made using conventional techniques. The social benefits of the model are that some individuals may be discouraged from starting a non-viable business. If it is assumed that the net social benefits of such individuals starting a firm are negative then use of the model could yield social benefits. If however the net social benefits of anyone, however unsuitable, starting a business are positive then the model could lead to welfare losses.

Clearly it is possible to make this analysis increasingly realistic by adding further assumptions such as which parties have access to the model, how the probability of successful prediction varies with the age of the firm etc. Nevertheless none of this extra sophistication overcomes the fundamental problem of being unclear whether, or under what circumstances, additional businesses in the economy necessarily lead to an increase in welfare.

This suggests that whether a predictive model of corporate failure leads to welfare improvements depends upon who uses it, the criteria which are used to identify companies predicted to be failures and non-failures and the alternative uses for the human, financial and other resources available. We must reiterate that, on *a priori* grounds, it remains unproven, even if a model could be successfully constructed, whether its predictions unambiguously lead to welfare improvements. Nevertheless, there may be clear private gains to financial institutions able to avoid investing in firms likely to fail.

THE CHARACTERISTICS OF FAILURE

With the above provisos in mind, the second half of this book has been devoted to a study of the characteristics of failed and non-failed companies with a view to examining whether there are any clear indicators of impending failure. Throughout the analysis it has been continually stressed that because failure rates are very high amongst small firms, and because so many die early in life, there are problems in assembling enough data to undertake a satisfactory time series analysis. In simple terms those firms which provide three years' information and then fail are the exception rather than the rule, and so analysis of such firms is *not* an analysis of the typical failing small firm.

Recognising these data problems, three of the chapters in Part Two have been devoted to studies of techniques. Chapter 6 used univariate analysis, Chapter 7 used multiple discriminant analysis (MDA), and Chapter 8 considered probit, logit and factor analysis. All of these chapters used ratios constructed from the Profit and Loss Accounts and the Balance Sheets of small companies. Finally in Chapter 9 the more qualitative aspects of small companies were investigated with a view to examining whether these can offer any useful insights into corporate failure.

Since each of the individual chapters is based upon the use of different statistical techniques it is now appropriate to assess the

319

extent to which the chapters, taken as a whole, provide a consistent picture of small firm failure. In so doing we assess the extent to which that picture changes depending on the choice of techniques.

Throughout Chapters 6 to 8 three major indices of potential failure were examined. Following the logic of Beaver profitability, liquidity and gearing are examined, on the assumption that businesses which were more likely to fail would have lower profitability, lower liquidity but be more highly geared. All of these hypotheses appeared to be supported, to different degrees using univariate analysis. Secondly it would be expected that as failure approaches there would be a deterioration in these ratios, but this was only found to be true for gearing ratios. This means that low profitability and a shortage of liquidity could be good long-term indicators of small company failure, together with increasing gearing ratios. However the variance of these ratios meant that they did not constitute a consistently effective decision rule.

To overcome these problems with univariate analysis, Chapter 7 employs multiple discriminant analysis (MDA). Here the 'best' prediction models include Cash Flow and Asset Structure ratios rather than the liquidity or profitability measures identified in the univariate analysis. However the correlations between cash flow and profits and between asset structure and liquidity illustrate the familiar problem with MDA of 'interpreting' the included variables.

To some extent this is supported by the results using logit analysis in Chapter 8 which re-emphasises the importance of profitability and liquidity in failure prediction. Gearing, however, does not appear to be a powerful variable.

Two other factors have been noted throughout our examination of small company failure — the age of the business and the sector in which it operates. Clearly, failure rates are higher amongst young companies of a given size than amongst older companies and there may also be differences between sectors, even within manufacturing. Nevertheless we have been unable to isolate these influences and formally incorporate them into a predictive model. In the case of age, whilst it is clear that very young companies have higher failure rates, it is difficult to include such businesses within the analysis since they do not have a 'track record'. Hence the present predictive models are only applicable to companies able to provide at least three years of financial data. In that sense they are irrelevant to predicting the performance of a substantial number of small firm failures.

In principle it would have been desirable to have separate predictive models for small companies in the printing industry or in bread-making etc. However, since only 636 companies were included in the analysis, it was not possible to produce separate sectoral models. The preliminary and sectorally aggregated analysis undertaken suggested there was little to be gained by sectoral decomposition, perhaps because the demise of small firms is more likely to be because of bad management which transcends sectoral considerations. It is our view, however, that there may be some advantage in undertaking a finer sectoral disaggregation but this could only be achieved by a substantial expansion in the number of cases included when the initial models are calibrated.

Several other general findings are also worth highlighting. First, that in terms of predictive power in hold-out tests the use of logit analysis yielded no improvement over the use of MDA. Any benefit obtained by the use of this technique was therefore in leading to an improved understanding of the factors associated with failure, rather than with any improvement in predictive power.

Second, it was consistently noted that a number of small companies did not, in all years in which they traded, submit accounts to Companies House. In Chapter 7 an attempt was made to incorporate this 'non-submission' information formally into the models by assuming that all firms not submitting accounts in year t actually failed in that year. This led to a considerable improvement in classificatory accuracy, and a major increase in the number of eligible cases, for the one-year-prior model, but no improvement for the three-year-prior model.

Finally, it will be noted that all the companies included in this book traded at some stage during the 1970s and a number of them failed in the mid 1970s. Since that time in the UK there have been major changes both in macro-economic conditions and in government attitudes to the role of small businesses in economic development. This may lead to a questioning of whether the results obtained by studying failures and non-failures, during what is now fondly regarded as days of prosperity, is relevant to current conditions. We strongly believe that, whilst macro-economic conditions have changed substantially,

321

the manifestations of small firm failure are unchanged since they reflect the difficulties of trading in a competitive market with inadequate financial and managerial resources. These problems remain unchanged in the face of different macro-economic conditions. Clearly changes do occur, both over the longer time period and, perhaps more significantly, over the trade cycle but these are only likely to be marginal. It must be remembered that the original Altman models, which were being used successfully in the late 1970s, were calibrated on firms, some of which failed in the early 1950s.

THE ROLE OF PREDICTIVE MODELS

The 'best' predictive model of small company failure provided in this book correctly classified 75.7 per cent of companies in a genuine hold-out test. Such a model is significantly better than would be expected by chance, and probably at least as good as could be achieved by 'panels' of experts. Nevertheless any study of small businesses, and of failure in particular, is a study of individuals and their management prowess. For any financial institution, in the public or private sectors, which is considering the use of such a model it has to be emphasised that this is supplementary to, and not a substitute for, the judgement of officials.

The value of the model is that it is able to screen new applications for funding and also to monitor the performance of existing businesses. This is particularly valuable to financial institutions having a large portfolio of small clients, since investigation by the institution's own staff is expensive and time-consuming and an 'early warning' system which enables potentially risky companies to be identified easily has clear benefits.

Small-firm failure models therefore are designed to identify, at low cost, the firms which are potentially 'at risk'. It will not diagnose the cause of that problem and it certainly will not identify the course of action which the company has to take to offset failure. Both these can only be accomplished by the financial institution working with the company, and possibly with other outside parties, to identify both the cause of any problems and a strategy for overcoming them.

QUALITATIVE FACTORS

Most corporate failure prediction models are calibrated on financial data, yet within publicly available records there may be additional 'qualitative' information which may supplement the financial data. Indeed changes in the UK Companies Act 1981 which enable companies to reduce their provision of information by producing 'Modified Accounts' mean that such qualitative information is likely to be of increasing relevance to those wishing to construct failure prediction models. To our knowledge qualitative data have only been extensively used in one major study (Peel *et al.*, 1986), but again the sampling frame was UK quoted companies. This study examined reporting lags, changes in directors and directors' shareholdings, and found them to be useful in supplementing ratio analysis.

Our studies showed that amongst small companies failure was positively correlated with companies having fewer directors, longer account submission lags and having loans secured by the banks. It also showed that the probability of failure was higher if the last year's submitted accounts were 'qualified' by the auditors and if no qualifications were made in the previous years.

These qualitative results are important for two reasons. First, because there is less opportunity for 'creativity' than in the provision of the financial statements. There is no opportunity for legally disguising the numbers of directors, whether they change, and whether they have other directorships. Equally, unless there is a conspiracy between the auditors and the business, it seems likely that the small companies 'at risk' will generally experience longer delays in submitting information than those where few problems arise. Second, qualitative data are important because the changes embodied in the Companies Act 1981 have reduced the availability of detailed financial data used to construct ratios.

The qualitative results also raise important questions about two groups intimately involved with small companies. First, as noted above, the finding that failure was positively associated with the presence of a secured bank loan might suggest that the banks are keen to 'pull the plug'. On the other hand it could also suggest that the only way in which the banks will undertake what they perceive to be risky loans is generally to take a floating charge on the assets of the business. Since it is these businesses that are more likely to fail this merely reflects the good judgement of the bank manager. These totally different interpretations of the same 'facts' indicate the need for further more detailed analysis.

A second group whose judgement is subject to scrutiny with qualitative data are the company auditors. It has been shown that many companies which fail receive no form of auditor qualification in their years immediately prior to failure. Small local accounting practices seem significantly less willing to issue qualifications to companies which subsequently fail than the larger national or international practices. Such marked differences ought not to exist, since a 'true and fair' view should not vary according to the size of the accountancy practice.

THE IMPLICATIONS FOR PUBLIC POLICY

The expectations of government for the small business sector are that it should be a source of new jobs, new wealth and new dynamism in the economy. For the owners of small businesses the objective is probably to maximise a time-discounted stream of income, possibly from a portfolio of businesses, subject to maintaining a satisfactory degree of ownership of the business. For the banking and financial sector its objectives may vary according to whether it is providing equity or loan capital. If it is providing the former it is interested in the growth prospects of the firm, primarily in terms of whether the business will have a share price which will enable the institutions to obtain a capital gain. On the other hand, when a loan is being made, the prime consideration is the continued viability of the business and its ability to repay the loan. Indeed rapid growth might be perceived as a disadvantage since it brings with it risks of overtrading on an inadequate capital base.

From this it should be clear that public policies which are frequently designed to assist the growth in employment in small business will be viewed with different levels of enthusiasm by the differing groups. For example it was shown in Chapter 5 that small companies which were growing rapidly, in terms of employment, were not necessarily growing any faster in terms of assets. That chapter also showed that there was only a weak relationship between trading profits and growth in employment, but that a much stronger relationship existed between retained profits and employment growth.

It is our view that UK public policy towards small businesses is seriously misguided because it appears unaware of the mechanism relating profitability, survival and non-survival, asset and employment growth in small firms — the mechanism being the aspirations, personal financial requirements and skills of the owner manager. As we noted in Chapter 5 policy is, and is becoming increasingly, designed to raise the trading profits of all firms in the small business sector. Unfortunately, as we show, only a small proportion of companies use this increase in profits in full to reinvest in expanding the business, either in terms of assets or employment. Given the variety of objectives which entrepreneurs have, many will use the windfall gain to finance personal consumption or, as we showed in Chapter 5, to reduce external borrowings. In short only a few businesses and businessmen have growth of the business, in terms of assets, as the overriding objective. Even fewer have the employment of additional workers as an objective.

A NEW PUBLIC POLICY TOWARDS SMALL FIRMS

A policy towards small business has to recognise from the outset that it will only have a modest impact upon employment in a country such as the UK over a period of one or two decades. It is far from clear, even in the United States, to what extent small firms generate new jobs, although recent UK experience suggests that the small firm sector is performing relatively well primarily because of the poor performance of large firms (Storey and Johnson, 1987).

Against that background it should also be clear that within an economy there are relatively few small firms which are both willing and able to create significant numbers of jobs. For example amongst every 100 Northern Region manufacturing firms which started in business after 1965, 30 per cent ceased trading within three years but amongst those surviving for 16 years two firms, at that stage, provided nearly one-quarter of all the jobs in that group of firms, and seven firms provided nearly half the jobs. The key point is that, in terms of job creation, only a few firms matter, and it is those firms which should become the focus of public policy. This reflects the limitations of individuals with limited managerial and financial resources, frequently relying on local markets and sub-contract work from the large firm sector. This inherent vulnerability stems from the fact that only a few individuals have either the ability or the desire to be the engine of economic recovery, irrespective of the sums of publis money and assistance-in-kind directed towards them.

The nature and form of such public policy changes are set out in detail elsewhere (Storey and Johnson, 1987), but the general thrust is that if there is to be a public policy designed to assist small businesses it has to be selective for several reasons. Firstly it has been demonstrated that significant job creation takes place in only a few firms. Secondly that if policies are to be effective they have to have a significant and clearly identifiable effect upon the performance of the firms. This involves a 'hands on' approach by public agencies rather than the current 'arms length' approach currently favoured. For example, many firms are unaware of sources of funds for expansion and there is a real need for financial packaging whereby the best possible deal is assembled by a loan packager. There are strong arguments that this service could be privately provided, but it is an extremely time-intensive service, since the packager has to have a full understanding of the requirements and position of the business which he represents. It means that an individual officer is only able to deal with a very few clients at any one time. Conversely it means, however, that the officer is then able, if the package is successfully assembled, to make a major contribution to the growth of the business. This contrasts with present policies whereby so many public agencies merely see their role as to provide 'arms length' advice on a wide variety of topics.

The use of a 'hands on' approach, in a situation in which there are fixed resources, implies that decisions have to be reached upon the few firms that will be helped, and the vast majority who will have to help themselves. In this sense both public and private initiatives should be targeted at the growers but, because the firms growing fast in terms of employment are not always the same as those growing fast in terms of assets or profitability, the same firms are not necessarily the target for public policy and private sector interest.

Bibliography

Accountancy (1983), 'Top Twenty Accountants by Fee Income', vol. 94, November, p. 23.

Aislabie, C.J. and Keating, G.R. (1976), 'Size, Industrial Classification and Growth of Australian Factories', *Economic Record*, vol. 52, March, pp. 82-93.

Altman, E.I. (1968), 'Financial Ratios, Discriminant Analysis and the Prediction of Corporate Bankruptcy', *Journal of Finance*, vol. 23 no.4, September, pp. 589-609.

—— (1982), *Corporate Financial Distress, a Complete Guide to Predicting, Avoiding and Dealing with Bankruptcy*, John Wiley, New York.

Altman, E.I. Avery R.B., Eisenbeis, R.A. and Sinkey, J.F. (1981), *Application of Classification Techniques in Business Banking and Finance*, JAI Press Inc. Greenwich, Conn.

Argenti, J. (1976), *Corporate Collapse — the Causes and Symptoms*, McGraw-Hill, London, New York.

Armington, C. and Odle, M. (1982), 'Small Business — How Many Jobs?', *Brookings Review*, vol. 1, pp. 14-17.

Aspin, A. and Welch, B.L. (1949), 'Tables for Use in Comparisons Where Accoucacy Involves Two Variances Separately Estimated', *Biometrika*, vol. 36, December, pp. 290-3.

Auditing Practices Committee, (APC), (1980), 'Auditing Standards and Guidelines', Institute of Chartered Accountants in England and Wales.

Bank of England (1982), 'Techniques for Assessing Corporate Financial Strength', *Bank of England Quarterly Bulletin*, June, pp. 221-3.

Bates, J. (1965), 'Alternative Measures of the Size of Firms' in P.E. Hart (ed.), *Studies in Profit, Business Saving and Investment in the United Kingdom 1920-1962*, George Allen and Unwin, London.

Bayldon, R., Woods, A. and Zafiris, N. (1984), 'Inner City Versus New Towns: a Comparison of Manufacturing Performance', *Oxford Bulletin of Economics and Statistics*, vol. 46, no. 1, pp. 21-9.

Beaver, W.H. (1966), 'Financial Ratios as Predictors of Failure', Empirical Research in Accounting: Selected Studies, *Journal of*

Accounting Research, Supplement to vol. 5 (1967), January, pp. 71-111.

Beaver, W. (1968), 'Market Prices, Financial Ratios and the Prediction of Failure', *Journal of Accounting Research*, vol. 6, Autumn, pp. 179-99.

Beesley, M.E. and Wilson, P.E. (1981), 'Government Aid to Small Firms in Britain', UKSBMTA Conference, London.

Binks, M. and Coyne, J. (1983), 'The Birth of Enterprise', Hobart Paper no. 98, Institute of Economic Affairs, London.

Birch, D.L. (1979), 'The Job Generation Process, MIT Program on Neighborhood and Regional Change', MIT Press, Cambridge, Massachusetts.

Birley, S. (1985a), 'New Firms and Job Generation', Paper presented to the Eighth National Small Policy Conference, University of Ulster.

—— (1985b), 'The small firm — set at the start', Cranfield Strategy and Enterprise Working Paper Series no. 10, Cranfield Institute of Technology.

Blum, M. (1974), 'Failing Company Discriminant Analysis', *Journal of Accounting Research*, vol. 12, January, pp. 71-111.

Bolton Committee, (1971), *Small Firms: Report of the Committee of Inquiry on Small Firms*, Cmnd 4811 HMSO, London.

Boswell, J. (1972), 'The Rise and Decline of Small Firms', George Allen and Unwin, London.

Carsberg, B.V., Page, M.J., Sindell, A.J., and Waring, I.D. (1985), *Small Company Financial Reporting*, Prentice—Hall, London.

Carlsson, B. (1985), 'Reflections on "Industrial Dynamics": The Challenges Ahead', Presidential Address to EARIE Conference, Cambridge, 13 September.

Casey, C. (1980), 'Variations in Accounting Information Load: The Effect of Loan Officers Predictions of Bankruptcy', *The Accounting Review*, vol. 55, January, pp. 36-49.

Chamberlin, E.H. (1933), *The Theory of Monopolistic Competition. A Re-orientation of the Theory of Value*, Harvard University Press, Cambridge, Mass.

Chesher, A. (1979), 'Testing the Law of Proportionate Effect', *The Journal of Industrial Economics*, vol. 37, no. 4, June, pp. 403-11.

Clarke, R. (1985), *Industrial Economics*, Basil Blackwell, Oxford.

Crasswell, A.T. (1985), 'Studies of the Information Content of Qualified Audit Reports', *Journal of Business Finance and Accounting*, vol. 34, Spring, pp. 93-115.

Cross, M. (1983), 'Small Firms in the United Kingdom', in D.J. Storey (ed), *The Small Firm: an International Survey*, Croom Helm, Kent.

Crum, W.L. (1934), *The Effect of Size on Corporate Earnings and Condition*, Harvard University Division of Business Research Studies, no. 8. Cambridge, Massachusetts.

—— (1939), *Corporate Size and Earning Power*, Harvard University Press, Cambridge, Massachusetts.

Dambolena, I.G. and Khoury, S.J. (1980), 'Ratio Stability and Corporate Failure', *Journal of Finance*, vol. 35, no. 4, September, pp. 1017-26.

Deakin, E.B. (1972), 'A Discriminant Analysis of Predictions of Business Failure', *Journal of Accounting Research*, vol. 10, March, pp. 167-79.

Department of Trade and Industry, (1985), 'Burdens on Business', HMSO, March, London.

Dewing, A.S. (1921), 'A Statistical Test of the Success of Consolidations', *Quarterly Journal of Economics*, vol. 36, November, pp. 84-101.

Diamond, H. Jr. (1976), 'Pattern Recognition and the Detection of Corporate Failure', Ph.D.Dissertation, New York University.

Droucopoulos, V. (1982), 'International Big Business 1957-77: A Sequel on the Relationship Between Size and Growth', *Journal of Economic Studies*, vol. 9, no. 3, pp. 3-19.

Dunning J.H. and Pearce, R.D. (1981), *The World's Largest Industrial Enterprises*, Gower, Farnborough, Hants.

Earl, M.T. and Marais, D.A.J. (1979), 'The Prediction of Corporate Bankruptcy in the UK Using Discriminant Analysis', Oxford Centre of Management Studies, Oxford, UK, Working Paper, 79/5.

Eatwell, J.L. (1969), 'A Stochastic Theory of the Growth of Firms: Some Analytics, Some Tests', Unpublished Seminar Paper, Harvard University.

Edmister, R.O. (1972), 'An Empirical Test of Financial Ratio Analysis for Small Business Failure Prediction', *Journal of Financial and Quantitative Analysis*, vol. 7, March, pp. 1477-93.

Eisenbeis, R.A. (1977), 'Pitfalls in the Application of Discriminant Analysis: A Classification', *Journal of Financial and Quantitative Analysis*, vol. 32, no. 3, March, pp. 887-93.

Foreman Peck, J. (1985), 'Seedcorn or Chaff? New Firm Formation and the Performance of the Interwar Economy', *Economic History Review*, Second Series, vol. 38, no. 3, August, pp. 402-22.

Fothergill, S., Gudgin, G., Kitson, M. and Monk, S. (1984), 'Differences in the Profitability of the UK Manufacturing Sector Between Connurbation and Other Areas', *Scottish Journal of Political Economy*, vol. 31, no. 1, February, pp. 72-91.9

Ganguly, P. (1982), 'Birth and Deaths of Firms in UK in 1980', *British Business*, vol. 29, 29 January, pp. 204-7.

—— (1983), 'Life-Span Analysis of Business in the UK 1973-1982', *British Business*, vol. 12, 12 August, pp. 838-45.

—— (1985), *UK Small Business Statistics and International Comparisons*, Harper and Row, London.

Geiser, J. (1981) *Unternehumensgrobenbezogene Wachstumschemmnisse mittelstandischer Industriebetriebe*, Gottingen: Verlag Otto Schwartz.

Gibrat, R. (1931) *Les Inegalités Economiques*, Paris, Sirey.

Gilbert, E.S. (1968), 'On Discrimination Using Qualitative Variables', *Journal of American Statistical Association*, vol. 63, December, pp. 215-34.

—— (1969), 'The Effect of Unequal Variance — Covariance Matrices on Fisher Linear Discriminant Function', *Biometrics*, vol. 25, September, pp. 505-15.

Hadon, T. (1977), *Company Law and Capitalism*, 2nd ed., Weidenfeld and Nicolson, London.

Hamer, M. (1983), 'Failure Prediction: Sensitivity of Classification Accuracy to Alternative Statistical Methods and Variable Sets', *Journal of Accounting and Public Policy*, vol. 2, no. 4, Winter, pp. 289-307.

Hart, P.E. (1962), 'The Size and Growth of Firms', *Economica*, vol. 29, no. 113, pp. 29-39.

—— (1965), *Studies in Profit, Business Saving and Investment in the UK, 1920-1962*, Allen and Unwin, London.

Hart, P.E. and Prais, S.J. (1956), 'The Analysis of Business Concentration: A Statistical Approach', *Journal of the Royal Statistical Society*, Series A, vol. 119, Part 2, pp. 150-91.

Hay, D.A. and Morris, D.J. (1984), *Unquoted Companies: Their Contribution to the United Kingdom Economy*, Macmillan, London.

Hertz, L. (1982), *In Search of a Small Business Definition: An Explanation of the Small Business Definition in the USA, UK, Israel and the People's Republic of China*, University Press of America, Washington.

Hull, C.J. (1985), 'Job Generation Among Independent West Germany Manufacturing Firms, 1974-80, — Evidence from Four Regions', *Environment and Planning; Government and Policy*, vol. 3, pp. 215-34.

Hutchinson, P. and Ray, G. (1986), 'Surviving the financial stress of small enterprise growth' in J. Curran, J. Stanworth and D. Watkins (eds.) *The Survival of the Small Firm*, vol. 1, Gower Aldershot, Hants.

Hymer, S. and Pashigan, P. (1962), 'Firm Size and Rate of Growth', *Journal of Political Economy*, vol. 70, no. 6, December, pp. 556-69.

Industrial and Commercial Finance Corporation (1983), *Small Firm Survey*, ICFC, London.

Johnson, P. (1986), *New Firms: An Economic Perspective*, Allen & Unwin, London.

Jones, W.T. (1969), 'Size, Growth and Profitability in the Mechanical Engineering Industry', NEDO, (Unpublished Documents), London.

Keasey, K. and Watson, R. (1986), 'Current Cost Accounting and the Prediction of Small Firm Performance', *Journal of Business Finance and Accounting*, vol. 13, no. 1, Spring, pp. 51-70.

—— (1987), 'The Non Submission of Accounts and Small Company Financial Distress', *The Accounting Review: The Quarterly Review of the American Accounting Association*. (Forthcoming).

Keasey, K and Wynarczyk, P. (1986), 'Ratio Stability and Corporate Failure: A Comment', Working Paper, Department of Industrial Economics, University of Nottingham, Nottingham.

Kennedy, H.A. (1975), 'A Behaviorial Study of the Usefulness of Four Financial Ratios', *Journal of Accounting Research*, vol. 13, Spring, pp. 97-116.

Kent, D., Sherer, M. and Turley, C.A. (ed) (1985), *Current Issues in Auditing*, Harper and Row, London.

Lawrence, E.C. (1983), 'Reporting Delays for Failed Firms', *Journal of*

Accounting Research, vol. 21, Autumn, pp. 606-10.

Lachenbruch, P.A., Sneeringer, C. and Revo, L.T. (1973), 'Robustness of the Linear and Quadratic Discriminant Function under Certain Types of Non Normality', *Communications and Statistics*, vol. 1, pp. 39-56.

Lee, T.A. (1981), *Income and Value Measurements, Theory and Practice*, 2nd Edition, Thomas Nelson & Sons Ltd, Surrey.

Levicki, C. (1984), (ed), *Small Business: Theory and Policy*, The Acton Society, Croom Helm, Beckenham, Kent.

Libby, R. (1975), 'Accounting Ratios and the Prediction of Failure — Some Behavioral Evidence', *Journal of Accounting Research*, vol. 13, Spring, pp. 150-61.

Lloyd, P. and Mason, C. (1985), 'Spatial Variations in New Firm Formation in the United Kingdom: Comparative Evidence from Merseyside, Greater Manchester and South Hampshire', in D.J. Storey (ed), *Small Firms and Regional Economic Development: Britain, Ireland and the United States*, Cambridge University Press, London.

Mansfield, E. (1962), 'Entry, Gibrats Law, Innovation and the Growth of Firms', *American Economic Review*, vol. 52, December, pp. 1023-51.

Martin, D. (1977), 'Early Warnings of Bank Failure', *Journal of Banking and Finance*, vol. 1, pp. 249-76.

McDonald, B. and Morris M.H. (1984), 'The Statistical Validity of the Ratio Method in Financial Analysis: An Empirical Examination', *Journal of Business, Finance and Accounting*, vol. 33, no. 1, Spring, pp. 89-97.

Meeks, G and Whittington, G (1975), 'Giant Companies in the United Kingdom, 1948-69', *Economic Journal*, vol. 85, December, pp. 824-43.

Meeks, G. and Whittington, G. (1976), 'The Financing of Quoted Companies in the UK', Background Paper to Report No. 2, 'Income from Companies and its Distribution', Royal Commission on the Distribution of Income and Wealth, HMSO, London.

Moiser, P. (1985), *Independence*, in Kent *et al.*(ed), pp. 33-4, *Current Issues in Auditing*, Harper and Row.

Moore, D.H. (1973), 'Evaluation of Five Discriminant Procedures for Binary Variables', *Journal of American Statistical Association*, vol. 68, pp. 399-404.

Moyer, C.R. (1977), 'Forecasting Finance Failure: A Reexamination', *Financial Management*, vol. 6, Spring, pp. 11-17.

Newbould, G.D., Stay, S.J. and Wilson, K.W. (1977), 'The Benefits of Company Size: The Case of Shareholders', *Scottish Journal of Political Economy*, vol. 24, no. 1, February, pp. 77-82.

Oakey, R.P. (1984), *High Technology Small Firms*, Frances Pinter, London.

Ohlson, J.O. (1980), 'Financial Ratios and the Probabilistic Prediction of Bankruptcy', *Journal of Accounting Research*, vol. 18, Spring, pp. 109-31.

Organisation for Economic Cooperation and Development (1985),

331

'Employment in Small and Large Firms: Where Have the Jobs Come from?', *OECD Employment Review*, September, pp. 64-82.

Page, M.J. (1984), 'Corporate Financial Reporting and the Small Independent Company', *Accounting and Business Research*, vol. 15, Summer, pp. 271-82.

—— (1985), 'The Auditor and the Smaller Company' in Kent *et al.* pp. 208-19.

Peel, M.J., Peel, D.A. and Pope, P.F. (1986), 'Predicting Corporate Failure — Some Results for the UK Corporate Sector', *Omega*, vol. 14, no. 1, pp. 5-12.

Pinches, G, Mingo, K. and Caruthers, J. (1973), 'The Stability of Financial Patterns in Industrial Organisations', *Journal of Finance*, vol. 28, May, pp. 389-96.

Pinches, G., Mingo, K., Carruthers, J., and Eubank, A. (1975), 'The Hierarchical Classification of Financial Ratios', *Journal of Business Research*, vol. 3, October, pp. 295-310.

Ramsey, J.R. and Foster, L.O. (1931), 'A Demonstration of Ratio Analysis', Bureau of Business Research, University of Illinois.

Rowthorn, R. and Hymer, S. (1971), *International Big Business 1957-1967: A Study of Comparative Growth*, Cambridge University Press, London.

Samuels, J. (1965), 'Size and Growth of Firms', *Review of Economic Studies*, vol. 32, pp. 105-12.

Schwartz, K.B. and Menon, K. (1985), 'Auditor switches by Failing Firms', *The Accounting Review*, vol. 60, April, pp. 248-61.

Shen, T.Y. (1965), 'Economies of Scale, Expansion Path, and Growth of Plants', *Review of Economics and Statistics*, vol. 47, November, pp. 420-8.

—— (1968), 'Competition Technology and Market Shares', *Review of Economics and Statistics*, vol. 50, February, pp. 96-102.

—— (1970), 'Economies of Scale, Penrose Effect, Growth of Plants and their Size Distribution', *Journal of Political Economy*, vol. 78, no. 4, July-August, pp. 702-16.

Singh, A. (1971), *Takeovers*, Cambridge University Press, London.

Singh, A. and Whittington, G. (1968), *Growth, Profitability and Valuation*, Cambridge University Press, London.

—— (1975), 'The Size and Growth of Firms', *Review of Economic Studies*, vol. 42, no. 1, January, pp. 15-26.

Steele, P. (1984), 'The Prediction of Small Company Failure Using Financial Statement Analysis: A Critique of Financial Statements and Previous Failure Prediction Studies', CURDS Discussion Paper no. 60, October, University of Newcastle Upon Tyne.

Stekler, H.W. (1963), *Profitability and Size of Firm*, University of California Press, Berkeley.

Storey, D.J. (1982), *Entrepreneurship and the New Firm*, Croom Helm, Beckenham, Kent.

Storey, D.J. (1985a), 'Manufacturing Employment Change in Northern England 1965-1978; The Role of Small Businesses', in D.J. Storey (ed.) *Small Firms in Regional Economic Development: Britain, Ireland and the United States*, Cambridge University Press, London.

—— (1985b), 'The Problems Facing New Firms', *Journal of Management Studies*, vol. 22, no. 3, May, pp. 327-45.

Storey, D.J. and Johnson, S. (1987), *Job Generation and Labour Market Change*, Macmillan, London.

Storey, D.J. and Wynarczyk, P. (1985), 'A Profile of Small Manufacturing Companies in Northern England: Profits, Jobs and Failures', CURDS Discussion Paper No. 64, February, University of Newcastle Upon Tyne.

Summers, H.B. (1932), 'A Comparison of the Rates of Earning of Large and Small Scale Industries', *Quarterly Journal of Economics*, vol. XLVI, May, pp. 465-79.

Taffler, R.J. (1982), 'Forecasting Company Failure in the UK Using Discriminant Analysis and Financial Ratio Data', *Journal of Royal Statistical Society*, vol. 145(3), pp. 342-58.

Taffler, R.J. and Tisshaw, H. (1977), 'Going, Going, Gone — Four Factors Which Predict', *Accountancy*, vol. 88, no. 1003, March, pp. 50-2 and 54.

Tamari, M. (1978), *Financial Ratio Analysis and Prediction*, Paul Elek, London.

Teitz, M.B., Glasmeir, A. and Svensson, D. (1981), 'Small Business and Employment Growth in California', Working Paper No.348, Berkeley, Institute of Urban and Regional Development, University of California.

Wahl, P.W. and Kronwal, R.A. (1977), 'Discriminant Functions when Covariances are Unequal and Sample Sizes Moderate', *Biometrics*, vol. 33, September, pp. 479-84.

Walter, J.E. (1957), 'Determination of Technical Solvency', *The Journal of Business*, vol. XXX, January, pp. 30-43.

Waterson, M. (1984), *Economic Theory of the Industry*, Cambridge University Press, London.

Watts, R.L. and Zimmerman, J.L. (1983), 'Agency Problems, Auditing, and the Theory of the Firm: Some Evidence', *Journal of Law & Economics*, vol. 26, October, pp. 613-33.

Wedervang, F. (1965), *Development of a Population of Industrial Firms*, Universitetsforlaget, Oslo.

Whittington, G. (1980), 'The Profitability and Size of U.K. Companies 1960-74', *Journal of Industrial Economics*, vol. 28, no. 4, pp. 335-52.

Whittred, G.P. (1980), 'Audit Qualifications and the Timeliness of Corporate Annual Reports', *The Accounting Review*, vol. 55, October, pp. 563-77.

Whittred, G.P. and Zimmer, I. (1984), 'Timeliness of Financial Reporting and Financial Distress', *The Accounting Review*, vol. LIX, no. 2, April, pp. 287-95.

Wilson Committee (1979), 'Committee to Review the Functioning of the Financial Institutions', Studies of Small Firms Finance, Research Report No. 3, HMSO, December, London.

Zavgren, C.V. (1983), 'The Prediction of Corporate Failure: The State of the Art', *Journal of Accounting Literature*, vol. 2, Spring, pp. 1-35.

—— (1985), 'Assessing the Vulnerability to Failure of American Industrial Firms: A Logistic Analysis', *Journal of Business Finance and Accounting*, vol. 12, no. 1, pp. 19-47.

Zimmer, I. (1980), 'A Lens Study of the Prediction of Corporate Failure by Bank Loan Officers', *Journal of Accounting Research*, vol. 18, Autumn, pp. 629-36.

Index